Creating Community

An Action Plan for Parks and Recreation

California Park & Recreation Society

Jane H. Adams

Editor

Human Kinetics

Library of Congress Cataloging-in-Publication Data

Creating community : an action plan for parks and recreation / California Park & Recreation
Society, Jane H. Adams, editor.
    p. cm.
  Includes bibliographical references.
  ISBN-13: 978-0-7360-6714-0 (soft cover)
  ISBN-10: 0-7360-6714-0 (soft cover)
  1. Outdoor recreation--California--Planning. 2. Parks--California--Planning. 3. Recreation and
state--California. I. Adams, Jane H. II. California Park and Recreation Society.
  GV191.42.C2C74 2008
  333.78'309794--dc22

2007040233

ISBN-10: 0-7360-6714-0
ISBN-13: 978-0-7360-6714-0

The Web addresses cited in this text were current as of November 2007, unless otherwise noted.

Acquisitions Editor: Gayle Kassing, PhD; **Developmental Editor:** Patricia Sammann; **Managing Editor:** Bethany J. Bentley; **Assistant Editor:** Anne Rumery; **Copyeditor:** Jan Feeney; **Proofreader:** Julie Marx Goodreau; **Permission Manager:** Dalene Reeder; **Graphic Designer:** Fred Starbird; **Graphic Artist:** Yvonne Griffith; **Cover Designer:** Robert Reuther; **Photograph (cover):** Courtesy of the City of Eugene Parks & Open Space; **Photographs (interior):** © Human Kinetics, unless otherwise noted; **Photo Asset Manager:** Laura Fitch; **Photo Office Assistant:** Jason Allen; **Art Manager:** Kelly Hendren; **Illustrator and Associate Art Manager:** Alan L. Wilborn; **Printer:** Sheridan Books

Printed in the United States of America   10 9 8 7 6 5 4 3 2 1

Human Kinetics
Web site: www.HumanKinetics.com

United States: Human Kinetics
P.O. Box 5076
Champaign, IL 61825-5076
800-747-4457
e-mail: humank@hkusa.com

Canada: Human Kinetics
475 Devonshire Road Unit 100
Windsor, ON N8Y 2L5
800-465-7301 (in Canada only)
e-mail: info@hkcanada.com

Europe: Human Kinetics
107 Bradford Road
Stanningley
Leeds LS28 6AT, United Kingdom

+44 (0) 113 255 5665
e-mail: hk@hkeurope.com
Australia: Human Kinetics
57A Price Avenue
Lower Mitcham, South Australia 5062
08 8372 0999
e-mail: info@hkaustralia.com

New Zealand: Human Kinetics
Division of Sports Distributors NZ Ltd.
P.O. Box 300 226 Albany
North Shore City
Auckland
0064 9 448 1207
e-mail: info@humankinetics.co.nz

This book is dedicated to the members of the California Park & Recreation Society and Karen McNamara, CPRS president from 1998 to 1999, who had the vision, insight, and passion to lead this amazing planning effort.

This book is also dedicated to the thousands of park and recreation professionals who create community through people, parks, and programs every day in communities across America.

A personal dedication is to Jack and Elnor Hipps, my parents; David, my husband; and Katherine, my daughter.

Contents

Foreword

People cannot discover new lands until they have the courage to lose sight of the shore.

—*Andre Gibe*

If you're reading this book, *Creating Community: An Action Plan for Parks and Recreation,* you should count yourself among the many proactive and insightful park and recreation professionals who have chosen to take command of the future of the profession. As a profession, we have continual challenges, and we must pull together and focus our energy on this excellent planning document. As California Park & Recreation Society (CPRS) president during the year the VIP Action Plan was created, I am so proud of the work we accomplished. Together we examined the future through the lens of the VIP Project.

We cannot direct the wind, but we can adjust the sails.

—*Dolly Parton*

In 1998, the CPRS board of directors made a commitment to the profession to lead the VIP Project by developing an action plan that would create a common vision of our future; identifying key trends that we need to address proactively; identifying and articulating our competencies, strengths, and values as a profession; seeking new market opportunities; and developing specific strategies to address the future. During project initiation, we developed the goals for the project, reviewed background material, and refined the work program. The consultant team worked closely with the CPRS Project Team and VIP Steering Committee to ensure that project outcomes would address the vision and concerns of all stakeholders. That was followed by an environmental scan (an analysis of existing conditions in parks and recreation, including the perceptions of those in the field of parks and recreation and those in allied professions). The scan included two major components:

1. Futurist Tapan Munroe (1999) wrote an analysis of major trends that are likely to affect park and recreation services.
2. More than 30 CPRS leaders administered a close-ended questionnaire to approximately 250 respondents, who were almost equally divided between park and recreation professionals and those in allied fields.

After the environmental scan, a VIP Summit was held to develop and review an action plan. Strategy teams of professionals reviewed the initial action-planning framework and developed a plan for eight strategic areas. Moore, Iacofano, Goltsman (MIG), consultants hired by CPRS, worked with the CPRS Project Team and VIP Steering Committee to produce a draft action plan. We unveiled the plan at the California and Pacific Southwest Recreation and Park Training Conference in Santa Clara in 1999. Attendees reviewed and commented on the plan in several interactive sessions. In other sessions we assisted members in applying the action plan and environmental scan information to their agencies.

After the conference, the draft plan was revised based on the comments received from members. The final plan was completed in April 1999, and implementation began in May. Many people helped deliver on the promise of the VIP Project, and now you have the opportunity to participate in the unlimited possibilities that exist for the profession. You have a blueprint that will guide you, both individually and collectively.

Even if you're on the right track . . . you'll get run over if you just sit there.

—*John Ray*

We need to be diligent in communicating the vision as articulated in the VIP Action Plan—it is our touchstone. We must stay positive and be willing to accept the challenges that the future holds. We must take responsibility for the future success of our profession. Critical thinking, insight, and planning are paramount in using the VIP Action Plan's strategy areas to create tangible outcomes that will showcase the profession as the vital link in creating community through people, parks, and programs.

The best way to predict the future is to create it.

—*Peter Drucker*

Karen M. McNamara
CPRS president, 1998 to 1999

Acknowledgments

1998-1999 VIP STEERING COMMITTEE MEMBERS

Current affiliation is noted.

Steering committee chair

Sheila Canzian, director of parks and recreation
City of San Mateo

Jay Beals, president and CEO
beals alliance, Sacramento

Bob Cardoza, president and CEO
NUVIS, Costa Mesa

Judy Kleinberg, city council member
City of Palo Alto

Lonald Lott, chief of police (retired)
City of Turlock

Anne Seeley, Active Communities coordinator (deceased)
University of California at San Francisco

Curtis Brown Jr., recreation superintendent
City of San Bernardino

Terry Jewell, administrator
Sunrise Recreation and Park District, Sacramento County

Karen McNamara, public services director
City of San Ramon

Jim Porter, director of parks and community services (retired)
City of Vista

Paul Romero, chief deputy director
California Department of Parks and Recreation

Mike Stallings, director of parks and recreation
City of Daly City

Veda Ward, Professor, department of leisure studies and recreation
California State University at Northridge

1998-1999 CPRS BOARD OF DIRECTORS

Affiliation at that time noted.

Karen McNamara, president
City of San Ramon

Curtis Brown Jr., president-elect
City of West Hollywood

Terry Jewell, vice president
Sunrise Recreation and Park District

Nancy Lerner, secretary-treasurer
City of Anaheim

Ken De Young, Region 1 representative
Carmichael Recreation and Park District

Barry Weiss, Region 2 representative
City of Palo Alto

August Hioco, Region 3 representative
City of Sanger

Donna Georgino, Region 4 representative
City of Duarte

Earleen Chandler, Region 5 representative
City of Yorba Linda

JoAnn Jones, council of sections representative
Vista Unified School District

Don Schatzel, council of sections representative
City of West Sacramento

STAFF

Jane H. Adams, executive director
  California Park & Recreation Society
  Sacramento

1999-2000 VIP ACTION TEAM

The CPRS board of directors created the VIP Action Team to direct this plan's implementation. Current affiliation is noted.

  Sheila Canzian, co-chair
    City of San Mateo

  Karen McNamara, co-chair
    City of San Ramon

  Don Allen (retired)

  Curtis Brown Jr.
    City of San Bernardino

  Dr. Rene Dahl
    San Francisco State University

  B.J. Grosvenor
    San Jose State University

  Terry Jewell
    Sunrise Recreation and Park District

  Mike Lopez
    City of Santa Ana

Stacia Mancini (retired)

Linda Rahn
  City of Coronado

Marcia Somers
  Town of Danville

Mike Stallings
  City of Daly City

Jesse Washington (retired)

Jane H. Adams
  California Park & Recreation Society

CPRS also extends a special thanks to CPRS members Pete Soderberg, Mary Burns, and Pete Dangermond, who had the insight to challenge the profession with the discussion paper they authored in 1997: "California Parks & Recreation Entering the 21st Century." Our appreciation goes to Sheila Canzian and Jane H. Adams for their leadership and hard work during 1998 and 1999 in making the VIP Project happen. We are grateful to Daniel Iacofano and Sally McIntyre from Moore Iacofano Goltsman, Inc., for their diligence and wisdom in shaping and writing the final plan. Finally, my deepest regards, respect, and appreciation go to all of the individuals and agencies who took the time to participate and who shared their passion for this incredible profession!

I

The VIP Action Plan

As a park and recreation professional, you set the strategic direction of your agency, division, or even special event. The California Park & Recreation Society has created a strategic planning model, the VIP Action Plan, as a tool you can use to position your agency and programs with your participants, citizens, and policy makers (see figure on page 2).

In chapter 1, we explain how the VIP Action Plan came to be and its purpose. We also consider the philosophy behind the Action Plan, the objectives and benefits of the VIP Project that developed the VIP Action Plan, and who can use the Plan and how.

Chapter 2 is where we delve into the core values, vision, and mission of the VIP Action Plan. After presenting the values and vision we support, we explain how you can use the mission to position your agency favorably and how to link the mission to your community. We offer several real-life examples of how park and recreation agencies have already put the values, vision, and mission to work.

A vital part of the VIP Action Plan is staying aware of trends in society and turning them into opportunities for our agencies. In chapter 3 we look at two large studies of current trends and their implications for park and recreation providers, and we consider how those trends might be converted into new opportunities.

The skills of agencies' staff will determine, to a large extent, what those agencies can accomplish. That's why in chapter 4 we discuss core competencies. After presenting our list of the competencies we believe park and recreation professionals need to have, we look at how those competencies might be incorporated into employee training and management. We also speculate on what new roles park and recreation agencies may need to take on in the future.

Our VIP Action Plan would not be complete without some specific strategies for you to use in accomplishing the values, vision, and mission. In chapter 5 we present

Effective Planning in Parks and Recreation

As a park and recreation professional, you must set the strategic direction of your agency, division, or even special event. CPRS has created a strategic planning model, the VIP Action Plan, for you to position your agency and programs with your citizens, policy makers, and participants.

Set your vision	Parks and recreation creates community through people, parks, and programs.
Operate with a sense of values	Inclusivity and accessibility, diversity of experience, spirituality, lifelong learning, service to community, environmental stewardship, personal development, healthy lifestyles, professional growth, fun and celebration.

Articulate the mission	Strengthen community image and sense of place	Foster human development
	Support economic development	Increase cultural unity
	Strengthen safety and security	Protect environmental resources
	Promote health and wellness	Facilitate community problem solving
		Provide recreational experiences

Ensure personal and professional development	Skills and competencies include strategic thinking, leadership, application of technology, research and evaluation, outcome-based management, political dynamics, understanding of ecosystems, human development, resource development, and prevention models.
Execute for the short, medium, and long term	Strategies to consider: improve communication, partnerships, workforce development; strengthen park and recreation ethics; focus on results and outcomes; document best practices, public policy, and resource development.
Measure your results	Community-based performance measures Professional-based performance measures

the eight strategies that we recommend, along with detailed lists of how you and your agency might implement each strategy in your community.

Chapter 6 focuses on the practical implementation of your VIP Action Plan. We tell you about how to form an action team and how that team can develop concrete action steps. We also look at choosing your goals and determining a way to measure them.

Once you've read through part I, you should have a solid understanding of what the VIP Action Plan is, how to use it, and what it can do for you and your park and recreation agency. We hope that you will find the Action Plan to be just the tool you need to develop effective programs and policies, position your agency as a leader, and show others the crucial role that our profession plays in creating healthy communities.

1

What Is the VIP Action Plan?

If you don't know where you're going, any road will get you there.

—*Lewis Carroll*

Knowing that 10 years from now the political, economic, and technological environment will be very different than it is now and, in all likelihood, we won't be doing things the same way, who *exactly* is looking 2 to 10 years into the future to assess the needs of the park and recreation profession? Who is determining the services that will be needed and desired by community residents? Who is developing an action plan for the park and recreation profession to ensure our continued existence? The California Park & Recreation Society (CPRS), in their VIP Project, provides a road map for the park and recreation profession.

VIP stands for these things:

Vision is the power of anticipating what will or may come to be and the ability to foresee what will happen. It is a mental image created by the imagination. It is intelligent foresight.

Insight is the capacity to discern the true nature of a situation.

Planning is a technique to formulate a detailed scheme, program, or method that leads to accomplishing a goal (or our vision).

The purpose of the VIP Project is to be proactive in determining the future of the park and recreation profession through development and implementation of a vision and action plan for professionals and the profession as a whole to create future success. The VIP Project developed a strategic planning tool called the VIP Action Plan, which is meant to accomplish these objectives:

- Place the park and recreation profession at the table when critical issues are framed and decisions are made.

- Proactively address future trends that will affect the profession.

- Meet the needs of a rapidly changing society.

- Give the park and recreation profession a common vision leading to our preferred future.

The VIP Action Plan positions park and recreation professionals as vital partners in building strong communities. By proactively addressing our future, we strengthen our profession and ensure future success. Other professionals, policy makers, and constituents will take notice of our presence and our purpose. Park and recreation professionals will be recognized for their vital role in creating healthy communities, families, and individuals.

Let's begin by looking at what the VIP Action Plan is and how you can use it to improve your work and your agency. We then examine the philosophies behind the plan and consider the objectives and benefits of the VIP Project that developed the Action Plan. Finally, we describe who can use the plan and how they can use it.

Providing creative and safe places for children to explore and imagine is part of the core mission of parks and recreation.

OVERVIEW OF THE VIP ACTION PLAN

Strategic planning is creating a vision of the future and working toward that expected future. It's a deliberate process that examines the past, where you are today, and where you want to be in the future. It's an effective process to ensure short-term decisions are made in order to accomplish long-term goals.

Strategic planning answers the three big questions:

1. Where are we today?
2. Where do we want to be in the future (vision, mission, and goals)?
3. What should we be focused on today (trends, implementation strategies, objectives, performance measures, tactics) in order to make it more likely we will be where we want to be in the future?

Strategic planning is a simple process that has incredible power to energize your organization and bridge the gap between long-term vision and day-to-day tactics. Ask anyone in your agency or department why they are doing what they are doing, and you will probably get one of two explanations:

- For 85 to 95% of the time they deal with day-to-day operations. They deal with the legacy of commitments to customers—offering programs advertised in the brochure or doing ongoing maintenance and operations of parks or facilities.
- The remaining 5 to 15% of the time they look to produce key results—those results, objectives, and outcomes that will make the future different and better. All employees must know what these key results are if they are to be achieved.

Accomplishing key results will literally change the status quo. The VIP Action Plan shifts our focus from the day-to-day operations to defining those key results (the vision and mission) and how we will achieve it. Figure 1.1 shows a flowchart of the VIP Action Plan.

The core values are combined to form a vision for park and recreation agencies and professionals: "We create community through people, parks, and programs." The ways in which we create community are listed in the nine mission statements. Examining key trends in society and locally leads to opportunities to meet the mission, especially when staff have the core competencies. Eight strategies can be used to accomplish our mission through the opportunities we choose, and we can measure how well we accomplish that mission by setting concrete goals and assessing them periodically. In each chapter in part I we look at a distinct part of the VIP Action Plan in more depth.

VIP ACTION PLAN AS A TOOL

The CPRS and its members charted new territory as we developed the VIP Action Plan. It is more than a plan for a single organization—the plan is meant for the entire park and recreation profession. By developing an action plan that articulates

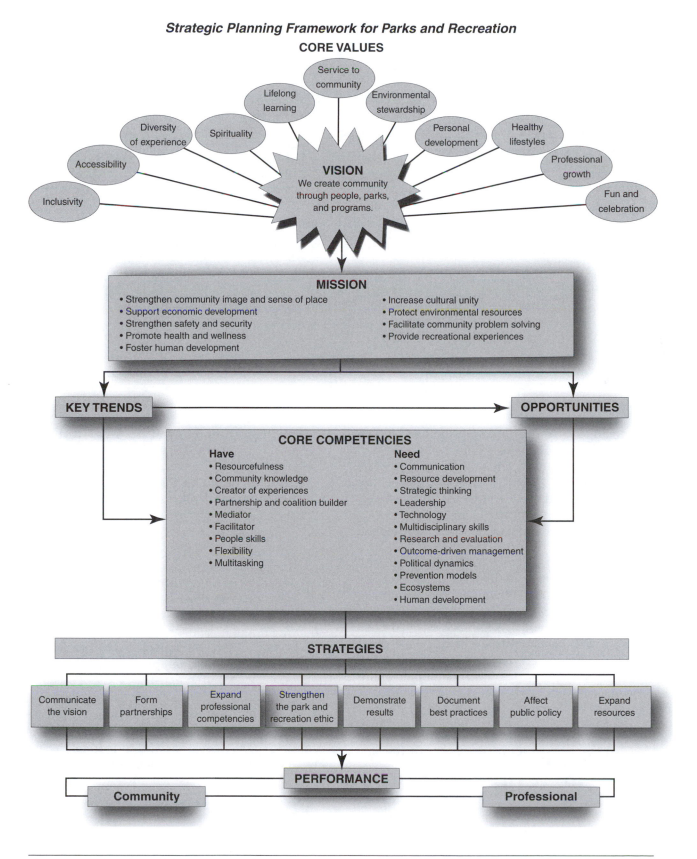

Figure 1.1 Flowchart of the VIP Action Plan.

VIP *in Action*

The San Carlos, California, Parks & Recreation Department started in 2000 by integrating the values, vision, mission, core competencies, and use of the implementation strategies to improve services, train staff, and create partnerships within the community. The department noted a 20% increase in its budget in the second year of a two-year budget cycle when normally only minor adjustments are made. The department received a 1% increase in its budget, despite the city's reducing the overall city budget by 12%; and the department received funding for two capital improvement projects during the 12% overall city budget reduction.

When discussing how to address the city's budget deficit, the city's police chief said he could not support a reduction in San Carlos Youth Center programs since it would mean an increase in his costs because the youth would have nothing posi-tive to do. City manager Michael P. Garvey stated, "The VIP Plan has raised the level of professionalism in parks and recreation. The community can now see that the services provided reflect professional planning. No longer do citizens see recreation leaders as 'people with whistles.' The average person now understands that careful planning is behind today's programs, programs that offer a richness and variety not seen before, and offer this right here in their own community" (personal communication, 2002).

The City of La Mirada (California) used the VIP Action Plan when developing a Community Services Needs Assessment and Community Services Model Plan. This effort helped guide the development of several major projects, including the $38 million "Splash" La Mirada Regional Aquatic Center (personal communication, 2007).

and demonstrates the outcomes provided by the profession, parks and recreation will be recognized as an essential community service. The park and recreation profession will become more self-sufficient and receive broader support, and consequently it will not be the first public service to be reduced or eliminated in difficult economic times.

The plan must be implemented through collaborative partnerships—including contributions that will be made by individuals; specific public, private, and nonprofit organizations; and state and national professional associations. Imagine the collective power that we can have by working toward a common vision and purpose, knowing that the strategies we use in our own communities and agencies will affect the profession as a whole.

CORNERSTONE PHILOSOPHIES OF THE VIP ACTION PLAN

The following philosophies guided the development of the VIP Action Plan:

• *Developing broad-based knowledge and support.* We looked inside and outside of the park and recreation profession to find answers, solutions, and partners. We recognized the diversity of our profession's service delivery system, so we sought out and called on our partners as we looked to the future of our profession.

• *Creating a vision that has relevance to all within the park and recreation profession.* The vision transcends agency boundaries and is relevant to professionals with diverse interests and who work in diverse settings—students and administrators; educators and practitioners; outdoor recreation professionals and programming staff; therapeutic, aging, and aquatic specialists; and citizen volunteers, park planners, park maintenance professionals, and park users.

• *Making the VIP Action Plan user friendly by offering a variety of implementation strategies.* The VIP Action Plan will be used to meet community needs and to strengthen the park and recreation profession. The plan is easy for individuals, organizations, and agencies to adapt for use.

VIP PROJECT OBJECTIVES

The VIP Project supports dissemination and use of the Action Plan and development of tools that support use of the plan. The objectives of the VIP

Park and recreation programs address many social conditions, such as the nation's obesity crisis.

Project are in italics. After each objective, the progress to date is described.

• *Create a vision for the future of the park and recreation profession that transcends agency boundaries and constraints and provides a common understanding of the profession's role in society.* The VIP Project includes a vision statement and defines the business of parks and recreation (the mission). This is the critical first step in bringing us together to capitalize on our collective strength as a profession. A number of agencies in California and other states have adopted this vision. Additionally, the VIP Action Plan is being taught at several California universities through management and program planning courses.

• *Bring together a diverse group of players in the park and recreation profession and related professions to create a common vision and shared strategies to prepare the industry for the 21st century.* The VIP Project has engaged professionals from the health care, public health, public safety, nonprofit or community-based, higher education, and economic development professions. In developing the VIP Action Plan, the professionals administered a questionnaire to both park and recreation professionals and allied professionals. One-on-one interviews were conducted with leaders in a vari-

ety of fields: public health, education, commercial recreation, government, and transportation. Interviewees included Derrick Crandall, president and CEO of American Recreation Coalition; Ester Feldman, Feldman Associates; Gary Yates, CEO of California Wellness Foundation; Marsha Mason, California Department of Transportation; Ted Gaebler, author and local government consultant; and Marian Bergeson, former California state senator and secretary, State of California Office of Child Development and Education.

• *Identify common and critical issues affecting the delivery of park and recreation services in California and develop strategies to address them.* The development process of the VIP Action Plan included interviews, questionnaires, a trend analysis, and workshops with professionals inside and outside the field of parks and recreation. Nearly 100 professionals participated in the VIP Summit held October 1998 to develop strategies that address the issues critical to our profession.

• *Identify trends affecting delivery of park and recreation services in the next 2 to 10 years, then develop strategies to address the most prominent and relevant trends.* A trends analysis for parks and recreation is discussed in chapter 3.

• *Identify opportunities to enable the park and recreation profession to affect the course of societal trends.* The trends analysis sets the stage for an emerging leadership role for park and recreation professionals. By taking strategic actions and pursuing the opportunities identified in the plan, we can affect the course of societal trends and our reactions to them.

• *Identify areas of research that are lacking or missing to support the future direction of the profession.* Research and evaluation are a specific implementation strategy area in the action plan.

• *Create tools and solutions, and identify opportunities that will assist park and recreation professionals and their organizations in maintaining relevance and value into the future.* Each year the California and Pacific Southwest Recreation and Park Training Conference includes educational sessions that teach the core competencies, market opportunities, and implementation strategies. CPRS has also created tools to assist park and recreation professionals in their implementation of the action plan. You can access these tools at www.cprs.org. For a listing of those tools, see appendix E.

• *Develop evaluation tools for the end user of the Action Plan, including recommendations for quantifying and measuring the success of organizational efforts.* The plan includes suggested performance measures that individuals, agencies, or organizations can adapt to measure their progress in achieving organizational goals and objectives.

OVERALL BENEFITS OF THE VIP PROJECT

Following are the benefits of the VIP Project to the park and recreation profession:

• *Tools for the future.* This extensive planning endeavor provides park and recreation students, educators, and professionals with tools to address the future of the park and recreation profession. VIP Action Plan concepts (such as the values, vision, and strategies) can be integrated into existing curriculums, particularly the courses focused on principles of park and recreation administration and program planning.

• *A common vision.* Park and recreation professionals, many of whom are CPRS members, participated in a planning process to develop a common vision for the future of the profession. This vision is intended for *all* professionals; it is the profession's vision. This common vision will prepare professionals to deal with future uncertainties. The vision is being applied in other states and has shown that it transcends geographic and demographic differences.

• *Higher-quality professionals.* As professionals develop a greater understanding of this larger vision for the future of the park and recreation profession, citizens will be better served. Partners, policy makers, program participants, and park users will benefit from park and recreation profes-

Children involved in an organized playground activity can learn essential social skills necessary for their development.

sionals who understand the overall outcomes of the parks, facilities, and programs they offer their constituents.

- *Ability to be proactive.* The VIP Action Plan is a tool for professionals and students to help them be proactive, not reactive. We are empowered as a profession when we acknowledge and support collectively a shared vision, values, and mission.

- *An adaptable, usable plan.* The plan can be adapted and used by individuals and park and recreation agencies to help guide and direct their own action-planning process locally.

WHO CAN USE THE VIP ACTION PLAN

Figure 1.2 shows the many ways to apply the VIP Action Plan. It takes the participation and interrelation of many groups to make the VIP Project's implementation a success. Consider these possibilities:

- *As an individual professional,* you are in control of your personal professional vision. What do you want to accomplish as a park and recreation

professional? What do you want to be known for in the community where you work? Do you want to be known as a person who runs the local swimming pool, or do you want to be known as a professional who creates community and promotes health and wellness or fosters human development? Do you want to be known as the park worker who plants the trees, or do you want to be known as the professional who creates the park and strengthens the community's image and sense of place or as the professional who protects the community's valued environmental resources?

- *As a student (full or part time),* you are in the optimal place when it comes to influencing the future of the profession. Learning how to express yourself about your career in parks and recreation will enhance your employability. People hire individuals who can communicate clearly and distinctly and have an understanding of the broad values, vision, and mission of the profession.

- *As an agency director,* you have the tremendous responsibility and opportunity to influence the community's health, safety, economic prosperity, and livability through the people, resources, and infrastructure you manage and direct. Employers are looking for leaders who know where they

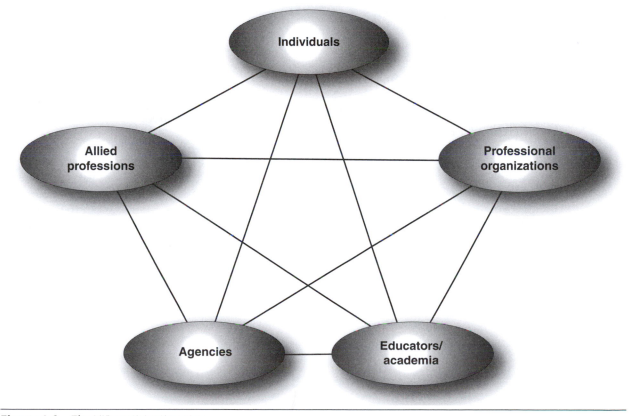

Figure 1.2 The VIP participation star.

are going and can express both short- and long-term goals clearly and with passion. Additionally, your agency will be sought as a place to work by the best and brightest professionals and students if you communicate clearly the vision and goals of the agency. The VIP Action Plan gives you those important goals, words, and tools. CPRS made the conscious decision that it would make the VIP Action Plan free to all agencies, individuals, educators, universities, and state and national park and recreation associations interested in advancing the shared values, vision, and mission of the VIP Action Plan.

• *As an association (local, state, or national),* individuals join associations for networking, professional development, tools, technical assistance, advocacy, and trends. The VIP Action Plan is a powerful professional development tool. It outlines core competencies needed for professional success and each of the implementation strategies can be applied to the association as well as an

agency. Several state park and recreation associations, including the Oregon Recreation and Park Association, the Michigan Recreation and Park Association, and the South Carolina Recreation and Parks Association, have already adopted the VIP Action Plan. Check to see if your state association is an adopter of the plan.

• *As an educator,* you influence students' thinking and learning. The VIP Action Plan has been integrated into program planning, park and recreation management, and student internship opportunities.

This chapter introduces you to the VIP Action Plan and its component parts. The VIP Action Plan is a strategic planning tool for anyone working in or studying the park and recreation profession. In this profession, we want to be known for what we can accomplish for (or provide to) individuals, families, neighborhoods, communities, and the nation as a whole. The VIP Action Plan transcends

Describing What You Do

Before you begin this exercise, have a pen and paper ready to answer the following questions.

You have many opportunities to share with others what you do for a living or what you are studying in college. How many times have you responded to the question "What do you do?" with an answer such as "I run a swimming pool" or "I'm director of a park and recreation department" or "I'm responsible for landscape planning and design" or "I run the special events"?

Write your standard answer to the question "What do you do?" or "What are you studying in college?" Write it without thinking about it.

Sometimes the person who asks the original question looks at you and asks again, "But, what do you *do*?" People are still perplexed about what we do because we usually answer with a job title or general responsibilities rather than accomplishments.

What if you responded to the question "What do you do?" with phrases such as these:

- "I foster human development" for the recreation supervisor, coordinator, leader, or senior center director.

- "I promote health and wellness" for the therapeutic recreation supervisor, park planner, aquatic director, or teen center director.

- "I create a sense of place and community identity" for the landscape planner, park and recreation director, or park superintendent.

- "I create community through people, parks, and programs" for everyone working in parks and recreation.

Each of these responses reflects a direct outcome of the VIP Action Plan's mission for parks and recreation (described in chapter 2). These responses express the outcome of the work, not the "doing" of the work. People are curious about the *why* of your work. These responses tell them why, and you can then follow up by sharing the programs, services, or products you are responsible for that bring about these outcomes.

Now, take a moment and rewrite your answer to the question "What do you do?" or "Why are you making parks and recreation your career?" Consider what the big-picture outcomes are for the work you do.

the profession's specializations (such as park planning, programming, aquatics, seniors, therapeutic recreation, and sports) as it provides consistency of values, vision, and mission, which we'll look at more closely in chapter 2. Understanding these key concepts will excite and motivate you to use them in your own work setting, whether it's agency-wide, within your division or department, or in your day camp program. As a student, you will deepen your understanding of the profession and what it can accomplish for individuals, families, and communities.

2

Core Values, Vision, and Mission

Park and recreation services are provided by a diverse community of people: volunteers; professionals; specialists in aquatics, aging, park planning, programming, youth sports; allied professionals; and nonprofit and for-profit organizations. Yet, those diverse professionals have a shared belief in certain principles and values. Those principles and attributes should guide all plans, partnerships, and activities. Such values form a foundation for parks and recreation that will meet the needs of your constituents.

In this chapter we describe the core values, vision, and mission for parks and recreation. The values shared here are unique: We are the professionals who bring those values to the communities we serve. We use the values in our decision making, planning, and programming. Here we show you how following the values, vision, and mission can help you to position your agency in a good light and link the work you do to the mission of parks and recreation. The examples of how various park and recreation agencies have used the elements will give you ideas for working them into your own agency and program planning.

ARTICULATING OUR CORE VALUES

The foundation of the VIP Action Plan, Creating Community in the 21st Century, is our professional values—those beliefs most valued by park and recreation professionals. These values are enduring, not transient. They communicate what we stand for and what is important to us. Our values also provide a framework for professionals to refer to and rely on in their effort to achieve their mission and vision.

Although we could have included many values in the VIP Action Plan, such as integrity, ethics, honesty, and teamwork, we focus on those values that are unique to the park and recreation profession. These are values that we bring to the community, not values you would expect from planning, public safety, or public works.

The following values were selected after much discussion, interviews, reflection, and finally, agreement:

Inclusivity

Accessibility

Diversity of experience

Spirituality

Lifelong learning

Service to community

Environmental stewardship

Personal development

Healthy lifestyles

Professional growth

Fun and celebration

For example, the profession's value of environmental stewardship is shown by preserving and protecting open space, riparian habitat, rivers, streams, lakes, and the coast; by agencies' conducting recycling programs and using

Courtesy of the Oregon Parks & Recreation Department

Protecting natural resources from development or degradation is the responsibility of local, state, and federal park agencies.

recycled products; by organizing community-wide clean-up of rivers, trails, streams, and the coast; and by providing environmental education and nature interpretation programs. The profession displays its value of spirituality by bringing people together in fellowship at community-wide events and by providing places for personal reflection, enjoyment, and peace, such as the vigils held in parks after the September 11, 2001, attacks on the World Trade Center and the Pentagon or classes in meditation, tai chi, yoga, and feng shui. Additionally, the agency may offer use of community facilities to faith-based groups at reduced fees or at no cost.

Harmony in values is necessary for success. Harmony in values means the values of the profession are compatible with each other and the behaviors of the professionals. Harmony in values provides these benefits:

- A sense of common direction for all professionals
- The social energy and esprit de corps to move the profession into action
- A framework for decision making and action
- A sense of stability and continuity in a changing environment

What Are Your Values?

Are the VIP values the same values that you hold? Figure 2.1 is a discussion guide to help you and others in your agency have a conversation about your core values. This guide can be used for a small planning group or for a staff retreat.

STATING OUR VISION FOR THE FUTURE

The vision statement describes the preferred future of the park and recreation profession. It uses language to convey a sense of how success will look and feel, and it reflects the unique concerns, goals, values, and aspirations of the park and recreation profession. It also shapes future efforts of the agency, organization, or profession.

The VIP vision statement is "We create community through people, parks, and programs."

This statement is described more fully in figure 2.2 (see page 16).

IDENTIFYING OUR MISSION

After identifying our values and creating our vision statement, we identified our mission. The mission is essential to building our future as a profession. A mission is defined as a specific task with which a person or group is charged, a calling or vocation, or a body of persons sent to perform a service

FIGURE 2.1

Discussion of Core Values

- ☐ Inclusivity
- ☐ Accessibility
- ☐ Diversity of experience
- ☐ Spirituality
- ☐ Service to the community
- ☐ Environmental stewardship

- ☐ Personal development
- ☐ Healthy lifestyles
- ☐ Professional growth
- ☐ Lifelong learning
- ☐ Fun and celebration

The core values in the VIP Action Plan, Creating Community in the 21st Century, can be linked to your day-to-day experiences in the workplace. The process of personalizing the values and hearing about the experiences of others will help you articulate the values to others in the profession.

The following questions are a guide for discussion. Have the group members answer the questions individually. Follow up with a small-group discussion of values. Participants should be encouraged to share what they are comfortable in sharing, and all should agree to honor confidentiality.

Tip: Provide index cards or notepaper for this exercise.

1. What values listed previously are the most important to you? How do you act on them in the workplace in relation to your colleagues and customers?
2. What values are fundamental to how your agency conducts its business and treats people?
3. Are these values demonstrated visibly day to day in your agency's philosophy, programs and personnel practices, customer service, and staff development? List some examples of how this is done.
4. What values would your customers say are demonstrated by your agency?
5. What values do you (and your agency) find difficult to demonstrate or articulate? Why?
6. What values do you intend to start acting on as an individual park and recreation professional? What values do you want your agency to demonstrate? How can you make this happen?
7. How can those values be manifested in the most diverse, broadest way possible?

Actions we will take as a result of this discussion:

_____

_____

_____

_____

_____

_____

_____

From California Park & Recreation Society, 2008, *Creating Community* (Champaign, IL: Human Kinetics).

FIGURE 2.2

The VIP Vision

Creating Community in the 21st Century is more than an action plan for CPRS and its members—it is a plan for repositioning the diverse profession of parks and recreation for the future. The plan reflects the values and beliefs of our diverse profession.

We

The park and recreation profession includes commercial and for-profit organizations, such as health clubs and equipment vendors; nonprofit organizations, such as the YMCA and Boys & Girls Clubs; natural resource agencies, such as the U.S. Forest Service, National Park Service, and county and state parks; therapeutic recreation agencies, such as hospitals, rehabilitation centers, and long-term care facilities; community colleges and universities that prepare our future professionals; adult education providers who offer lifelong learning opportunities; park professionals who preserve the natural environment, enhance safety, and protect our valuable resource investment; special districts and local recreation agencies that provide park and recreation opportunities to local residents; students who are the professionals of the future; and citizen volunteers who provide many direct services. All are part of the vision for the future.

Create

To create is to bring into being or to cause. This word emphasizes the active role of parks and recreation in the task of creating community.

Community

Community is a sense of belonging, ownership, and common purpose that develops among people who live or work together as a social unit. Within the park and recreation profession, a community may be a city, county, hospital unit, park and recreation district, senior center, national park, neighborhood, for-profit business, or nonprofit agency. It includes both your coworkers and the clients you serve.

Through

Park and recreation often delivers services through people. Our staff and volunteers make connections with our clients and residents to improve lives. It is this person-to-person contact that relieves the loneliness of senior citizens, reduces the stress and isolation of working adults, and inspires and teaches youth to become productive community members.

People

Park and recreation professionals mobilize people to celebrate, learn, and solve community problems—including building trails, coaching sports leagues, and tutoring youth at risk. We are the essential connection to people and their needs in the communities and settings that we serve.

Parks

As a profession, we are known for our parks and open space. They are the green infrastructure that is essential to our economy—from the peaks of Yosemite National Park or the valley of the Grand Canyon National Park to a neighborhood park in the midst of New York City. We provide relief from urban development, preserve the environment, and provide opportunities for recreation through our facilities. In addition to parks, we provide many types of facilities today to meet the needs of our customers—water parks, health clubs, wilderness areas, skate parks, and community centers. In the vision statement, the word *parks* can be interpreted as any facility provided by parks and recreation to meet needs.

Programs

Programs can be recreation activities, services, or organizational structures designed to produce specific outcomes or benefits to our clients. Historically, our programs have also been an important means of connecting with clients and creating community. As such, these programs must be acknowledged in our vision statement.

or carry on an activity. A mission statement simply describes why an organization or profession exists, its calling, or its specific tasks. A mission statement states a common direction. It mobilizes people, students, volunteers, agencies, educators, and colleges and universities around why we do what we do and how we do it.

The mission statement describes the intended outcomes to be provided by parks and recreation. Those outcomes are necessary for developing healthy individuals and communities. This mission of parks and recreation was crafted from feedback obtained by professionals, allied professionals, local and state policy makers, and educators throughout the action-planning process.

The following is the mission of parks and recreation:

- *Provide recreational experiences.* Through programmed and self-facilitated recreation, a variety of benefits to individuals and society are achieved. Recreational experiences also are important as an end in themselves for personal enjoyment.

> Values are fun and celebration, diversity of experience, and personal development.

- *Foster human development.* Park and recreation services support and facilitate social, intellectual, physical, and emotional development of all ages and abilities.

> Values are personal development, spirituality, lifelong learning, and professional growth.

- *Promote health and wellness.* Participation in recreation activities and programs improves physical, mental, social, and emotional health.

> Values are healthy lifestyles, accessibility, and inclusivity.

- *Increase cultural unity.* Parks and recreation increases cultural unity among individuals, neighborhoods, and communities through programs and community-based events that promote cultural understanding and celebrate diversity.

> Values are diversity of experience, inclusivity, and accessibility.

Courtesy of California Park & Recreation Society

Bringing residents together to celebrate historical or cultural events can help to strengthen the social fabric of the community.

Courtesy of the City of Eugene Parks & Open Space

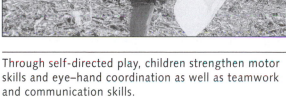

Through self-directed play, children strengthen motor skills and eye–hand coordination as well as teamwork and communication skills.

Courtesy of City of Eugene Parks & Open Space

Public park and recreation agencies at all levels of government are key to maintaining the integrity of our natural world so future generations may experience all that nature has to offer.

• *Facilitate community problem solving.* Park and recreation professionals and agencies facilitate and lead to resolve community-wide problems. Examples are park and recreation agencies' coordinating free transportation service for youth, disabled, or senior residents; removing graffiti throughout the community; and providing before- and after-school care for working parents and caregivers.

Values are service to community and inclusivity.

• *Protect environmental resources.* By acquiring and protecting valuable resources such as open space, rivers, streams, greenways, view sheds, forests, and other habitat areas, natural resources are protected, and habitats required for the survival of diverse species are preserved.

Values are environmental stewardship and spirituality.

• *Strengthen safety and security.* Park and recreation professionals provide safe environments for recreation activities and design programs and services specifically to reduce criminal activity. Through park and facility design, we work toward eliminating injuries and accidents. Park and recreation professionals teach skills and supervise activities such as swimming, diving, and safe boating. We provide park rangers or officers to ensure the public's safety.

Values are service to community and accessibility.

• *Strengthen community image and sense of place.* Parks, recreation facilities, programs, and community events are key factors in strengthening community image and creating a sense of place. Parks often define a city or community (consider Millennium Park in Chicago, Golden Gate Park in San Francisco, Forest Park in St. Louis, and Central Park in New York City).

Values are service to community, inclusivity, accessibility, spirituality, and personal development.

• *Support economic development.* Recreation programs and facilities attract and retain businesses and residents as well as attract tourists. Parks and recreation provides jobs and generates income for the community and for local businesses.

Values are service to community and personal development.

Positioning Your Agency

The term *positioning* is gaining prominence in parks and recreation because of the research of Dr. John L. Crompton from Texas A&M University's department of recreation, parks, and tourism sciences. According to Crompton, positioning is the *process* of fostering a desired state of the park and recreation agency in the minds of citizens and elected officials relative to their perception of other services that are the field's competitors

VIP *in Action*

The City of Myrtle Beach (South Carolina) Culture & Leisure Services regularly communicates the VIP mission. The following excerpt details just some of their summer 2007 programs, events, and accomplishments:

Strengthened Safety and Security

- The Recreation Division saved 2,297 lives by teaching people how to swim!
- The Recreation Division worked to eliminate "latchkey" kids by providing a safe after-school and summer camp environment for 467 children ages 5 to 12.
- Pepper Geddings offered a free skateboarding clinic at the Matt Hughes Skate Park on Tuesdays and Thursdays from 3:30 to 5:30 p.m. We had 33 youths age 11 and under learning to skate in a fun and safe environment.

Promoted Health and Wellness

- We had 2,995 daily visitors to our recreation centers. This number includes daily visits for fitness workouts, lap and open swim, and open gym time for basketball and volleyball. We had 180,272 daily visitors this past fiscal year.
- We sold 64 memberships in one week, and we sold 3,738 memberships during FY 2006/2007.
- We had 2,136 participants registered in instructional classes, fitness classes, and events this past fiscal year.

Fostered Human Development

- The Recreation Division provided youth sports leagues and clinics for 2,555 children this year. These programs keep kids active and productively involved.

- The Myrtle Beach Swim Team Senior Training Group participated in four swim meets in four weeks. They achieved 75 new personal best times!

Protected Environmental Resources

- Field Maintenance "aerified" fields 1, 2, 3, 4, 5, 6, & 7 at Meyers Avenue Complex on the base to reduce field compaction to create more airflow to roots. This enhanced root growth.
- Maintenance sprayed 23-0-23 liquid fertilizer with iron on Doug Shaw Stadium and sprayed 34-0-0 ammonium nitrate on the Myrtle Beach High School practice field and Ashley Booth Youth football field to enhance growth and "green up" these fields.
- The Parks Division took care of 25,000 trees. An average tree soaks up about 1,271 gallons of storm water annually, saving most cities more than $500,000 in infrastructure costs.

Provided Recreational Experiences

- At Crabtree Gym, we offered evening and morning cardio-kickboxing/body sculpting classes, Wallyball open play, skills-n-drills youth basketball clinics, Xpress fitness workout cards, personal training with the Crabtree Crew, and senior volleyball and senior fitness classes.
- In youth programs, we provided 317 summer day camp participants with recreation experiences in sports, organized games, and arts and crafts.
- In adult sports, we had 54 teams participating in men's softball. We had five men's basketball teams and seven women's softball teams participating in the summer leagues.

Adapted, by permission, from City of Myrtle Beach Culture & Leisure Services.

for public money (Crompton, 2007). Positioning your park and recreation agency requires that you understand, provide, and highlight the work you do that is important to policy makers and constituents. This strategy is necessary because of the fierce competition for tax money among other public services, such as police, fire, planning, public works, health and welfare services, and redevelopment. We, as park and recreation professionals, must recognize this fierce competition and articulate the outcomes associated with our services, programs, and parks in language that

Making the Mission Real

Think about how you can incorporate the VIP mission statement into your agency's programs and communications efforts. Use the interactive exercise in figure 2.3 to help you and other staff consider how to apply the statement to your current and future activities.

conveys that the *entire* community benefits from these expenditures rather than only the individual who registers for a class, uses a recreation facility, attends an event in a park, or lives by a park. For instance, the mission of parks and recreation as defined in the VIP Action Plan addresses broader community-wide issues:

- Promoting health and wellness
- Protecting environmental resources

- Facilitating community problem solving
- Strengthening safety and security

Historically park and recreation providers have focused on the public benefits of parks and recreation, particularly in making budget presentations and in doing community outreach. Private outcomes also can be accrued from park and recreation services that might not be promoted as widely as the public benefits, yet they have a place in communicating the benefits of park and recreation services. This does not imply an "either–or" nature to the benefits; it is simply an acknowledgment that park and recreation providers must be able to articulate both the private and public benefits to a variety of audiences, including the policy makers, community organizations, the general public, and even the agency's own staff.

Table 2.1 displays the differing private and public outcomes of park and recreation services.

FIGURE 2.3

Understanding the Mission of Parks and Recreation

1. How does your agency currently promote the business of parks and recreation?
2. How can you promote your services to communicate and implement the vision of creating community through people, parks, and programs?

Here are some statements of how park and recreation agencies can carry out the VIP Action Plan's mission statement. You can use these statements in marketing your programs in your program brochures, press releases, annual reports, and reports to policy makers. Agencies can also organize their budgets around these statements and demonstrate how expenditures are going toward health and wellness, cultural awareness, safety and security, and so on.

Provide Recreational Experiences

For the sheer fun and excitement of it, we offer active and passive recreation experiences for young and old, individuals, families, and groups.

Foster Human Development

Whether it be dancing, cooking, or playing bridge, learning a new skill in a recreational class fosters personal growth as well as social and emotional development. The opportunity to meet new people and socialize with friends in recreation activities fosters social development and self-esteem.

Promote Health and Wellness

Active people are healthy people. Exercise, fitness, and sport programs enhance physical and emotional health and prevent illness. Social recreation programs for older adults offer companionship and can prevent premature institutionalization.

Increase Cultural Unity

Interpretive programs communicate the value of a community's cultural heritage and can enhance cultural awareness and the community's identity. Special events showcase cultural heritage building, community pride, and cultural understanding.

Table 2.1 Private and Public Outcomes

VIP mission: private outcomes	VIP mission: public outcomes
Provide recreational experiences • Belong to a group • Provide challenging opportunities • Provide socialization opportunities • Provide opportunities for creative expression	Provide recreational experiences • Keep youth occupied during nonschool hours • Meet parental safety concerns • Reduce juvenile delinquency • Provide support network for seniors
Promote health and wellness • Improve cardiac conditioning • Reduce risk of diabetes and other illnesses • Reduce depression, obesity • Reduce stress • Maintain physical and mental health • Reduce health care costs to seniors	Promote health and wellness • Reduce health care costs to employers • Make community more attractive for being active • Reduce costs for social service agencies
Protect environmental resources • Provide natural spaces for rest, play • Provide scenic-view sheds • Increase environmental awareness • Provide interaction with nature	Protect environmental resources • Provide shade trees to improve air quality • Protect watersheds for drinking water • Preserve native plants and animals • Enhance property values • Attract tourists • Reduce automotive traffic and consumption of fuel • Manage storm water
Facilitate community problem solving • Residents feel safe in the community • Youth have employment opportunities	Facilitate community problem solving • Connect neighbors to neighbors • Build relationships with and between businesses • Reduce cultural differences • Engage nonprofit organizations
Support economic development • Youth learn work skills • Keep retirees connected with community • Support small-business owners	Support economic development • Create jobs • Promote retail sales (recreational products, equipment, clothing) • Rejuvenate downtown • Improve neighborhood quality
Foster human development • Support positive character development • Learn skills transferable to school and work • Provide opportunity for social expression • Provide opportunity for creative expression	Foster human development • Develop work skills • Keep youth out of trouble
Strengthen community image and sense of place • Provide opportunity to meet neighbors	Strengthen community image and sense of place • Increase community pride • Promote the community to others, which attracts business relocation and new residents

VIP in Action

One way in which park and recreation agencies can aid their communities is by helping them to tackle the growing obesity crisis. Park and recreation agencies, along with urban development, transportation, and planning, can play an important role. For instance, one factor that contributes to obesity is that in many places a car is required for almost all aspects of life. Public health experts are now urging urban planners, park and recreation professionals, and policy makers to consider how they can make changes that compensate for the problems caused by this situation. Community agencies can recognize how development and sprawl create a lack of spaces for physical activity, auto emissions cause air pollution, driving causes stress among those who must drive often, and those who can't drive or afford a car may not have access to places to exercise. A study by the International City/County Management Association and the National Association of Counties Center for Sustainable Communities in 2004 revealed that policy makers consider park and recreation departments as one of the key governmental services to lead their communities' active living efforts. Yet, park and recreation professionals seldom articulate and demonstrate the role they can play in increasing physical activity and thereby reducing the subsequent related health care costs (Frumkin, Frank, & Jackson, 2004).

Following is the VIP Action Plan's positioning strategy:

By taking a customer-driven, outcome-oriented, and collaborative approach, the park and recreation profession can continue to play a central role in maintaining and improving quality of life in our communities.

This strategy recognizes that parks and recreation provides significant benefits to both individuals and communities. It acknowledges that public parks, recreation facilities, trails, open space, forests, wildlife refuges, and a rich mix of recreation programs and services enhance a community's competitive advantage as a place to live and to do business.

An agency's positioning strategy will rely on its ability to communicate and execute programs and services that are targeted to those issues that are important to policy makers and constituents. Failure to do so will weaken that agency's place within the community and may lessen its fiscal and human resources support.

Linking Mission to Your Community

The opportunities through which you carry out the mission must be consistent with the values and vision of your community. For example, if youth involvement is a priority of policy makers and the community, your agency should plan and promote the following aspects:

- *How it fosters human development* by offering before- and after-school programs and summer enrichment opportunities, internships, and junior camp counselor and other employment opportunities

- *How it strengthens safety and security* by engaging youth in meaningful activities led by trained professionals, particularly during nonschool hours

- *How it supports economic development* by hiring youth or hosting community, regional, or statewide sports tournaments

- *How it promotes health and wellness* by preventing alcohol and drug abuse and teen pregnancies by providing programs, spaces, and places for youth

- *How it provides recreational experiences* through all the youth activities you offer

Applying the mission articulated in the VIP Action Plan to community wants and needs can position your agency as a vital player in creating a vibrant and livable community.

USING THE VALUES, VISION, AND MISSION

Here are ways in which your agency can communicate the VIP values, vision, and mission:

- Place the vision on your activity guide and program fliers.

- Create "short takes" (one-page descriptions) that give pertinent information about the agency—make the vision prominent.
- Put the vision on the sleeve or back of your staff shirts or program participant shirts.
- Put the vision on a welcome mat inside each facility's entrance.
- Put the vision on your agency's vehicles.
- Share the values, vision, and mission when you meet with developers. One director told developers that she is in the "creating community" business, which has helped developers understand that adding parks, trails, shade trees, medians, and lakes creates a sense of place and improves the community's image.
- Include your values, vision, and mission on job announcements. Agencies that have done so have indicated an increase in the number of good applicants.

The City of Tracy, California, Parks and Community Services Department incorporated the VIP vision into the following statement about their 2001 strategic plan:

The Tracy Parks and Community Services Department is valued as the primary agency that creates community in Tracy through people, parks, and programs. We have positioned ourselves as an integral part of the city's services to the community. The department's services and programs are woven into the fabric of what makes Tracy an excellent place to live and work. The benefits of parks, recreation, and community services are understood by the community and other city departments as a result of our skills and abilities in articulating and measuring the impacts and outcomes of our programs and services. We are recognized as key players in promoting health and wellness, fostering human development, strengthening safety and security, protecting natural resources, supporting economic development, increasing cultural unity, and reinforcing Tracy's community image and sense of place.

As a staff, our expertise and input are sought out by community leaders, residents, business leaders, education leaders, and other city staff. In all cases, we deliver what we promise, and people can count on us as a department that understands and meets the needs of the community. The department is included as a partner in solving issues that are important to the community. We are known as a team of staff that are resourceful, flexible, multidisciplined, action oriented, and profes-sional. We capitalize on our strengths in these areas and continually strive to improve our inefficiencies and weaknesses.

As professionals, we use current and cutting-edge techniques and service delivery models. We understand how to stay ahead of the changes that will transform how we offer and deliver services to the Tracy community over time. We are able to be at the table with other professionals in facilitating community and organizational problem solving. We hire only the best people, and everyone wants to work for us. Our peers respect us as a proactive, trend-setting organization.

As leaders, we come to the table with solutions and a commitment to holding each other accountable for the department's successes and failures. We have positive influence over key decisions that are made that affect the quality of life for the citizens of Tracy. We build links and partnerships with other agencies in Tracy who also play a role in creating community. We speak out for and defend the availability and access of recreation and community services to all segments of the population.

As a team, we value each other's contributions and know that our strength lies in our diversity. We understand that we all play a role in strengthening the department's position in the community. We can count on each other to work together to make the department the best in Tracy and in the state.

Reprinted, by permission, from City of Tracy, California, Parks and Community Services Department.

RECOGNIZING THE IMPORTANCE OF VALUES, VISION, AND MISSION

Reprinted, by permission, from P. Harnik, 2003, *The excellent park system: what makes it great and how to get there* (Washington D.C.: Trust for Public Land), 16.

Peter Harnik (2006), in *The Excellent City Park System: What Makes It Great and How to Get There*, states that park systems don't "just happen." He identifies the seven measures of a great park system:

1. A clear expression of purpose (or vision)
2. Ongoing planning and community involvement
3. Sufficient assets in land, staffing, and equipment to meet the system's goals
4. Equitable access
5. User satisfaction
6. Safety from physical hazards and crime
7. Benefits to the city beyond the boundaries of the parks

In having a clear expression of purpose, Harnik (2006) states, "A failure to develop this definition [purpose or mission] and to periodically check whether it is being followed can lead to departmental drift due to political, financial, or administrative pressures" (p. 16). The City of Long Beach, California, states this as its mandate, mission, and core values: "We create community and enhance the quality of life in Long Beach through people, places, programs, and partnerships." Although not a word-for-word use of the VIP Action Plan vision, it does embody the key elements. According to Harnik, "This phrase emphasizes that parks and natural areas are a conduit through which community is strengthened—a means to the end, not the end itself. Parks and recreation can involve anything from economic development to facilitation of community problem solving to promotion of health and wellness to protection of environmental resources" (2006, p. 16).

In this chapter the profession's values, vision, and mission are explained in detail. Examples of how agencies and individual professionals are applying the values, vision, and mission are provided. In chapter 3 we take a look at the future and the implications for parks and recreation. Watching and studying trends should become a regular part of your education and ongoing professional development. Being familiar with trends will enable you and your agency to be proactive rather than reactive.

VIP *in Action*

Pamela Yugar, director of parks and recreation in Bell Gardens, California, stated in an e-mail to the author on December 16, 2004, "I . . . used the VIP Action Plan to sell the points of how our [park and recreation] department increased economic development, safety and security, increases home values, health and wellness. I demonstrated through measurement outcomes and performance numbers that we indeed were creating community throughout the city. Long story short, as a result of this [strategic plan] presentation, our department was granted two new full-time positions; we were able to acquire golf course operations that were contracted and we are hiring several new part-time staff to assist with this. Thank goodness for the VIP Action Plan. It really helped me to create a better strategic plan."

Reprinted, by permission, from Pam Yugar, City of Bell Gardens.

3

Key Trends and Opportunities

As a student or professional, you need to be aware of the trends that are affecting how citizens live, work, and play. Knowing the trends can help you position your services with your constituents, staff, policy makers, and stakeholder groups. During the VIP Action Plan planning process, we identified trends that will have a major impact on parks and recreation in the future and will best use distinctive professional competencies. We describe here many demographic, social, and environmental trends. Based on these trends, we then examine their implications for park and recreation providers and target specific marketing opportunities that have growth potential for the future. Since the impact of trends will vary depending on your geographical location and the character of your community, evaluate the trends and marketing opportunities in light of your local needs and priorities.

SUMMARY OF VIP TRENDS ANALYSIS

The *Trends Analysis for Parks & Recreation: 2000 and Beyond* was originally conducted for the California Park & Recreation Society by Tapan Munroe (1999), policy consultant and former chief economist for Pacific Gas & Electric. He studied the political, social, demographic, and government trends in six main areas and identified their implications to parks and recreation:

• *Topic 1: The changing California economy.* This trend recognized the essential role of parks and recreation as a key economic force in the world's seventh-largest economy. Parks and recreation is an integral part of the state's tourism industry (Munroe, 1999).

• *Topic 2: Community economic vitality and other economic impacts.* This trend identified parks and recreation as critical to the economic vitality and livability of a community. It underscored the importance of parks and recreation in attracting and retaining businesses and residents, and as an employer of thousands of workers.

• *Topic 3: Demographic, social, and cultural trends.* This trend documented the growth and change in the California population and the increased demand for park and recreation services. The park and recreation profession also needed to respond to an increasingly diverse customer base as their community's population diversified. Several potential roles for the park and recreation profession emerged from an evaluation of business and social trends: advocate for the underserved, contributor to community safety and security, partner in K-12 education, provider of for-profit services, and promoter of healthy, balanced lifestyles.

• *Topic 4: Political and legislative trends.* This trend area identified major issues at the forefront of California's political climate. Park and recreation professionals must always be prepared for inconsistent public funding by partnering and forming alliances with nonprofit organizations, businesses, and other government departments. Other opportunities under this trend area included participating in the revival of interest in education issues by partnering with K-12 schools and linking park and recreation funding initiatives to other infrastructure issues. In November 2006 California voters passed Proposition 1C, the Housing and Emergency Shelter Trust Fund Act of 2006. This act primarily provides funding for emergency shelters for battered women and homeless families, affordable homes for seniors and working families, and homes for former foster youth. Yet, park funds were included for the acquisition, development, and rehabilitation of parks, recreation facilities, and open space due to policy-maker recognition of parks' relationship to neighborhood development and efforts by park and recreation professionals and advocates.

• *Topic 5: Changing technology and the communications revolution.* This trend area identified the impact of technology in the home, city, and workplace. Potential market opportunities for the park and recreation profession that respond to this trend included providing technology-based recreation and dispersing recreation services to meet changing recreational needs.

• *Topic 6: The fundamental issue—America's time-use pattern.* This final topic area looked into the lives of individual Americans to observe behavior patterns suggesting that people increasingly feel a need to be productive at all times, whether at work or at play. Average TV viewing time is 12 hours per week (Munroe, 1999), which points out that the greatest percentage of our leisure time is spent watching television. Stress reduction, customer satisfaction, and helping customers develop balanced lives will be roles for the park and recreation profession in the future.

VIP ACTION PLAN TRENDS REVISITED

In the development of the VIP Action Plan, noted economist and policy consultant Tapan Munroe conducted a trends scan. He made several projections that have come to pass. For example, he identified, through the "couch potato syndrome," that people would spend their free time in passive activities. He identified that park and recreation agencies should play a major role in educating the public about the health consequences of such a passive lifestyle. Many park and recreation agencies are now active and vocal proponents of healthy and active lifestyles. With the continuing concern about the obesity epidemic that is prevalent in youth, park and recreation professionals must continue their efforts in educating citizens and offering places, programs, and services that promote a healthy and active lifestyle. With the fast pace of change in our society, an updated trends analysis is necessary.

What will be the future of parks and recreation? That question is difficult to answer. The amount of time and money available for discretionary pursuits as well as the nature of those choices will reflect the changes in the world in which we live. So the better question would be how the world will change over the ensuing years and influence the lives of people. This query leads us to the real area of our interest in parks and recreation, another good question with no absolutes. How will these changing patterns and preferences unfold? What possible roles will parks and recreation play in the future? How will parks and recreation meet the needs and interests of people?

Park and recreation trends don't spring out of thin air. Rather, they reflect the myriad of shifts and changes in society that ultimately affect how people live, work, learn, and play. Those types of changes will be used in developing a list of possible directions, challenges, and opportunities for the field. The changes used as a basis for these projections include the following:

• *Who will we be?* Who are we today and how will the demographic changes and social and behavioral shifts related to changing demographics and other environmental factors change the face of our world?

• *Where and how will we live?* Will some parts of the country grow in population and popularity while other regions decrease? Will we be more likely to live alone or in larger, extended groups of friends and families?

• *How will environmental factors affect us?* A myriad of external factors, often referred to as environmental factors, shape people's lives, organizations, and society as a whole. These include economic, legal, political, and science and technology.

Let's look at these changes and what they mean in terms of challenges, opportunities, and suggestions for our field.

Who Will We Be?

What will be the similarities and differences among our population? The most concise descriptor contains four words: younger, older, more diverse.

The United States, like most developed nations, is an aging society. When the aging population is coupled with extended life expectancy, the percentage of the aging population and the diversity related to health and independent living ability among that aging population will increase as well. The population becomes older as childbearing rates are expected to remain low at about the same time that baby boomers begin to age.

In May 2007, a U.S. Census Bureau report indicated that the number of nonwhite Americans reached the 100 million mark. This increased level of minority representation in the United States is due in part to the increased number of Latinos. When you couple the low median age of Latinos with the increased numbers in the 60-plus age group (which is predominantly white), you can begin to see how this country is becoming both older and younger, and more diverse, with diversity in both ethnicity and age (Fulbright, 2007). At the same time, we are experiencing the growth of a widening gap between the wealthy and the poor.

By 2016, we'll be in the throes of demographic shifts that will upend our political, economic, and technological priorities and redefine our markets. (Zolli, 2006, p. 67)

Changes in Life Stages

Even the projections of the changing demographics will not fully paint a picture about who people will be and what their lives will be like in the future. Because of a myriad of factors, the ages and behaviors traditionally associated with various life stages in the industrial era have changed and continue to evolve. The changes include what it means to be a senior citizen, a child, and an adolescent.

Various Faces of Aging

Getting older is a life stage that is changing in a number of ways. As the baby boomers move through this life stage, it is certain that they will change this life stage just as they have every other one that they've experienced. The leading edge of

Courtesy of the City of Eugene Parks & Open Space

As baby boomers begin to turn 60 years old, park and recreation agencies should adapt their programs to address the needs and interests of this demographic segment, or cohort.

the baby boomers turned 60 in 2006, which in turn will mean that this cohort group begins turning 65 in 2011. Some of the factors to keep in mind about the changes in aging include the following:

- The old become even older as the percentage of Americans aged 85 and older becomes one of the fastest-growing groups.

- The values and attitudes of the baby boomers' parents and the baby boomers themselves are very different and will seriously influence preferences and behaviors related to leisure pursuits.

- The maturing baby boomers are changing the definition of what it means to be old as they strive to remain healthy and active.

- A common adage circulating is "60 is the new 40" or even 30 as baby boomers pursue health and vitality to maintain a youthful outlook.

- This new generation of older adults will not retire in the traditional manner as many of them continue to work for financial reasons or the need for health insurance as well as desires for socialization and mental stimulation.

- Memberships in health clubs among the 50-plus generation as well as participation in senior sport programs such as tennis and softball continue to grow.

- Many housing developers have already begun building retirement communities in nontraditional areas not in the sun belt as many of the new older adults will age in place.

Other changes in the definition and parameters of aging include the redefinition of retirement and the new concept referred to as *aging in place.* The decline in traditional retirement is due in part to changes in the workplace agreement related to benefits and lifelong employment. Aging in place is an emerging trend among baby boomers in which they elect to remain in their existing homes or perhaps downsize to a smaller residence within the general geographic area where they have long lived rather than choose to move to warmer climates as previous generations often have done. In fact, the traditional picture of the elderly in the United States, whether it is envisioned as the frail older woman living on a fixed income or a fairly healthy couple living in a retirement community, will not be the case. The extended longevity of people, when coupled with other factors such as money, health, personality, and support systems, will lead to the creation of entirely new groups of older adults. The interaction of the four factors (money, health, personality, and support systems) will create a range of needs based on level of independent functioning. Extroverted older adults in good health with a reasonable amount of financial resources will likely not require specialized services from park and recreation providers, while older adults with health complications, limited finances, and few friends or family members nearby will require more specialized services. Age may end up not being as much a determining factor as will individual preference to be extroverted rather than introverted. Physical health may be a more significant predictor of need than wealth as the old paradigms related to senior centers and nursing homes are replaced by the new ways of aging.

Changing Dimensions of Childhood and Adolescence

The older life stage is not the only one that has changed. The traditional behaviors and expectations of childhood, adolescence, and young adulthood have changed, and previous aspects of these three life stages have blurred. Children now play a large role in family purchasing decisions, even influencing purchases of higher-priced cars and vacations. Young adults are now spending more time residing with parents rather than leaving home to live independently (Howe & Strauss, 2006). The following are some of the observations and projections about these life stages:

- Children seem to become older sooner because of the heightened pace of physical maturing, the growing concerns for personal safety, and the increased level of responsibilities they assume for household chores because of working parents.

- The life stage of adolescence has become increasingly longer. Teens and young adults take longer to leave home, marry at later ages, and spend more time in college or employment searches.

- According to KIDS COUNT, funded by the Annie E. Casey Foundation (2004), one of four young adults in the United States is "at risk" for not making a successful adult transition. Imagine the impact of almost 25% of the population not being able to support themselves financially or emotionally.

Children are now influencing family purchasing decisions, including equipment for leisure time activities.

The increasing diversity of roles and expectations within these previously distinct life stages will significantly influence the actions and activities of discretionary time preferences. The "at risk" identification of a sizeable portion of young adults will become a growing concern to all and a potential focus for public parks and recreation.

Ethnic Diversity

Diversity generally refers to ethnic differences in the population. The U.S. Census Bureau tracks current patterns and makes projections related to how the diversity within the country will change and grow. Following with that "more diverse" label identified as two of the four words describing the future, the population as a whole will become less white and more diverse with particularly large increases in the proportion of people who are of Hispanic and Asian origin. Here are some statistics on this issue (Facts on File, 2001):

- From 2000 to 2050, the numbers of the non-Hispanic, white population are projected to increase from 195.7 million to 210.3 million, representing an increase of 7%. However, the *proportion* of non-Hispanic whites is projected to decrease in the 2040s, which would result in non-Hispanic whites being 50.1% of the total population in 2050, compared with 69.4% in 2000.

- Nearly 67 million people of Hispanic origin (who may be of any race) are projected to be added to the population between 2000 and 2050. Projected growth is from 35.6 million to 102.6 million, *an increase of 188%*. Their share of the nation's population would nearly double, from 12.6% to 24.4%.

- The Asian population is projected to grow 213%, from 10.7 million to 33.4 million. That would double their proportion of the population from 3.8% to 8%.

- The black population is projected to increase from 35.8 million to 61.4 million in 2050, an increase of about 26 million, or 71%. That would raise their share of the country's population from 12.7% to 14.6%.

The Haves and Have-Nots

The term *haves and have-nots* is one that people have used frequently over the past few decades, and the term is generally perceived as referring to those people who are wealthy and those who are not. Mishel, Bernstein, and Allegretto, authors of the 2005 book *The State of Working America, 2004/2005,* maintain that, in spite of a recent economic recovery, many Americans are still dealing with problems and trends associated with the previous economic downturn. They identify the following areas to support this trend:

- *More inequality among family income.* Between 1979 and 2000, households in the top 20% of earners saw real income increase by 70% while households in the bottom 20% experienced a 6.4% increase.

- *Stagnant wages and longer hours.* Middle-income families experienced a 2.2% drop in real wages with an increase in the number of hours spent working.

- *Wealth inequality.* The distribution of wealth is even more unequal than income distribution. The wealthiest 1% of Americans controlled more than 33% of the wealth in the country, while the bottom 80% of Americans controlled only 16%, and an additional 17.6% of households had no wealth or negative wealth control.

- *Poverty increases.* The poverty rate among Americans continues to rise, albeit slowly: 11.1% in 1973, 11.7% in 2000, and 12.1% in 2002.

- *Widespread job shortages.* In 2003, there were 36 states that had fewer jobs than they had previously.

- *Worldwide comparisons.* How does the United States compare to other OECD (Organisation for Economic Co-operation and Development) countries? The United States has a higher per capita income, less mobility from poverty, and the lowest rate of social spending represented as a percentage of the Gross Domestic Product (GDP).

The conditions covered by the term *haves and have-nots* have expanded and grown more diverse as well. *Haves and have-nots* can refer to wealth, health, social support, and other aspects of the human condition. Consider the following variations in this term:

- Increased mobility among society results in an increase in children of aging parents living far from parents, limiting the amount of ongoing support those older adults receive.

- The aging of the population as well as medical advances can lead to an increased number of people with limited mobility.

- The variations in working patterns have created new categories, including overworked, underworked, unemployed, and underemployed.

- The rise in single-parent households reduces the amount of social and emotional support available for both the adults and children in those households.

Where Will We Live?

Several factors influence where people live. One of the key factors is the economy. People cannot live in areas where they cannot find employment that supports their basic needs. This economic necessity related to work results in two patterns: rapid growth in areas where a strong economy flourishes and outmigration from areas where people cannot afford to sustain themselves or a preferred standard of living.

Economic research indicates that the United States is poised to embark on a sizeable economic growth spurt; $25 trillion will be expended by 2030, which is more than twice the size of the current economy (Kaihia, 2005). Planner Robert Lang, as cited in Kaihia's article, predicts that the majority of that investment will be made in 10 major metropolitan areas that he calls "megapolitans." These megapolitans will undergo surging growth in areas that often cross state boundaries and sometimes follow major highways. The following are the 10 megapolitans identified:

Cascadia (Seattle and Portland)

Norcal (Sacramento and San Francisco)

Southland (Los Angeles and Las Vegas)

Valley of the Sun (Phoenix and Tucson)

Gulf Coast Belt (Houston and New Orleans)

Atlantic Seaboard (Boston, New York City, and Washington)

Interstate 85 Corridor (Raleigh-Durham and Atlanta)

Southern Florida (Tampa and Miami)

Great Lakes Horseshoe (Chicago, Detroit, and Pittsburgh)

Interstate 35 Corridor (San Antonio, Dallas, and Kansas City

There is little doubt that certain areas of the country will experience population increases while other areas will find themselves plagued by outward migration of their residents. It has been occurring over the last few decades in certain states in the Northeast: Massachusetts, Pennsylvania, and New York have lost Congressional representation while the megastates, such as California, Florida, and Texas, gain greater representation.

As the population in the United States recently reached the 300 million mark, and 400 million residents are projected over the next 30 years, the issue is not where to find space for the population but rather how to disperse the population throughout the country. Currently, Americans are clustered around major metropolitan areas close to coastlines or bodies of water. Some other interesting patterns have been developing. There appear to be disconnects in proportions of diversity throughout the United States: A large number of various ethnic groups are represented

As cities become larger, providing spaces for active living and play becomes more difficult because of rising land prices. Kids and adults are learning to make do with what is available to them.

in only certain parts of the nation while other segments of the country remain largely untouched by growing diversity. For example, the percentage of foreign-born individuals living in the United States counted in the last census was 11%, while the percentages for California and New York were 26% and 20% respectively. And at the other end of the spectrum were states similar to Vermont and South Dakota, with foreign-born percentages of under 4% and under 2%, respectively (Kaihia, 2005).

The choice of locations within metropolitan areas is changing as well. In areas of the country with increasing growth and high-priced housing, people are moving beyond the suburbs of the urban centers and creating new pockets of growth. As suburbs become more expensive and acquire some of the issues of urban areas, the further migration is quite understandable.

The excitement of the 1990s with the rebirth of America's cities may have been a bit premature. While the relocation of young professionals and

empty-nest suburbanites has occurred, it is not as widespread as initially projected.

How Will We Live?

The size of households has become smaller in this country as the number of people living alone has risen. Some interesting shifts in this category are likely as the aging of parents and the traditions of new cultures in the United States may give rise to more extended family living situations with three generations under one roof. At the same time, the number of nonfamily households may grow and become more varied as aging, nonrelated, single baby boomers form households for economic and social reasons and immigrants entering the States through the more traditional coastal gateways find that they need to put several families under one roof to survive.

Many Americans were shocked when the Census Bureau announced that, if current patterns continue, before the end of the next decade unmarried adults will be the new majority for living arrangements in the United States. These living arrangements are varied: Some people are living alone; others are unmarried, such as single parents; and others are unmarried partners or adult relatives living together.

How Will Environmental Factors Affect Us?

Factors external to individuals and organizations are referred to as *environmental* and include such focus areas as economic, legal and political, science and technology, sociodemographics, competition, and organizational and operational trends. Each of these focus areas is addressed in the ensuing section. Please note that changes or directions in one area can significantly influence other environmental factors.

Economic Factors

This category includes the state of the economy, both global and national, as well as the patterns and shifts within the work world.

Global Economy

There is little doubt that we live in an age of a global economy where the business practices, demographics, and consumption patterns of people all over the world influence the economic outlook in the United States. Although it is apparent that the shift of manufacturing to various developing countries has left some Americans unemployed or underemployed, it simultaneously provides most Americans with access to inexpensive goods. Manufacturing is not the only area of the economy where jobs have been transferred to other parts of the world—the same is true of outsourcing in certain segments of the service economy. Customer-service call centers in various areas around the world are one such example.

While the growth and expansion of a global economy have resulted in an increase in purchasing power for some Americans at the expense of decreased purchasing power for others, the full extent of the global economy has yet to be revealed. Many economists believe that the change to a global economy will result in two types of work opportunities: service and value added. The service sector of the economy encompasses wait staff, day care supervisors, and home health care workers. These occupations that require site-specific contact will continue to be present within our shores. The value-added portion of the global economy will seriously challenge previously lucrative professions, such as attorneys, accountants, and engineers. Software that enables people to complete income tax forms, construct simple wills, or redesign houses will force professionals in many specialized areas to add value to their products and services.

Shift From Information to Conceptual Economy

The growing need for professions and services to add value that cannot be easily replicated in a less expensive version somewhere across the globe will result in a shift to another new type of economy: from the information to the conceptual economy. Daniel Pink is among those recognizing such a shift. The statistics Pink cites in his book *A Whole New Mind* (2005) include projections to reinforce this economic focus:

- One out of four existing information technologies will be outsourced to individuals and companies outside of the United States by 2010.
- A minimum of 3.3 million white-collar jobs along with $136 billion in wages will move from the United States to low-cost countries such as India, China, and Russia by 2015.

Pink cites three major forces behind this economic shift: abundance, Asia, and automation. Abundance refers to the plethora of choices our world provides. For example, while cars consist of an engine and four wheels to transport us from place to place, the choices among companies, models, styles, options, and even colors are almost limitless. This type of abundance moves "right-brain" thinking characterized by creativity into the forefront. Abundance exists in life experiences as well, complete with various ways to conceive children, give birth, celebrate birthday parties, and even hold funerals.

Right- and Left-Brain Thinking

Right-brain thinking is random, intuitive, and holistic, with a focus on looking at situations or challenges as a whole and synthesizing suggestions and ideas. Left-brain thinking is logical, sequential, and rational, with a focus on looking at individual aspects of a situation or challenge.

The Asia factor cited by Pink reflects the ease with which processes and procedures previously requiring high levels of professional competence or expertise can and are being outsourced—often to Asia. This holds even for highly trained and skilled professionals such as accountants and engineers.

The final factor is automation. The automation that Pink cites is everywhere. Those knowledge services that once were considered individually developed for each person have given way to Internet divorces for $200 and do-it-yourself will drafting, among other services. His premise also incorporates a need to shift from left-brain thinking to right-brain thinking in the belief that creativity will lead to innovations and value-added components of the conceptual economy. Implications for changes in the way children learn and play will result from this shift as well.

Many of the traditional approaches to games and activities more closely correspond to left-brain thinking, such as identification of one clear winner; prescriptive rules and directions most likely provided by an outside source; and logic being involved in successful strategies. Play that incorporates right-brain thinking is usually more fluid and flexible, with no individual clearly winning. It is implemented in a structure that invites suggestions and directions from participants. Also, creativity is recognized and appreciated. One such example would be the difference between traditional board games such as Monopoly where there is a lock-step sequence of progress around the board; each purchase follows a set of guidelines, and at the end of the game it is clear who has prevailed. Cranium, a more right-brained game that incorporates different activities, is sold in the same aisle as the more traditional board games but boasts that it is a game for the "whole brain." While it has the traditional board and team approach, the majority of its activities involve group problem solving as well as more artistic renditions through art and drama.

Changes to the Work Agreement

The world of work and careers has changed significantly in a relatively short time. Gone are the days when people worked for one employer for their entire working lives. The unwritten agreement between employees and employers has eroded, resulting in unemployment and underemployment for many Americans. In addition, the change in the work agreement reduces employee loyalty, resulting in Americans' changing jobs more frequently.

Some of the technological improvements and the impact of the global economy have resulted in people's not just changing jobs but changing careers as well.

Changes to Our Way of Living

Many people complain about not having enough time and cite an extensive list of the activities and responsibilities that get shortchanged. Enter the Take Back Your Time initiative, a project of the Center for Religion, Ethics and Social Policy (CRESP) at Cornell University and an initiative of the Simplicity Forum, a leadership alliance for the Simplicity Movement. While the industrial era led to the creation of OSHA to protect employees from accidents and other unsafe working conditions, the Take Back Your Time initiative may provide a similar type of function for the information and conceptual economies.

Our current working patterns and practices continually consume more of people's waking hours, thus eroding quality of life for workers, their health, family relationships, and sense of community. The Take Back Your Time initiative identifies several facts reflecting the state of today's work world (Simple Living Network, 2004):

- Americans are working longer hours now than in the 1950s.
- Current working conditions have us toiling longer than medieval peasants did.
- Americans actually work longer hours than employees in the other industrial countries.
- Americans, on average, work nearly nine full weeks (350 hours) *more* per year than most Western Europeans do.
- Most working Americans average slightly over two weeks of vacation time annually.
- Some American workers get no paid vacation at all; 37% of working women making under $40,000 do not receive a paid vacation.
- Europeans average five to six weeks of vacation each year.

The United States has long been regarded as the center of free enterprise. Americans in all walks of life feel as if they are on a treadmill running as fast as they can and getting nowhere. We have become a nation of overworked, overscheduled, overstressed, and overwhelmed people. We are paying a high price as individuals, communities, and society for this work pace. According to Take

Back Your Time, time stress has these consequences (Simple Living Network, 2004):

- Leads to fatigue, accidents, and injuries
- Reduces time for physical activity
- Supports consumption of high-fat, high-sugar fast foods
- Contributes to job stress and burnout, costing the U.S. economy over $300 billion each year
- Results in less time (and more guilt) with fewer hours to care for children and older parents
- Reduces the sense of community because we have less time to get to know and spend time with the neighbors
- Means fewer hours for volunteering in the community
- Leaves us with less time to be active, knowledgeable, and involved with the community and the decision-making power of voters
- Reduces employment levels because fewer people work longer hours, eliminating the need for additional full-time positions
- Leaves little or no time for people's self-development or spiritual growth
- Contributes to further destruction of the environment as lack of time leads to use of convenient, throwaway products and reduces recycling

Retirement Revisited

Both the concept and reality of retirement as previously practiced in this country will be significantly reconfigured. There was a time when retirement occurred at 65 and retired individuals were "set out to pasture" with Social Security benefits and pensions from employers. In some cases the retirees lived only a few years past their retirement dates.

Today the landscape of retirement is quite different. There are no guarantees that pensions will be an ongoing employment benefit or even that pensions will be there as would-be retirees anticipated, not to mention that Social Security is an ongoing debate at the federal government level. Retirement will take on an entirely new focus in our society. There are so many factors playing into this change, including the uncertainty of today's economic outlook, lack of health insurance coverage until the age of 65, the lack of savings for retirement among the baby boomer

What it means to be a "senior citizen" is evolving due to social, political, and demographic factors. Many senior citizens stay young by choosing active, enriching leisure activities.

generation, extended longevity, and of course the global economy. In fact, many experts call for the "retirement" of retirement.

It is likely that the aforementioned factors, when coupled with baby boomers' desire to stay mentally active and socially involved, will result in several scenarios for retirement in the future, including ongoing part-time employment, flexible working opportunities provided in the years between 60 and beyond, development of business opportunities where boomers can determine their own working conditions, new career options, and periods of work followed by periods of sabbatical on a cyclical basis.

Legal and Political Factors

The role and changes in public opinion and resulting public policy are certain to play a significant role in our future in parks and recreation. While the terms *legal* and *political* are often used together when conducting a critical review of existing information on trends (an environmental scan), differences do exist. *Legal* refers to actual laws and regulations, whereas *political* refers to the process of and attitudes toward various aspects of governing. So future regulations related to the use of snowmobiles in national parks and the sale of mineral rights in national forests are examples of the legal aspect in this category. The discussion by lawmakers and the public, often heated, related to whether any of these policies should be enacted encompasses the political aspect of the process based on and influenced by the public's perceptions and opinions.

Presidential elections and some referenda at the local levels illustrate the sharp divide among Americans. These vastly different sets of opinions and approaches suggest that attitudes and values of Americans will continue to create great political chasms. Discussions in the recent past and present make the case that people in this country continue to feel sharply divided on a variety of important issues. Some version of "red" and "blue" states as seen in the 2004 presidential election is likely to continue and, as it relates to many issues, similar divisions will occur at the local levels. Three areas of particular interest to those in parks and recreation are the growing concerns about environmental issues, promises in public policy funding, and actual policy decisions.

Heightened Interest in Environmental Issues

On the national level, policies such as what activities are suitable in national parks and what types of uses should be permitted in national forests are among those that will generate strong feelings and lobbying efforts between very different constituent groups. The environmental aspects of planned burning and reduction or reintroduction of certain species of wildlife into natural areas will also draw their fair share of differing opinions.

While the United States appears to be divided on environmental issues on the national level, as evidenced by two differing views on global warming, there is a strong sense of cohesion on the local level. The purchase and protection of natural and open space have become a priority in many local communities. According to a press release issued by the Trust for Public Land, after the 2004 elections voters at the state and local levels favored land conservation, as revealed by the 120 communities in 26 states that passed ballot initiatives endorsing $3.25 billion for further protection of land for parks and open space. Since 1997, 1,000 out of 1,301 conservation ballot measures passed, resulting in a 77 percent rate of passage. Trust for Public Land suggests this signals a mandate for land conservation among Americans (2004). However, the underlying causes of environmental erosion and aspects such as global warming will likely assume a front-and-center position in the

Protecting environmental resources is a key mission of parks and recreation. Without concerted efforts at protection, many of our natural areas may be lost to development or pollution.

near future. (See the section titled Natural Environment later in this chapter.)

Promises in Public Policy Funding

Regarding the legal side of an environmental scan, particularly one focused on public parks and recreation, trends in government expenditures are worth noting, as those trends determine the availability of and priority for public funding. Any other requirements that detract from government funding for open space or recreational provisions are areas of concern. The following data provide a sense of priority and trends in this area, including justice services, health care costs, and of course the coming attractions related to government guarantees to older Americans:

- Local, state, and federal governments spent a record $167 billion on justice services in 2001 ($254 per capita for police protection, $130 per capita for judicial and legal services, and $200 per capita for correctional services) (Bureau of Justice Statistics, 2004).
- The overall expenditures in justice activities jumped 366% since 1982. That's nearly 400% in just 20 years; although when adjusted for real money, the increase is "only" 165%. Local governments funded nearly 50% of all direct justice system costs, and states kicked in an additional 35% (Bureau of Justice Statistics, 2004).
- National health care costs have soared over time, rising from 7% of the gross domestic product in 1970 to 14% by 2001, and the end is not in sight. The Department of Health

and Human Services has projected that the national health expenditure will grow to $3.4 trillion by 2013, almost twice as much as the 2004 projection of $1.8 trillion (Library Index, 2004).

- In 2002, the estimated cost for treating diabetes was $132 billion; that is the equivalent of $1 out of every $10 spent on health care. The cost of health care for people with diabetes averaged $13,243 in contrast to health care costs of $2,560 for people without diabetes (Centers for Disease Control and Prevention, 2007).

Just how much will it cost the government to fulfill the retirement benefit promises made to older adults in the United States? A research analysis conducted by *USA Today* (Cauchon, 2006) compiled a list of all taxpayer-based liabilities at the federal, state, and local levels and estimated that each taxpayer will owe over a half-million dollars to each older household. The analysis further enumerates that these government obligations represent a $57.8 billion liability, which is five times the personal debts of Americans.

The following are areas of expenditures contributing to this liability:

- Medicare, the health care program for older Americans, experienced a $4.5 trillion increase in its deficit since 2004.
- The Social Security benefits expended for individuals currently in the system experienced a $2.5 trillion increase in its deficit since 2005.
- Governments at most levels have underfunded the promised pension benefits for military and civil servants.

One overall projection for this public policy, economic picture, includes the following calculation: Social Security, Medicare, Medicaid, student loans, food stamps, farm subsidies, and other entitlements now cost over $1.3 trillion and will cost more than $2.5 trillion in 10 years, even though most baby boomers will not yet be retired (Kotlikoff & Burns, 2005).

Public Policy Decisions

This area is fraught with change and societal wishes and whims. The future in this area will be determined by many issues:

- Who will be voting in large numbers
- Whether we will expend money on the "growing" or the "goldening" (young versus old)

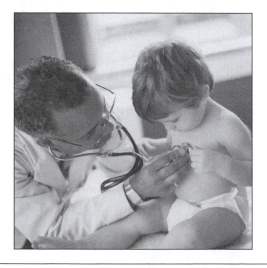

Instilling the importance of health and wellness from a young age is a key mission of parks and recreation.

- What and who will govern the regulations about life and death
- Whether we will decide to ration medical services on the basis of age or conditions

Science and Technology

The progress within the closely related fields of science and technology has significantly changed the ways in which we live, work, learn, and play in this country. The progress produces mixed results along with forward motion. Consider that those born at the turn of the last century had a life expectancy of the mid-40s, and the advent of antibiotics and other medical advances has added years to the average life span. Visualize the impact of those medical advances on the increases in worldwide population and the subsequent challenges arising from such increases.

Imagine how difficult it would have been to create and live in suburbia without the widespread manufacture of affordable automobiles. Then also consider the proliferation of the automobile and how that invention has contributed to air pollution, depletion of natural resources, and possibly the growing levels of obesity in the developed world because of lack of walking in our daily lives and activities.

While the overlap and blurring between science and technology exist, it is also necessary to recognize that science and technology have effects in two distinct but related areas: the natural environment and the human condition. New technology advances also affect how we relate to each other on a daily basis.

Natural Environment

A discussion of science would not be complete without consideration given to environmental concerns around the world. The depletion of natural resources, the population growth creating increased need for clean water and food, the impact of acid rain, and the controversy over global warming are all issues of a scientific nature. These issues have also become political footballs and the subject of great conjecture in public policy circles.

Americans' dependence on various energy sources and preference for acquiring material goods contribute to overall threats to the natural environment. Environmental impact and issues are both macro and micro. The big-picture concerns over global warming and greenhouse gases capture the attention of the world while prolonged dry spells in certain regions of the country and the decrease in fish counts and the sooner-than-expected arrival of spring birds or flowers bring the issues to the local level.

The counterbalance to environmental concerns has given way to the local outcry for communities that are friendlier for walking, biking, and other forms of alternative transportation. The push through local referenda to purchase, protect, and preserve open space that is disappearing due to development's agenda is on the increase. The recognition being afforded urban areas, particularly in cities such as Chicago, where planting trees and restoring parks and natural spaces have become a high priority in public policy, will move this agenda.

The failure of the United States to sign the Kyoto Agreement has resulted in several states' recognizing and implementing the components in the agreement. The independent, nonprofit, and nonpartisan Pew Center on Global Climate Change (2006) endeavors to bring credible information and innovative solutions to the issue of global climate change. The center released a comprehensive plan targeting reduction of greenhouse gas emissions for the United States. One of the key conclusions of this report is that no single policy, sector, or technology can address this issue. Organizations such as Pew will continue to highlight important environmental issues; provide accurate, nonpartisan information; and move this environmental agenda. The future of the natural environment will manifest itself in a truly "glocal" approach where the global issues are addressed in some ways at local levels.

Human Condition

Yes, scientific advances have extended the life span of people in developed countries, resulting in more people living longer and better at the same time. These advances will create new life stages. Older adults (many of them baby boomers) will live, work, and play in the same ways as adults in general do, perhaps with additional time and money to expend. Senior adults will be those who choose to seek primarily social and entertainment alternatives with people of their own age. The frail elderly will be a growing group of Americans whose health conditions curtail even basic life activities and place them at risk for even greater erosion of their health. Such stages will lead to a need for greater and new services for many older people. Consider the impact on today's senior centers and programming.

The extension of life expectancy represented through medical advances also plays a prominent

Public awareness about the lack of physical activity in our society is increasing the demand for bike trails and highway bike lanes.

role in diseases that people contract that cause them to die. At the turn of the 20th century, most of the premature deaths were most likely due to inadequate medications or immunizations for various diseases. Currently people living in developed countries no longer die from typhoid and diphtheria. Today people are more apt to die from causes brought about by a combination of personal choices, genetics, and environmental factors. In this case, environmental factors refer to the physical layout and systems approach inherent in today's society. For instance, in most communities it is nearly impossible to walk rather than drive to do simple errands. The use of all sorts of technology, including TV remote controls, the Internet, and preferences for fast food, has contributed substantially to this new era of disease in the developed world.

The myriad of chronic diseases that are associated with physical inactivity and obesity include cardiovascular diseases, diabetes, and some forms of cancer; these diseases greatly contribute to

rising health care costs. The rapid increase in obesity among children and the near-epidemic levels of type 2 diabetes among youth are significant indicators of the ways in which we live, and those factors affect quality of life and government expenditures on health care.

For our ancestors, the hunters and gatherers, the adrenaline rush created by stress (the "fight or flight" phenomenon) was a positive reaction that enabled them to fight or flee accordingly, thus saving their lives. We carry that stress reaction over to modern life but lack the same types of life-threatening situations. The toll that stress takes in this country continues to surface. There is growing evidence that some reactions to stress contribute to the growing obesity crisis and other behaviors and conditions such as depression and various forms of substance abuse. Several studies have indicated an association between psychopathology, including depressive symptoms, and high body mass index (BMI) or obesity (Chapman, Perry, & Strine, 2005).

The development of medications that potentially extend life expectancy by reducing the risks associated with high blood pressure, cholesterol, and other predictors of cardiovascular disease are welcome additions from the scientific community. However, the flip side of the medication picture is the growing number of Americans who are prescribed medications to alter mood and behavior and deal with stress and anxiety, conditions exacerbated by the pace of modern life.

Technology and Human Relations

Technology is the other half of the science category and has had widespread ramifications on how we live, work, learn, and play, and it's affected us in ways that were only imaginable a short time ago. Technology has led to a paradox of behavior that can be called "connect–disconnect." People check cell phone messages and e-mail from beaches and ski lifts. Young people are connected to people all over the world via the Internet and yet may not even have friends within their local social sphere for connecting and interacting. There is some evidence that suggests that Gen Wired may be losing their ability to converse via speech while their text-messaging skills are growing.

The emerging 21st-century network model, which includes networks such as MySpace.com, changes the face of social interaction. The growing use of blogs as a way to communicate fact, fiction, and opinions will lead to radical shifts in how politics, public opinion, and advertising are conducted around the world. While the 20th-century networks focused on content, this emerging network will go well beyond content and create nonphysical communities that shape values and attitudes and, subsequently, behavior.

The other part of the connect–disconnect equation is the disconnect. Human beings are increasingly becoming disconnected from actual physical human contact and greatly removed from the natural environment. Richard Louv's book *Last Child in the Woods* has struck a chord among many segments of society with his enumeration of the benefits missing from the lives of children and adults because of lack of contact with the natural environment. Studies by the Alfred P. Sloan Foundation between 2001 and 2005 attest to the dearth of real contact among family members. In one such four-year study conducted by UCLA at their Center on Everyday Lives of Families, researchers observed the daily life of households in Los Angeles. The households consisted of both parents working outside the home. They paid a mortgage, had two or three school-age children, and were representative of Los Angeles' diversity. Some of the initial UCLA study findings are of interest to parks and recreation (Wallis, 2006):

- Parents and children live virtually apart from one another during the work week with only a few hours at the end of the day to connect.
- Together time is motion time: Families are involved with lessons, classes, games, or shopping.
- Most family purchases and decisions are driven by the activities of the children; thus the minivan is so popular.
- It appears as if we are moving from a child-centered to a child-dominated society.
- Life and relationships are overscheduled and outsourced with little room for spontaneity.

Sociodemographics

The environmental factor referred to as *sociodemographics* contains almost limitless trends attributed to the intersection of demographic basics such as birth rate and life expectancy, which are then coupled with economics, public opinion, and technology. These come together to change the ways in which we live. Sociodemographics is critical to projecting how people will work and

play in the future, and it is also difficult to assess because of the complex interdependence among the variables within this category.

The close of the 20th century and the onset of the 21st century have shown us that generational differences between the boomers and Gen X have led to a range of issues from child-rearing practices to conflict in the workplace. Household composition is another sociodemographic factor that was dramatically altered and now includes people living alone, blended households, and the increase in same-sex marriages and civil unions. The role of religion in the United States has significantly influenced the political process while technology has blurred the ways in which we work and has resulted in our being connected to the office 24/7.

To limit the sheer number of alternative trends and shifts within this category, it may be more expedient to provide a framework in which park and recreation professionals can monitor such changes more closely and remain aware of emerging patterns and preferences. Four subgroups of factors exist in the web of relationships leading to sociodemographic trends:

- *Core* is the demographic attributes you acquire at birth, such as sex and race.
- *Culture* is shaped by social surroundings and experiences, including religion, education, and income.
- *Choice* is related to both core and culture. It identifies aspects of an individual based on values and attitudes that form preferences and behaviors.
- *Change* is an element that interacts with and substantially influences culture and choice, with factors such as important life events and the more natural rhythms of life stages.

This 4C view of people and the trends accompanying our times can lead to some interesting situations such as these:

- Core: The ability to save babies born with once-debilitating conditions creates issues well beyond whether one is male or female.
- Culture: The growing income and education gaps in the United States, when coupled with the rapid increase in diversity, are certain to become major forces in public policy decision making and service delivery.

- Choice: Limits in today's society are rarely placed on this construct as evidenced by the number of people choosing to live alone or remain childless or become vegetarian. Those examples are only the tip of the iceberg.
- Change: One of the more significant aspects in this category is related to life stage as people marry later, finish school later, and have children later. These changing patterns heighten the importance of life stage as a predictor of patterns and preferences.

Competition

There was a time in the late 20th century when competition in public parks and recreation was perceived as coming from other sectors of the same industry (nonprofit organizations, community-based organizations, private providers, or commercial enterprises). The 21st-century version of competition does not include other providers as much as it does competing forces that shrink the available resources that people and families have for leisure pursuits.

In addition to American adults' increased work hours and decreased time for leisure pursuits, as previously discussed, children are experiencing similar time constraints. Today's children are likely to be overscheduled and therefore have less time for real leisure pursuits. Latchkey children confined to their homes because of parents' instructions and safety concerns are deprived of time that once was spent in outdoor play and recreation.

The other culprit of time erosion for leisure is technology. We are becoming a nation of "screenagers" as ever-increasing numbers of Americans of all ages and income levels are spending more time in front of a screen—computer, TV, video game, and even cell phone. The Kaiser Family Foundation's study (2003) of the role electronics play in the lives of children is enlightening. Here are some of the results from the survey of youth between the ages of 8 and 18 years:

- Youth spend about 6.5 hours per day in front of or plugged into something.
- Youth are spending about the same time watching TV as they did 5 years ago, but they've added newer technology to their daily patterns.
- They spend relatively little time reading or doing homework.
- When multitasking is added to the mix, children are involved with media for about 8.5

hours a day, almost an hour increase from 5 years ago.
- 68% of those surveyed had TVs in their rooms.
- Youth with TVs in their rooms watched about 90 minutes more TV per day and did less reading and homework.

And let's not overlook the most common 21st-century practice referred to as *multitasking*. This term is now a regularly accepted part of American life. We talk on the phone while we check e-mail. We oversee or undertake household chores and child rearing with one eye on the television. Business people make sales calls or hold conference calls from the sidelines of their children's sports games or practices. Multitasking has become a well-regarded practice. People boast about their proficiency, one that results in distractions leading to car accidents, lack of concentration causing some people to suspect early dementia, and further erosion of meaningful social interactions.

Organizational and Operational Trends

A discussion of trends influencing parks and recreation or any entity functioning in the 21st century would not be complete unless the organizational and operational trends brought about by economic and technological changes were cited. Organizations—public, nonprofit, private, corporate, and commercial—do not function in the same manner as they have in the past. The shift in the economy from industrial to information and the array of technological advancements have created new patterns for how organizations conduct their business. The ways in which consumer-oriented companies deliver products and services to people have evolved. Starbucks provides some of the best examples of several of these changes:

- Mass marketing has given way to mass customization. Think of Starbucks and its impact on the once-generic commodity, coffee. Starbucks now boasts nearly 20,000 product variations, and they are all quickly and cordially fulfilled on the basis of individual preference.
- The organization as a creator of products and services for people has given way to the organization and customer as collaborators in preferred experiences. Starbucks does it again.

If McDonald's was the consumer king in the service sector for the industrial era, then Starbucks is the role model for consumer-based organizations in the informational and conceptual economies. Table 3.1 shows how they differ from one another and reinforces the shift in the ways organizations operate.

Many lessons are to be learned and trends taken from the similarities and differences between these two wildly successful consumer companies developed during two different eras.

IMPLICATIONS FOR PARK AND RECREATION PROVIDERS

Trends are actually of very little value unless the information they provide and the shift they suggest are put into practice. This section encompasses an analysis for the industry, suggested organizational changes, and methods for continuing to monitor trends as they develop.

Table 3.1 McDonald's Versus Starbucks Organization Patterns

McDonald's	Starbucks
Conveniently located and seemingly everywhere	Conveniently located and seemingly everywhere
Reasonably priced, prototyped food served inexpensively	High-priced coffee served exactly to the customer's specifications
Emphasis on not having the process take much time	Emphasis on creating a "third place" where people want to spend more time

Techniques for Trend Tracking

No one source can continue to monitor the proliferation of statistics and information being generated, just as no one person can possibly track all changes in society. Professionals will need to become adept at tracking trends in society and adapting their organizations accordingly. Following is a series of activities and alternatives, adapted from O'Sullivan and Spangler (1998), that may help park and recreation professionals fulfill that responsibility:

- *Seek stars.* Observe practices and changes at businesses or organizations that are attractive to consumers and others who attract and retain large numbers of people, such as Starbucks.

- *Go surfing.* In the past, this would have been channel surfing, which can still be the case, but be sure to include surfing the Web to uncover the needs of various target market segments.

- *Watch friends and family.* Observe and make note on changing behaviors and interests among friends and family members. Those emerging interests and changes often identify underlying trends that can be acted on.

- *Make new friends.* As the world becomes more diverse and our lives become smaller because of technology that enables us to remain at home, make a concerted effort to go places and do things that will bring you into contact with people outside of your normal sphere of influence.

- *Observe new words and terms.* Our world is awash in new words and terms, so be aware of them and be sure to discover their meaning and the trends leading to their development.

As always, although many interesting trends are presented here, they will be useful to you only if you take action based on them. Choose one or more of these activities and see if the trends you find can be applied to the programs and policies you use at your agency.

Adapted, by permission, from E. O'Sullivan and K. Spangler, 1998, *Experience Marketing* (State College, PA: Venture Publishing), 390.

Let's frame the following questions in a SWOT analysis:

S: What strengths or values does the park and recreation profession bring with it as we proceed into the 21st century?

W: What are the weaknesses within our industry?

O: What are the emerging areas of opportunity that parks and recreation will encounter?

T: What threats or challenges can parks and recreation capitalize on?

Any list responding to these questions could be extensive, but table 3.2 shows some of the most critical responses.

Strengths

While individuals, organizations, and movements all have particular strengths, four areas of strength inherent in parks and recreation are cited here. In the case of parks and recreation, these particular strengths are sometimes overlooked or not given the focus of consideration warranted:

• *Clean air and water.* People in general seem to value having trees and green space as part of their landscape. The role of parks and recreation in procuring, protecting, and preserving as it relates to the essential nature of life—clean air and water—is one of our strongest assets. Park and recreation agencies provide the green infrastructure for cities, urban areas, and suburban communities.

• *Public places and spaces.* People flock to the many public places and spaces that fall within the operational purview of parks and recreation. Where do people gather for concerts and community events? Where do our nation's youth pursue athletic competition? We are the keeper of the keys for these community assets, and we should leverage their use to address critical social needs.

• *Universal human need.* Once the basic human needs for subsistence are addressed, the need to pursue growth, social interaction, and achievement is universal to all human beings across all life stages. We have long been associated with alternatives and opportunities for all age groups.

• *Recognize our roots.* The profession of parks and recreation is rooted in the good deeds of individuals such as Joseph Lee, Frederick Law Olmsted, Jane Addams, and Luther Gulik. Just as those people recognized the critical needs of society as we evolved from an agricultural to an industrial nation, the recognition and application of a return to our roots are essential to our future.

Weaknesses

All aspects of life have their weak areas that can contribute to their downfall or certainly play a part in their lack of success.

Table 3.2   SWOT Analysis of Parks and Recreation

Strengths	Weaknesses
Clean air and water	Credibility
Public places and spaces	Direct services
Universal human need to grow	Focus on activity over outcome
Recognizing our roots	Fees and charges
Opportunities	**Threats**
Contributions to society Health and wellness	Current way of American life
Adult transition	Competing priorities for time and money
Independent elderly	Escape and entertainment
Building community	Preference for intrinsic leisure activities available within one's residence

Providing spaces for spontaneous and unstructured play gives children opportunities for social interaction.

• *Credibility.* In parks and recreation, one of the most ongoing and critical weaknesses holding us captive is the lack of understanding that people and society have about the value of our services. This will remain our Achilles' heel unless we make progress in this arena. The VIP Action Plan clearly addresses the values, vision, and mission for the profession. Consistently applying these will help us build our credibility as a profession.

Additional aspects that may be related to this lack of credibility and understanding are our reliance on direct services, our preference for activity over outcome, and the proliferation of fees and charges:

• *Direct services.* The focus on providing direct services consumes significant amounts of resources, including staff time and facility capacity, and continues our focus upon individuals rather than society overall. Other roles an agency may play include facilitator, advocate, or partner.

• *Preference for activity over outcome.* It comes as no surprise when decision makers call on park and recreation departments to undertake an unusual request or address an emergency situation because

we seem to have an internal compass that seeks out action. This can be a weakness because it takes away from communicating the important community and social outcomes such as positive youth development, health, and sense of community achieved through park and recreation services.

• *Fees and charges.* There is nothing wrong with people paying to use certain facilities and participate in various activities. The weakness in this area centers on the reliance that park and recreation services have on fees and charges as well as the lack of differentiation between essential services that should be available at no or low cost and those opportunities that should carry with them a break-even or revenue-generating price tag.

Areas of Opportunity

One should never be discouraged or misled by the weaknesses or threats to parks and recreation because the current situation facing individuals, communities, and society overall at this time bodes well for our future contributions. While many challenges face society, those challenges are actually opportunities for our profession.

• *Health.* Today we include a myriad of issues under health. Clean air and water, community design, availability of sidewalks and public transportation, overweight and obesity, and stress reduction and substance abuse are some of the issues. The unique role that parks and recreation can play in helping people find positive pursuits and pastimes supports the overall health of a community and society.

Mission: Promoting health and wellness

• *Successful adult transition.* High school dropout rates are only one indicator that leads to what leaders in the greater Los Angeles area refer to as "social dynamite." Social dynamite brings to our attention that as many as one of every four young adults in the United States is at risk of making a successful adult transition (Annie E. Casey Foundation, 2004). Parks and recreation can assume a powerful role in helping this group acquire needed skills and relationships to ensure their future.

Mission: Fostering human development

• *Independent life stage of elderly.* What is society to do with the large number of older Americans, not

to mention the large group of aging adults (i.e., the baby boomers born between 1946 and 1954) following on their heels? A review of current expenditures and projected services strongly suggests that as a society we may not be able to afford growing old in this country. Involvement in physical activity, social interaction, mental challenges, and new experiences among older Americans will contribute to their ability to remain healthy and live independently for most of their years. Parks and recreation is a core service provider in those areas.

Mission: Fostering human development and facilitating community problem solving

• *Building community.* Americans in the past decades have become a mobile society. It's not so common for a person to marry someone who lives within three blocks of their childhood home, just as it is common for grandparents to live thousands of miles from their grandchildren and adult children who could potentially serve as caretakers for them. Robert Putnam's work suggests that being anonymous within a community leads to greater incidences of juvenile crime, lower turnout for elections, and public debate (2000). The very

Physical activity is now easier to integrate into our daily lives with the number and variety of classes available at park and recreation facilities.

fabric of a society is its ability to bring people together to recognize common aims. While this is a critical issue in a values-divided America, it also represents an opportunity for parks and recreation.

Mission: Strengthening community image and sense of place

• *Parks and recreation as the real thing.* Faith Popcorn, the futurist who coined the term *cocooning*, is suggesting that our current culture is suffering from "experience deficit" (Popcorn & Marigold, 1996). The availability of online knowledge and simulated experiences results in people having experiences that are only secondary. Fantasy football is popular, but does it replace a group of friends getting together and watching or playing football? Talking to grandparents over the Internet is good family communication, but does it replace actual bedtime story reading? Visiting the Serengeti via Disney World or IMAX is a powerful experience, but does it replace the actual contact with the natural setting? No.

Mission: Providing recreational experiences

Threats

One of the underlying assumptions of planning is that if you can identify the threats to your situation, then you can dissipate those threats by choosing to make them opportunities. If only it were that straightforward. The threats in this instance include those that will greatly challenge the assets and abilities of this profession:

• *Current way of life.* Prescriptions for mood-altering medications continue to increase. The amount of time Americans spend commuting increases as well. Family time decreases while weight increases and the blurring of work and life escalates. Americans from many segments of society are caught in a seemingly endless trap of materialism, technology, growing debt, and health risks.

Mission: Promoting health and wellness

• *Competing priorities.* While dealing with competing priorities, such as police and fire, are not new conditions for parks and recreation, it becomes apparent that the competition for public funds and support will escalate. Will the country assign scarce resources to youth or older adults? What about the public policy promises related to Medicare and Social Security? It will come down

to a serious, bottom-line-driven, results-oriented agenda that requires parks and recreation to consistently communicate the outcomes of our services, parks, and facilities.

Mission: Facilitating community problem solving

• *Escape and entertainment.* Money and time run neck and neck as the most important commodity in this country. Americans are decreasing the amount of time they spend in outdoor pursuits, while the time and money expended on fantasy sports and gambling are rapidly increasing. It appears as if Americans, either out of choice or lack of time, are opting to pursue escape and entertainment over some of the more traditional benefits of parks and recreation.

Mission: Providing recreational experiences

ORGANIZATIONAL CHANGES

Park and recreation organizations can no longer operate in the same ways that have proven successful for them in the past. Society is changing, and the park and recreation profession must change as well. While McDonald's once served only burgers and fries and anticipated that people would drive up in their cars, order, and leave, the company, reflecting changes within society, has expanded its menu and now offers healthier selections. They also offer Wi-Fi, bocce ball, and playgrounds to encourage customers to hang around.

Park and recreation departments are not immune or oblivious to such societal changes, and just as restaurants and bookstores and other types of businesses have changed, the same changes need to occur in the park and recreation profession. Trends apply not just to public policy and programs but to the ways in which we conduct our operations as well. Two possible changes are from providing full services to facilitating them, and from delivering services to society to transforming it (O'Sullivan, 1999).

From Full-Service Provider to Facilitator

Adapted, by permission, from E. O'Sullivan, 1999, *Setting the Course for Change* (Ashburn, VA: National Recreation and Park Association), 9-10.

The shift from mass production to mass customization, when coupled with the growing diversity of society, means that one organization cannot possibly afford to be all things to all people. This will result in many other organizational shifts as well:

- Moving from sole provider of services to willing partner with other organizations will ensure opportunities for the masses.
- Moving from professionally centered organizations where the employed staff deliver the majority of programs and services to participant-collaboration relationships whereby the department assumes a facilitative role by providing education and direction will enable participants to satisfy their own goals.

From Delivering Services to Transforming Society

The societal challenges and economic priorities of the country suggest that park and recreation services in the public and nonprofit sectors cannot survive in the future unless they move beyond what they do for individuals in favor of what they make happen for the good of the community. Here are other shifts included in this change:

- Moving from activity-centered to outcomes-based programs will allow activities to serve as the means to an end for the overall well-being of society. For instance, after-school programs are promoted as safe places for children to be during nonschool hours; adult sport activities can reduce high blood pressure and high cholesterol levels; senior centers provide nutrition services and grief counseling.

- Moving from a nicety to a necessity is a mandatory change if we are to maintain public support for our efforts. The challenges associated with overweight kids being disconnected from their families, one another, and nature and the challenges of keeping three or more older generations healthy and vital members of the community emphasize the need to be a part of transforming society.

Just as General Motors, once the solid base of the economy, finds itself needing to change their practices in order to survive, the same will be true for public and nonprofit parks and recreation.

OPPORTUNITIES

Now that we've examined trends that are likely to affect our profession and how we do our work, let's look at the possible opportunities that those

trends afford us. We also briefly consider how to choose opportunities that both respond to trends and meet community needs.

Opportunities Based on Trends

As stated previously, the *Trends Analysis for Parks & Recreation: 2000 and Beyond* was conducted specifically for the California Park & Recreation Society by Tapan Munroe (1999). Munroe also identified 19 opportunities in 4 categories that responded to key trends that were expected to affect the profession and build on core competencies of the park and recreation profession (see chapter 4 for more on core competencies).

Target Markets

Anticipated demographic changes were most frequently mentioned by VIP Questionnaire respondents as the trend that will have the greatest impact on the provision of park and recreation services.

Providing accommodations for people of all ages and abilities is a core value of the park and recreation profession.

Children and families are becoming more of a focal point for increased services aimed at improving youth resiliency, maintaining healthy family relationships, reducing obesity and inactivity, and preventing and reducing crime. Other groups, such as seniors, will make up a greater percentage of the total population than ever before. Some groups, such as people with disabilities, have been underserved in the past and require programs and facilities to meet their needs. Additionally, the population of the United States is becoming more diverse. This diversity points to the fact that park and recreation professionals must respond to the needs of an increasingly diverse customer base. This customer base also may provide a new group of advocates for parks and recreation.

Specific target markets included the following:

- Dependents (children under 12 years of age, people with disabilities, and frail elders)
- Youth (children and youth up to 18 years old)
- Seniors (active to frail)
- Ethnic populations
- People with disabilities
- Families

Social Trends

Parks and recreation must recognize and address significant social trends and changes in how people live today and will live tomorrow.

The following are social trends that were strongly supported by the VIP Action Plan trends analysis:

- Health and wellness
- Lifelong learning
- Technology-based recreation

Community Planning and Development

Respondents to the VIP Questionnaire reported that creating community or quality of life is, after services and facilities, the most important value of parks and recreation. Community planning and development services offer professionals an opportunity to contribute actively to their community and use core competencies, such as leadership and community involvement skills.

The following are community planning and development opportunities:

- Park and recreation facilities
- Cultural arts

Providing recreational experiences is a key mission of the park and recreation profession. Other outcomes associated with classes can include improvements in physical, emotional, and social health.

- Economic development and tourism
- Model neighborhoods
- Partnerships with education (K-12)
- Partnerships with libraries
- Community problem solving

Environmental Awareness and Stewardship

Parks and recreation will continue to play an important role in educating citizens about the significance of the environment and preserving and protecting the environment. Citizens value their natural environment, but increasingly portions of the nation's natural resources are threatened by development. Through environmental education and outdoor recreation experiences, people learn the value of our natural environment firsthand and become better users of and advocates for natural resources.

Environmental awareness and stewardship market opportunities include the following:

- Outdoor recreation
- Nature tourism
- Environmental stewardship and open space

You can find specific opportunities for each of these opportunity categories in appendix A.

Opportunities That Fit Our Communities

Although we need to be aware of what societal trends will affect our park and recreation agencies, equally important are the opportunities we choose as we react to the trends. Each agency must determine how it can best serve its community in response to a given trend. For example, with the aging of baby boomers, the senior population is expected to grow and to be active. Opportunities that result from this trend could include trips for seniors, dependent care for frail elders, nutrition services, medical assistance, fitness and wellness services, and volunteering. For example, Agency X has confirmed through a census review that the senior population is expected to grow in their community. However, the local Area Agency on Aging operates the senior centers in this community, and additional centers are not needed. Agency X has an excellent outdoor recreation staff, and a community survey has identified a demand for senior outdoor programs. Agency X decides to contact local outfitters to develop a partnership to provide a variety of outdoor recreation programs for seniors, such as skiing, canoeing, and tours to state and national parks. A senior advisory group is formed to help plan the activities. The program is so successful that Agency X and the outfitters'

Courtesy of California Park & Recreation Society

Providing meaningful opportunities for volunteering can position the park and recreation agency as a key partner in facilitating community problem solving.

VIP in Action

The City of San Carlos (California) park and recreation staff studied the demographics of the city and heard from a variety of speakers in law enforcement, community development, and social services about what San Carlos will be like in the next 5 to 10 years. Four significant market opportunities were identified: baby boomers, millennial generation (the group born in the late 1980s and 1990s who will come of age in the new millennium), environmental concerns, and volunteerism. Staff task forces formed to address each market opportunity. *It's Your Turn to Play* programs were developed and printed to address the baby boomers. In fall 2002, the staff task force developed a "boomer bonanza" focus in the quarterly activity guide. The Boomer Bonanza page highlighted programs appealing to baby boomers, including a boomer brainstorm bash, sea kayaking, theater trip, and introduction to wine class. The brainstorm bash was an evening wine and cheese event with opportunities to network and learn more about program offerings, and it served as a community focus group to give feedback to staff. The staff then developed a direct-mail piece and complimentary brochure. The *It's Your Turn to Play* brochure advertises "programs to fit your lifestyle" and shows choices in outdoor activities, fitness, education, art and culture, and future programs.

To develop this program, the agency staff first developed a form to help them identify the opportunities within the trend of changing demographics (see figure 3.1 on page 50).

Reprinted, by permission, from City of San Carlos Parks and Recreation.

professional association are recognized for their contributions to tourism goals in several regions of the state.

Agency Y is also evaluating how to respond to the projected growth trend in the senior population. Agency Y is in a new community that is composed primarily of families with young children. Agency Y decided after its census review that the level of growth in the senior population that the community will experience will not require new senior centers or many programs targeted at the senior population. However, a community survey has identified a need for intergenerational programs. When Agency Y becomes involved in developing a community center for a new neighborhood, plans are made to serve all age groups and to develop intergenerational programs in partnership with the local Area Agency on Aging.

Agency Y becomes known for creating caring families in the community.

Here we have addressed trends in the areas of who we are, where we will live, where we will work, and even how we will spend our leisure time. As you can see, trends are dynamic and affect each aspect of our lives personally and professionally. As a student and professional, you need to pay attention to trends and regularly talk to your peers about what they are experiencing and how they are reacting.

Chapter 4 looks at the competencies you need to develop in your field as a student or as a professional in order to ensure your success. As a profession, we can no longer rely only on specific competencies related to parks and recreation if we are to manage in a complex and ever-changing world.

FIGURE 3.1

Exploring Market Opportunities

Trend: _____

Programs, services, and facilities needed:

Typical clients:

Strategic partners:
(List both current and potential partners and the services and resources they are willing to provide.)

Competitors:

Other resources needed:

Which opportunities are the highest priority, based on community need and our strengths?

4

Core Competencies

Core competencies are the special skills and abilities that park and recreation professionals need in order to deliver services in an ever-changing market. Adapting to changes is paramount to the future success of our profession.

We need professionals who are willing to develop skills and savvy and who have the courage to lead our profession into the next decade. Those who will survive are those who respond to the issues proactively by providing services that our communities and customers value. They will weave a complex web of stakeholders and coalitions into a force that achieves our vision and mission.

The professionals who will succeed in the next decade are those who

- understand and can articulate our role in creating community;
- master the political process to achieve their goals;
- have compassion for people;
- not only respond and react to changes and trends but are trendsetters;
- have relevant, honed communication, leadership, and decision-making skills;
- broker resources and bring coalitions together; and
- are leaders who are called to the table when important decisions are made.

Those who prefer the status quo and do not recognize the forces that shape us will flounder in the profession.

Given the importance of competencies, we look here at the professional competencies discovered during the development of the VIP Action Plan and how those competencies can be used in training and assessing students and employees. We also discuss the new roles park and recreation professionals can expect to play in the future.

IDENTIFYING PROFESSIONAL COMPETENCIES

During the development process of the VIP Action Plan, participants identified distinctive skills of the park and recreation profession today and skills that should be developed to ensure our future success. The following are some competencies attributed to park and recreation professionals today:

- Resourcefulness
- Community knowledge
- Creating experiences
- Partnering and building coalitions
- Mediating
- Facilitating
- Orientation toward people
- Flexibility
- Multitasking

Professionals will need these additional skills in order to maintain a vital and relevant profession in the new millennium:

- Action planning
- Community building
- Communication
- Resource development
- Strategic thinking
- Leadership
- Use of technology
- Use of multidisciplinary skills
- Research and evaluation
- Outcome-based management
- Political dynamics or acumen
- Use of prevention models
- Understanding ecosystems
- Knowledge of human development

These competencies are further described in figure 4.1.

A chain is only as strong as its weakest link. We need all individuals in our profession to take responsibility for developing new skills, shedding irrelevant and outdated work habits, learning new paradigms, and accepting future challenges to move us closer to our common vision. You play a role in strengthening the park and recreation profession—whether you are the department head in your organization, a recreation therapist in a hospital or community setting, or a student just beginning your career.

INCORPORATING COMPETENCIES INTO EMPLOYEE TRAINING AND MANAGEMENT

One of the best ways a profession can identify and disseminate the competencies desired by entry-level employees is through professional organizations. When an agency cares about the performance of its employees and the quality of services it provides, it can compare its performance on a variety of criteria to benchmarks from the professional organization in its field. This can be a very cost-effective and time-saving way to determine how and where to improve performance. The VIP Action Plan list of competencies can be used as a benchmark for hiring and managing employees and training students for jobs in parks and recreation.

Agencies that recognize the importance of staff development can increase the skill sets or knowledge of their workforce as well as improve goal setting.

CALIFORNIA PARK & RECREATION SOCIETY

7971 Freeport Blvd
Sacramento, CA
95832-9701
916/665-2777
FAX 916/665-9149

Contact:

Jane Adams,

Executive Director

916/665-2777

CPRS provides

the leadership

to advance the

positive impact

and value of

the profession

FACT SHEET

Professional Competencies

In 1999 the California Park & Recreation Society released the VIP Plan, "Creating Community in the 21st Century." The VIP plan has set a vision and direction for California's park and recreation profession. While creating the VIP Plan it became clear that park and recreation professionals will need to develop different core competencies if we are to be successful as a profession:

- professionals who understand and can articulate our role in creating community
- individuals who master the political process to achieve their goals
- leaders in their own communities
- individuals who have a compassion for people
- professionals who are trendsetters
- innovative professionals who have relevant, finely honed skills
- multi-faceted individuals who can broker resources and bring coalitions together
- leaders who are called to the table when important decisions are made

The VIP Plan calls for park and recreation professionals to improve their core competencies in several areas. These areas have been defined further in order to develop training and professional development programs that address these competencies. Skill in these core competencies will help us do a better job in hiring, developing staff, communicating, clarifying roles, and evaluating performance. Improving our performance in these competencies will enable us to work more effectively in a rapidly changing society.

So what are the new core competencies that California park and recreation professionals need to have? Fourteen skills have been identified in the VIP Action Plan *"Creating Community in the 21st Century"*. We have organized the competencies using a "meta" leadership competency model used by corporations. A brief description of each of the core competencies as outlined in the VIP Action Plan follows:

Business Acumen

Action [strategic] planning

Knowledge of the development and implementation of strategic change initiatives to produce change (external related to the organization's products, services, revenues, and relationships and/or internal related to capacity building, strengthening community leadership, or enhancing the planning process); ability to be a change-agent when a new course or direction is dictated.

Ecosystem management

Ecosystem management implies a holistic approach to the use and safeguarding of the natural resource base. It recognizes the need to protect or restore critical ecological components, functions, and structures to permanently sustain resources. It requires understanding of the natural world and natural features (forests, waters, geological features, wetlands, riverbanks, etc) for protection and visitor management. Managing these resources requires restoration, maintenance, and enhancement of the resources.

Human development

Ability to understand the life-long development process of a person that recognizes the physical, psychological and sociological needs of an individual. It is the ability to program and design facilities to account for the inter-relatedness between generations. It is understanding of the role of recreation and play in meeting human physical, psychological and sociological needs. It is the ability to plan activities based upon the appropriate stages of human development (i.e., pre-school, youth, teens, adults, and seniors) and familiarity with various human development models (i.e., Maslow, Piaget). It is the ability to recognize the community's demographic groups and how to meet desired outcomes.

(continued)

Figure 4.1 CPRS fact sheet.

Figure 4.1   *(continued)*

Resource [management and] development

Understanding of the financial, information, technology, and space resources of the community and the organization. Responsibly allocates and leverages resources, including staff, technology, equipment, facilities, and monies to increase resources. Integrates resource management into strategic planning and program development. Develops ways to measure effective and efficient use of resources. Ability to leverage resources towards desired outcomes.

Strategic thinking

Analyzes and evaluates information and situations for problem solving, decision-making, and conceptualizing. Synthesizes ideas and integrates information resulting in holistic versus fragmented perspectives and action. Ability to link the long term vision with short term goals to achieve desired results.

Technology

Understanding advances in technology to facilitate information gathering, sharing information; and its use in effective decision-making; use of Internet to expand public awareness and support.

Communications & Marketing

Communications

Knowledge that communications is a management tool that supports the organization's mission and strategic plan, provides a framework for making competent decisions, assists in efficient day-to-day operations and enables effective relationships with multiple and diverse audiences. As a process, it is exchanging information, impacting ideas, and making oneself understood by others. Skills include speaking, listening, choosing an appropriate style and forum for a message, presenting information clearly and concisely, giving and receiving feedback, and facilitating.

Facilitation

The ability to enable groups and organizations to work more effectively to collaborate and achieve synergy. The ability to serve as a "content neutral" party who by not taking sides or expressing or advocating a point of view, can advocate for fair, open, and inclusive procedures to accomplish the group's work. Knowledge of the facilitation processes and skills. It involves exceptional interpersonal skills, keen observation, insight, and tact.

Mediation

The ability to bring individuals and/or groups to agreement through "informed consent." Requires understanding of mediation concepts and qualities, collaboration, group process, and group decision-making. It is the ability to build win-win situations and constructive agreements among stakeholders.

Planning & Evaluation

Creator of Experiences

The ability to create experiences that involves people directly while engaging their psyche in the process to make the right kind of thing happen for their customers. Knowledge of the values and trends in the experience industry; understanding the differences between products, services, and experiences; and incorporating the heightened consumer preference for personalization.

Outcome driven management

Management that focuses on outcome measures to report results (or the quality) of the service being provided. Outcome measures indicate the impact on the problem the program was designed to address and they indicate the difference made by the program in qualitative terms. It is understanding the methods and use of various evaluation tools and methodology.

Prevention models [knowledge of and use of]

Understanding that multiple levels of prevention and intervention are critical in developing and sustaining healthy individuals and communities and understanding the link between prevention and early intervention and the long term solutions that approach provides. It is the ability to calculate and articulate the long term cost savings associated with the preventative nature of recreation and community services. It is the ability to focus service delivery on preventing social problems as defined by the community or agency. It is the ability to design measurement or evaluation tools that focus on the preventative nature of the program or service. It is the knowledge that long term health of a community relies upon community involvement and collaboration and the development of a comprehensive, integrated plan.

Research and evaluation

Evaluation is a management tool of obtaining objective data to make better management decisions, to promote programs and to assess performance. Evaluation is the process of determining the effectiveness of current practices, procedures, and plans. Types: (1) outcome evaluation – measures the effect of a service on the client; (2) process evaluation – focuses on the conduct of the program (has it been done in an efficient, legal, and ethical manner)

Community Relations

Community knowledge

Knowledge of constituents and stakeholders and their diverse needs; knowledge of the community's hierarchy and its physical, human, and fiscal resources. Community knowledge is applied to provide services and to look for solutions. Understands that service reaches beyond immediate and obvious constituencies and that service affects relationships and other aspects of community life.

Figure 4.1   *(continued)*

54

Community building

Knowledge of governance, environment, culture, processes, procedures, and how decisions are made. Involves understanding of community's values, traditions, power structures, use of resources and roles. Involves consultation with stakeholders and constituents before making decisions affecting them. Knows who the community's leaders and decision makers are and is familiar with community's organizational structure. Uses relationships and partnerships to accomplish goals.

Partnering and coalition building

Techniques and skills to develop voluntary agreements, cooperative ventures, joint arrangements, alliances, collaborations, coalitions, and work forces based on common, or at least compatible, goals to maximize resources for the long term. Partnership skills include understanding the qualities that influence partnership success (personal characteristics, interpersonal characteristics, organizational characteristics, and operational characteristics), barriers to productive partnerships, policy considerations, and staffing.

People-orientation

An understanding of human development needs and the ability to motivate people. Includes self awareness, listening, giving feedback and assessing performance (paid and volunteer), understanding and valuing diversity, developing and coaching staff, effectively implementing the hiring and selection process, and preventing and resolving conflict. Supports people's efforts to develop skills, knowledge, and abilities that contribute to organizational or community goals. Recognizes people for their contributions to the success of the organization/community.

Political dynamics/acumen

Understanding of the governance, environment, culture, processes, procedures, and how decisions are made locally, at the state level, and nationally. Understands the relationship between community sectors, voters, constituents, and stakeholders.

Leadership & Management

Flexibility

The ability to adapt and deal with situations and manage expectations during periods of change. It is the ability to work with many different people over time, develop new methods and technologies to perform the work and to be spontaneous and responsive to unpredictable demands placed on individuals or the organization. It is the ability to see new possibilities, be reflective, and able to handle ambiguity proactively

Leadership

Ability to commit people to action, convert followers into leaders, and convert leaders into agents of change. Sets direction and makes decisions, displays willingness to take action, understands the accountability that accompanies leadership, sees larger organization view as opposed to own view. Makes decisions that are aligned with vision, mission, and goals and values of organization; models integrity in decisions, communication, and treatment of people, places organization's best interest before own best interest; thinks holistically; has vision for the future and communicates it to others; and mentors and develops others.

Multi-tasking

The ability to handle multiple projects simultaneously and to create linkages between all the stakeholders. It requires knowledge of time management, setting priorities, and managing ambiguity.

Resourcefulness

The ability to identify and maximize the use of human, financial, technical or organizational resources to accomplish the desired results. The ability to define and communicate organizational objectives and goals to stakeholders. The ability to handle conflict and to cope with finding solutions.

Figure 4.1 *(continued)*

Here are several practical ways that the desired competencies suggested by the VIP Action Plan can be translated into components of the employee training and selection process:

- Use items to compose a self-assessment checklist to be administered to employees (or students) at the entrance and exit from their jobs (or the major).

- Use the list as discussion points between supervisors and employees, or students and faculty advisors, to decide on training preferences or elective courses.

- Use the list to identify matching preparation for a position, whether in prior paid or unpaid work experience or in courses.

- Employing agencies can use these criteria to create target outcomes to be accomplished by student interns during field placement.

- Translate the competencies into selection criteria when hiring new full-time employees.

- Use the list as part of the language in position descriptions when searching for new employees.

- Discuss the criteria with recreation, park, and tourism professors, and have them use these criteria as part of their self-assessment during the retention, tenure, and promotion (RTP) or the posttenure review process. This is a way of keeping academicians connected with the field and employer expectations.

- Use the competencies as criteria to compare candidates competing for the same position.

- Use the competencies to identify training needs and priorities.

Agencies may wish to add more detail to the list of competencies. For example, what does the competency "use of technology" include? The ability to use computers and word-processing programs is a very small part of an ever-changing world of technology. Should you add other emerging forms of technology? And what is the skill of grant writing—a stand-alone skill or one that is woven into the competencies of community or coalition building or communication? The VIP list of competencies is not a one-size-fits-all model; the point is to use the list items and tailor them to suit the needs of your agency or your own professional development plan. Each competency can be broken down into sets of specific skills to be acquired at various stages of a career, and the emphasis on certain competencies might change over time as your agency shifts focus and priorities or as you advance in your career.

One example of how VIP Action Plan core competencies could be woven into training is through internships. The NRPA Council on Accreditation for Recreation, Park Resources, and Leisure Services Education has established 1,200 hours as a minimum number of field placement hours to be amassed by undergraduate students (in accredited programs). Students and their academic departments document both the content of the students' experience and the quality of the students' actual performance.

As the number of accredited agencies increases, as well as the number of experienced and college-trained practitioners who supervise interns, it would be helpful to develop a common set of expectations for student interns and a core training that would apply to all agency supervisors. Additional requirements could be tailored to the

unique characteristics of the agency, state and local needs, or demographics.

The City of West Sacramento integrated the VIP Action Plan core competencies into not only their training for recreation interns but also their employee selection process. Figure 4.2 shows a resource exercise based on the VIP Action Plan that they had their interns carry out. Figures 4.3 and 4.4 (see pages 59-61) show examples of the interview questions and evaluation sheets used for both interns and the senior recreation supervisor position. All are based on assessment of the core competencies.

Figure 4.5 (see pages 62-64) is a sample competency assessment form that can be used to assess students' abilities before and after an internship. This form could easily be adapted to apply to staff members as well.

Interns may also wish to create or add to portfolios of their work during their internship. Many employers at agencies now want to see portfolios for students who have just graduated in order to better assess each candidate's competencies. Students may choose to organize their portfolios into categories based on the core competencies. (See appendix D for more on the use of portfolios for student assessment.)

All students enrolled in professional preparation baccalaureate degree programs clearly want (and expect) universities and employing agencies to establish consistent requirements, whether for further education or fitness for work. Particularly at the undergraduate level, students want reassurance that classroom expectations match qualifications identified by employers in entry-level position descriptions. Internships and schooling are most valuable to students when university faculty and agency practitioners get together and examine the relationship between student learning and preprofessional employment preparation. To ensure first-class student training, schools should create "ambitious content standards [such as the VIP Action Plan core competencies] as the basis for assessment and accountability, set demanding performance standards, and ensure that schools, teachers, and students have something at stake for meeting those standards" (Linn, 2001, p. 2). For many of today's students, there are no higher stakes than the promise of full-time employment (with benefits) in their chosen field. And it's great if that field happens to be the one for which their academic program prepared them!

Employee Evaluations

Traditionally, employee evaluations have focused on generic skill and behaviors such as decision making, initiative, or timeliness. If we are to move forward as a profession, we must assess our skills in the core competencies identified in the VIP Action Plan. Pick one or two of the competencies and begin to assess your own performance or skill level and that of your employees. Following that assessment, provide opportunities to receive training (formal or informal), coaching, and be given work assignments that call for those competencies.

FIGURE 4.2

Resource Exercise for Recreation Interns

City of West Sacramento (California) Parks & Recreation Department

As a recreation intern, you will be exposed to the duties, routine, and challenges of a recreation supervisor. We want that experience to be positive and effective, so we have created an exercise that functions as a resource tool containing information about the value of parks and recreation. The City of West Sacramento Parks & Recreation Department is responsible for providing you with an experience that helps prepare you for a full-time career in our profession. We think that this exercise will make your experience more meaningful.

Step 1

- Get a three-ring binder with clear sleeves that allow you to slip paper in for a customized cover. Include in your binder labeled dividers so you can clearly separate each set of documents. A binder and dividers should be available in the office supplies section of the department workroom.

- Go to the California Park & Recreation Society's Web site (www.cprs.org) and print out and review the 68-page document titled VIP Action Plan: Creating Community in the 21st Century (www.cprs .org/pdf/cc21.pdf). Place the document in a small binder. Print a second copy of the document's cover and place it in the front of your binder. Because this will take some time to print, please do so when the printer seems least busy.

- Open up the VIP Action Plan Framework. This document is huge, so you'll need to save it to your computer. Once you've done that, open it up as a separate document. You should be able to print it out as a one-page color document. Once printed, place it in the back cover of your new VIP binder.

- Make a label for the spine of your binder.

- Print out a copy of the Executive Summary of the VIP Action Plan: Creating Community in the 21st Century (at www.cprs.org/pdf/VIPSummary.pdf) and place it in a separate section of your binder.

- Print out a copy of the Mission Areas of the VIP Action Plan (www.cprs.org/creating-mission.htm) and place it in a separate section of your binder.

- Print out a copy of the Leading to Promote Health & Wellness (at www.cprs.org/membersonly/ Health&Wellness.pdf) and place it in a separate section of your binder.

- Print out a copy of the Leisure Education Policy (at www.cprs.org/membersonly/P&REdPolicy.pdf) and place it in a separate section of your binder.

If you are a CPRS member, you will have easy access to everything on the CPRS Web site. If you are not, your access will be limited. This exercise is designed for nonmembers, so everything you need should be available to you. It might take some time to find what you need, but you will find it.

Next, go to the National Recreation and Park Association's Web site at www.nrpa.org. In the Search window, type "stats & facts" and find your way to the Stats & Facts page. Once there, go to "Programs

(continued)

Figure 4.2 *(continued)*

and Partnerships, Step Up to Health," where you will find numerous documents pertaining to parks and recreation and health under "Resources and Health Information." Documents include the following:

- Overweight and Obesity Statistics
- Overweight/Obesity and Physical Activity Background Information
- Health Benefits of Parks and Recreation

Print out these three items and place them in separate sections of your binder with labeled binder dividers.

Step 2

Write a one-page, single-spaced memo to your supervisor explaining the contents of the binder and why it will be a valuable resource for you. Include in your memo an example of how you could use some of the enclosed information to help explain why the program is beneficial to local residents. Be sure to cite the section of your binder and the page number of the document.

Step 3

- Submit the binder to your supervisor for review and request a few minutes to discuss your findings with him or her.
- Be prepared to expand and modify your binder. As you come across other resources during the duration of your internship, you may want to create new sections for this information or merge them with information your already have. Be sure to share with your supervisors the information you've discovered, because it may be new information to them.

Reprinted, by permission, from City of West Sacramento Parks & Recreation. Created by Andre Pichly, MS, CPRP, recreation superintendent, City of West Sacramento. From California Park & Recreation Society, 2008, *Creating Community* (Champaign, IL: Human Kinetics).

FIGURE 4.3A

Interview Questions for Recreation Intern

City of West Sacramento (California) Parks & Recreation Department

Core competencies we are looking for:

- Leadership
- Communication
- Partnership and coalition building
- Outcome-driven management

- Resource development
- Research and evaluation
- Strategic thinking

1. Describe your college experience thus far as it relates to the pursuit of an internship and ultimately a career. Describe how your education (and training, if any) have prepared you for an internship with a public agency.

2. How would you describe your leadership style? Cite a specific situation that shows how your leadership style helped to gain closure on a problem or challenge.

3. Describe your ideal recreation intern experience. How would such an internship benefit the park and recreation department and residents of West Sacramento?

4. Describe how you motivate others and build team spirit with classmates or coworkers. Give examples.

5. What experience do you have working in a recreation and park setting, whether it was private or public?

6. If I spoke to your current or former boss or instructor, what would he or she say your greatest strengths and greatest weaknesses are?

7. When you begin to work with new people, how do you get to understand them? Are you successful in predicting or interpreting their behavior? Give examples.

8. Describe your experience, successes, and difficulties, if any, in developing programs and resources or accomplishing projects.

9. Describe any success you have had in seeking outside donations, sponsorships or partnerships, and other resources.

10. Explain your experience working with members of the community.

That is the end of our questions. Is there anything you would like to add to your interview that would assist the department in assessing your qualifications for this position?

Do you have any questions or comments?

Reprinted, by permission, from City of West Sacramento Parks & Recreation. Created by Andre Pichly, MS, CPRP, recreation superintendent, City of West Sacramento. From California Park & Recreation Society, 2008, *Creating Community* (Champaign, IL: Human Kinetics).

FIGURE 4.3B

Interview Questions: Senior Recreation Supervisor

City of West Sacramento (California) Parks & Recreation Department

Core competencies we are looking for:

- Leadership
- Communication
- Partnership and coalition building
- Outcome-driven management
- Resource development
- Research and evaluation
- Strategic thinking

---

1. Describe your current role in the department and your responsibilities. Describe how your education, training, professional involvement, and experience have prepared you for this position.

2. How would you describe your leadership style and management skills? Cite a specific situation that shows how your leadership style helped to gain closure on a problem or challenge.

3. What does customer service mean to you? How would you implement your philosophy as a senior recreation supervisor?

4. Describe how you motivate staff and build team spirit with coworkers. Give examples.

5. Articulate your vision for this department. How would you go about sharing that vision with other staff?

6. What evaluation tools and techniques have you used to evaluate programs and measure their success?

7. If I spoke to your current or former boss, what would he or she say your greatest strengths and your greatest weaknesses are?

8. When you begin to work with new people, how do you get to understand them? Are you successful in predicting or interpreting their behavior? Give examples.

9. Describe your experience, successes, and difficulties, if any, in developing partnerships and coalition building.

10. Describe your budget skills and what success you have had in seeking outside donations, sponsorships, and other resources.

11. Explain your experience working with boards, commissions, neighborhood groups, and members of the community.

That is the end of our questions. Is there anything you would like to add to your interview that would assist the department in assessing your qualifications for this position?

Do you have any questions or comments?

Reprinted, by permission, from City of West Sacramento Parks & Recreation. Created by Andre Pichly, MS, CPRP, recreation superintendent, City of West Sacramento. From California Park & Recreation Society, 2008, *Creating Community* (Champaign, IL: Human Kinetics).

FIGURE 4.4

Internship Interview Evaluation Sheet

_____   _____
Candidate's name   Position applying for

Instructions: Based on the definitions and your observations and judgment, use the following rating scale to determine a grade for each job dimension and observed personal qualities for this candidate. Place a number grade for each dimension in the space provided. Use the comment space liberally.

Rating Scale

Observation	*Rating*
Excellent	4
Good	3
Fair	2
Poor or improvement needed	1
Unsatisfactory	0

_____

Job Dimensions	*Rating*
Leadership	_____
Communication	_____
Partnership and coalition building	_____
Outcome-driven management	_____
Resource development	_____
Research and evaluation	_____
Strategic thinking	_____

Personal Qualities	*Rating*
Oral communication skills	_____
Situational reasoning and problem-solving ability	_____
Interpersonal skills	_____
Assertiveness and initiative	_____
Flexibility	_____
Creativity	_____

Comments: _____

_____

_____

_____

_____

_____   _____
Date   Evaluator's signature

FIGURE 4.5

Pre- and Postinternship Competency Assessment

This form is to be completed at the points indicated. A final copy shall be placed in the student's advising folder at the conclusion of Recreation and Tourism Management (RTM) (by the student) and at the conclusion of the internship experience (600 hours or more). Use the following scale (whole numbers only). Face-to-face meetings with second parties are required and should be scheduled by the students *well in advance of the due date*. Wherever possible, identify one or more courses in the major (or embedded experiences) that address that competency or standard. Note evidence of each competency.

4 = outstanding   3 = above average   2 = average or acceptable   1 = below average or unacceptable

Competency	Self-evaluation	Advisor	Preinternship assignments	Postinternship
Competencies Required by a Park and Recreation Professional				
Action and strategic planning				
Ecosystem management				
Human development				
Resource management and development				
Technology				
Communication				
Mediation				
Facilitation				
Creator of experiences				
Outcome-driven management				
Prevention models				
Research and evaluation				
Community knowledge				
Community building				
Partnering and coalition building				
People orientation				
Political dynamics and acumen				

Created by Veda Ward. From California Park & Recreation Society, 2008, *Creating Community* (Champaign, IL: Human Kinetics).

Competency	Self-evaluation	Advisor	Preinternship assignments	Postinternship
Competencies Required by a Park and Recreation Professional *(continued)*				
Flexibility				
Leadership				
Multitasking				
Resourcefulness				
Use of multidisciplinary skills				
Internship Preparation				
Career and internship information				
Cover letter				
Resume or curriculum vitae				
Self-assessment				
Interview techniques				
Presentation skills				
Facilities (design, operations, risk management)				
Job or internship search strategies				
Budget preparation				
Group process				
Group work				
Program skills				
Civic engagement				
Individual responsibility and self-management				
RTM Core				
Leisure in society				
Program and event planning				
Therapeutic recreation and special populations				

Created by Veda Ward. From California Park & Recreation Society, 2008, *Creating Community* (Champaign, IL: Human Kinetics).

(continued)

Figure 4.5 *(continued)*

Competency	Self-evaluation	Advisor	Preinternship assignments	Postinternship
RTM Core *(continued)*				
Recreation and community development				
Promotion of recreation experience				
Entrepreneurial ventures				
Models of play, leisure, and recreation				
Evaluation research				

Professional memberships, training, and certifications

_____

_____

_____

_____

Field experience (600+ hours)

_____

_____

_____

_____

Non-RTM coursework (electives or general education)

_____

_____

_____

_____

Other

_____

_____

_____

_____

Created by Veda Ward. From California Park & Recreation Society, 2008, *Creating Community* (Champaign, IL: Human Kinetics).

EVALUATING EMPLOYEES BASED ON THE COMPETENCIES

Traditionally, employee evaluations have focused on generic skills and behaviors such as decision making, initiative, and timeliness. If we are to move forward as a profession we must assess our skills in the core competencies identified in the VIP Action Plan. We must first understand what each of the competencies means, and then we need to decide which behaviors or actions will demonstrate that the employee has those competencies. To assist agencies in moving toward a VIP-based competency-based evaluation, we have developed a position evaluation tool (see appendix F). We suggest that agencies choose one or two of the competencies and assess their employees' current performance or skill level. Following that assessment, agencies can provide opportunities to receive formal or informal training and coaching, and give work assignments that will help develop those competencies.

TAKING ON NEW ROLES

Another reason to promote new competencies for park and recreation professionals is that, in a rapidly changing society, the role of parks and recreation in the community is changing. The ability to respond to needs with the flexibility of a variety of roles or delivery models will be essential. More than ever before, we must recognize that no one agency working alone can meet all the recreational needs of a community. Park and recreation professionals will be more likely to work as members of a multidisciplinary team than in a group of like professionals. Historically the park and recreation profession has been best known as a direct provider of services and facilities, and that role will likely continue. However, as early as 1991, Murphy, Niepoth, and Williams predicted that park and recreation agencies will also serve as facilitators, advocates, and educators. This change in our possible roles is caused by reduction in fiscal resources, recognition that government cannot be all things to all people, and constituents' moving from greater dependence on the park and recreation provider for recreational experiences to greater self-sufficiency and independence (Murphy et al., 1991).

The following are potential roles of the park and recreation provider (see figure 4.6):

- *Direct service provider/technician.* A centralized agency provides services directly to customers.

- *Information/referral provider.* An agency develops partnerships to meet recreation needs and shares its knowledge of resources with customers. This model recognizes the role of the entire community in meeting needs.

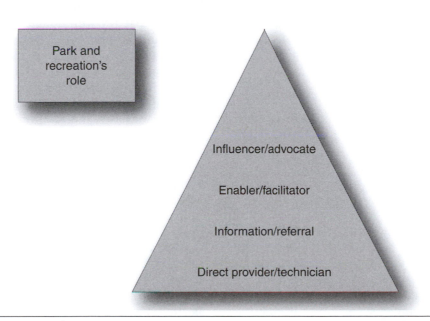

Figure 4.6 Delivery pyramid.

Determining the role that agencies wish to play for service delivery will determine the competencies needed by the agency's staff.

What Roles Can We Play?

To see what roles your agency could be playing in your community, see figure 4.7 for a worksheet you can use to assess your current roles in each area where your agency is active.

- *Enabler/facilitator.* An agency works with customers to improve their skills through developmental activities.
- *Influencer/advocate.* An agency actively represents the needs of its constituency and is a leader in community problem solving.

Agencies will not play only one of those roles. As an example, an agency may be the direct provider in the area of youth programs as it offers a variety of after-school and summer day camp programs, runs the teen center, and provides a variety of recreation classes geared for children and youth. But in the area of services for older or mature adults, the agency may be the information or referral provider, as it has decided to partner with the nonprofit organization in town that offers an array of senior services and programs. In this case, the agency would include the name of the center and its programs in its promotional materials and encourage seniors to use the center.

Various competencies will be needed for park and recreation students and professionals to ensure the outcomes of the profession are recognized as integral to addressing the complex and ever-changing world in which the profession must operate. Even seasoned park and recreation professionals should evaluate their strengths and areas that need improvement in the competencies identified in the VIP Action Plan.

In chapter 5, we describe implementation strategies that park and recreation professionals can undertake individually or within their department, division, or entire agency. It is only through action that the values, vision, and mission can be communicated to citizens, policy makers, strategic partners, and the media.

FIGURE 4.7

Determining Your Agency's Role

As a park and recreation agency, you can fulfill several roles:

Direct service provider/technician provides the service directly to customers.

Information/referral partners with others to share knowledge.

Enabler and facilitator works with customers to improve skills.

Influencer/advocate actively represents the needs of the community and leads in problem solving.

Use this form to assess the current situation and identify the best role your agency can play in addressing the particular need.

1. Define the community issue or need. (Be as specific as possible; draw on available data and current resources.)

_____

_____

2. Identify organizations, government departments, or individuals who are aware of or who are currently involved in the issue. If possible, list the resources they are bringing to the table. Rate them on a scale of excellent to poor in your estimation of the impact of their current efforts.

Agency	Their resources	Impact of their work

3. Identify any of your current efforts and rate your impact (scale of excellent to poor) currently being made by your agency with this issue.

Resources	Impact of your work

4. Articulate and estimate what is needed in order to address the issue more completely (time, staff, community awareness, policy).

_____

_____

5. Review the analysis and determine your role in the issue.

_____

From California Park & Recreation Society, 2008, *Creating Community* (Champaign, IL: Human Kinetics).

5

Strategies for Achieving the Vision

The next step in the VIP Action Plan is implementation, which help in achieving our professional vision: to be known as the profession that creates community through people, parks, and programs. The implementation strategies are the methods, resources, processes, and systems we will deploy to achieve success.

Each of the eight strategies links with the vision of creating community through people, parks, and programs and with the mission components. The strategies and their related opportunities might suggest a different approach than what your agency is currently doing. Comparing what you currently do to the strategies can help focus the direction of your agency. And the strategies and opportunities you select can help you respond to emerging trends in your community, meet underserved demands, or discover better ways to do business. Concentrating resources in the strategies will position your agency for success amid social, political, and technological change. The opportunities you choose should be ones that build on the profession's competencies and strengths and take into account current trends and issues; they may even lead to an expanded role for your agency. We recommend you do a local assessment to select the appropriate strategy and opportunities for your agency, because trends will have different effects attributed to local conditions. In this chapter we present examples of how you can implement the VIP Action Plan at the local level, but it is up to you to seize the opportunity.

Park and recreation agencies can help create the community's image and sense of place. Parks are natural places for residents to gather.

THE EIGHT STRATEGIES

Following are the eight strategies of the VIP Action Plan:

1. Communicate the vision.
2. Form partnerships.
3. Expand professional competencies.
4. Strengthen the park and recreation ethic.
5. Demonstrate results.

6. Document best practices.

7. Affect public policy.

8. Expand resources.

The strategies do not have to be used in this order; they are presented as a menu to use to position parks and recreation as vital in a community. For instance, the park and recreation agency needs to regularly communicate its vision to the community, its policy makers, and its constituents. Through communicating, the agency can explain what the public can expect from the park and recreation programs and services. The intent of the communication is to ensure that residents understand the value of park and recreation services and the agency's efforts to partner with others in the community. Chapters 9 and 10 present specific techniques for communicating to your intended audiences.

One more caution is that the strategies are not intended as a list for you to check off and move on. They are long-term strategies for positioning parks and recreation as vital resources. You may find that your agency is already focusing on one or more of the strategies listed. In fact, we expect most park and recreation agencies are now forming partnerships. If that is the case for your agency, select a strategy that you currently are not using, such as strengthening the park and recreation ethic (among your community's residents) or affecting public policy.

Short-, medium-, and long-term time lines are suggested for each implementation strategy. Time lines serve as goals for completion. For example, a long-range action item (4 or more years) does *not* mean that action will not start for at least 4 years, but rather that it is estimated to take at least 4 years to reach the *goal* for that action item. Short-, medium, and long-range action items may all be running concurrently. The time lines are as follows:

Short range: 0 to 2 years to complete

Medium range: 2 to 4 years to complete

Long range: 4 or more years to complete

STRATEGY IMPLEMENTATION PLANS

To achieve a plan that encompasses the entire park and recreation profession, people are needed at many levels:

- Individual professionals
- Park and recreation agencies
- State and national organizations

- Allied professionals
- Educators and academic institutions

The charts that follow in figure 5.1 spell out the implementation responsibilities for each of the eight VIP Action Plan strategies. They suggest potential roles for you, your agency, your university, and your professional organizations.

A Note About Execution

A good plan, violently executed now, is better than a perfect plan next week.

General George S. Patton

Strategies do not become alive until they are executed or acted upon. More and more is being written about execution and its importance in reaching goals. In their book, *Execution: The Discipline of Getting Things Done,* authors Larry Bossidy and Ram Charan give three points about execution: 1) execution is discipline, and integral to strategy; 2) execution is the major of the business leader; and 3) execution must be a core element of an organization's culture.

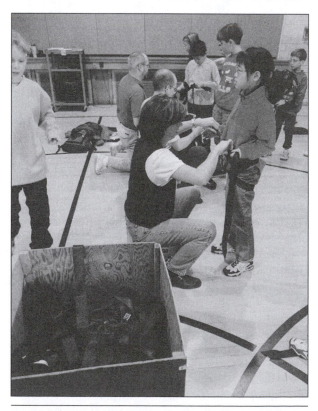

In addition to inspecting equipment, facilities, and park sites, park and recreation agencies also provide trained staff.

FIGURE 5.1

Implementation Responsibilities for VIP Action Plan Strategies

1. Communicate the Vision

Communicate the vision, values, and mission of parks and recreation to members of the profession.

Trends Reference

External environmental factors

Competition for public funding

Technology

Organizational and operational changes

	Individuals	Agencies	Professional organizations	Allied professions	Educators/ academia
Short-range steps					
1. Create an internal ambassador program to communicate the vision and value of parks and recreation and the VIP Project to members of the profession.	X	X	X		X
2. Adopt the VIP vision as an individual professional, as an agency, and as an organization.	X	X	X		X
3. Conduct action-planning processes in individual agencies modeling the VIP Action Plan framework (see appendix B).	X	X	X		X
Medium-range steps					
4. Review, analyze, and evaluate agency organizational structures to determine how well those structures support the values, vision, and mission stated in the VIP Action Plan.	X	X			X
5. Designate individuals who have implemented the plan to serve as mentors to assist agencies.	X	X	X		
Long-range steps					
6. Establish a recognition program for those who promote the VIP vision.			X		

(continued)

From California Park & Recreation Society, 2008, *Creating Community* (Champaign, IL: Human Kinetics).

Figure 5.1   *(continued)*

What possible steps (short, medium, or long range) could you and your agency undertake? Brainstorm with others, then list your ideas here and indicate the estimated time frame.

Idea	Time frame

2. Form Partnerships

Develop partners and allies by communicating the vision and value of parks and recreation to allied professionals, citizens, the media, and policy makers.

Trends Reference

Who will we be?

Where and how will we live?

External environmental factors

Organizational and operational changes

	Individuals	Agencies	Professional organizations	Allied professions	Educators/academia
Short-range steps					
1. Cultivate and strengthen relationships with local media. (See chapter 8, Developing a Communications Plan.)	X	X	X		X
2. Participate actively on citizen boards and in allied professional organizations to promote the profession's values, vision, and mission.	X	X	X	X	X
3. Promote the value of parks and recreation to target audiences.	X	X	X		
Medium-range steps					
4. Create an external ambassador program to communicate a consistent message to target audiences.	X	X	X		

From California Park & Recreation Society, 2008, *Creating Community* (Champaign, IL: Human Kinetics).

	Individuals	Agencies	Professional organizations	Allied professions	Educators/ academia
Long-range steps					
5. Design and implement a phased-in statewide public relations program in public and professional media. • Select spokespeople to champion the park and recreation vision. • Create stories that describe the relevance of parks and recreation. • Cite research data on the outcomes provided by parks and recreation.	X	X	X	X	X

What possible steps (short, medium, or long range) could you and your agency undertake? Brainstorm with others, then list your ideas here and indicate the estimated time frame.

Idea	Time frame

3. Expand Professional Competencies

Build capacity within the park and recreation profession by providing professional and continuing education that increases skills in the core competencies for success in the future.

Trends Reference

Who will we be?

External environmental factors

Competition

Organizational and operational changes

(continued)

From California Park & Recreation Society, 2008, *Creating Community* (Champaign, IL: Human Kinetics).

Figure 5.1 *(continued)*

	Individuals	Agencies	Professional organizations	Allied professions	Educators/ academia
Short-range steps					
1. Recruit and develop park and recreation professionals to reflect local and state demographics.	X	X	X	X	X
2. Engage park and recreation professionals, allied professionals, and educators in analyzing university curriculum for its relevance to the park and recreation profession.	X	X	X	X	X
Medium-range steps					
3. Develop core competencies and skills needed by park and recreation professionals.	X	X	X		X
4. Gather, expand, and disseminate university curriculum materials that support the VIP Action Plan.			X		X
Long-range steps					
5. Develop a professional training program in areas identified in an occupational analysis for the park and recreation profession that need further development.			X		X
6. Develop and market a continuing education requirement for park and recreation professionals.			X		X

What possible steps (short, medium, or long range) could you and your agency undertake? Brainstorm with others, then list your ideas here and indicate the estimated time frame.

Idea	Time frame

From California Park & Recreation Society, 2008, *Creating Community* (Champaign, IL: Human Kinetics).

4. Strengthen the Park and Recreation Ethic

Integrate the park and recreation ethic into aspects of the K-12 educational experience.

Trends Reference

Who will we be?
Where and how will we live?
External environmental factors

	Individuals	Agencies	Professional organizations	Allied professions	Educators/academia
Medium-range steps					
1. Develop, gather, expand, and disseminate K-12 curriculum materials that demonstrate the value of parks, recreation, and leisure, as well as help children develop strong leisure skills; implement those in K-12 schools statewide by providing curriculum to teachers and giving classroom presentations by recreation professionals, students, and educators.	X	X	X	X	X
Long-range steps					
2. Educate schoolchildren about leisure benefits, values, and skills; integrate the park and recreation ethic into aspects of the school experience.	X	X	X	X	X
3. Participate in school facility planning and design to ensure that educational facilities are conducive to recreational and leisure uses by the community.	X	X	X	X	X

What possible steps (short, medium, or long range) could you and your agency undertake? Brainstorm with others, then list your ideas here and indicate the estimated time frame.

Idea	Time frame

From California Park & Recreation Society, 2008, *Creating Community* (Champaign, IL: Human Kinetics).

(continued)

Figure 5.1 *(continued)*

5. Demonstrate Results

Conduct research to document the value of parks and recreation, influence public opinion, and set policy.

Trends Reference

External environmental factors

Organizational and operational changes

	Individuals	Agencies	Professional organizations	Allied professions	Educators/ academia
Short-range steps					
1. Develop an ongoing benchmarking program to establish performance standards for park and recreation operations.	X	X	X	X	X
2. Develop a research agenda to commission research in areas that support the VIP Action Plan.			X	X	X
3. Increase access to relevant research studies.			X	X	X
Medium-range steps					
4. Strengthen students' and practitioners' skills in collecting and using research data.	X	X			X

What possible steps (short, medium, or long range) could you and your agency undertake? Brainstorm with others, then list your ideas here and indicate the estimated time frame.

Idea	Time frame

6. Document Best Practices

Identify, develop, and document new or current practices that demonstrate the outcomes of parks and recreation as described in the mission.

From California Park & Recreation Society, 2008, *Creating Community* (Champaign, IL: Human Kinetics).

Trends Reference

External environmental factors

Organizational and operational changes

	Individuals	Agencies	Professional organizations	Allied professions	Educators/ academia
Short-range steps					
1. Establish criteria for identifying VIP demonstration projects related to the mission.		X	X		X
2. Identify and promote best practices, including project models, organizational structures, and partnership arrangements from the most successful demonstration projects.	X	X	X	X	X
Medium-range steps					
3. Create and fund demonstration projects that demonstrate the power of the VIP Action Plan.		X	X	X	X
Long-range steps					
4. Document and publicize the measurable outcomes of demonstration projects to illustrate the power of the VIP Action Plan concepts.	X	X	X	X	X

What possible steps (short, medium, or long range) could you and your agency undertake? Brainstorm with others, then list your ideas here and indicate the estimated time frame.

Idea	Time frame

(continued)

From California Park & Recreation Society, 2008, *Creating Community* (Champaign, IL: Human Kinetics).

Figure 5.1 *(continued)*

7. Affect Public Policy

Affect public policy at the local, state, and federal level in accordance with the values of parks and recreation.

Trends Reference

External environmental factors

Organizational and operational changes

	Individuals	Agencies	Professional organizations	Allied professions	Educators/ academia
Short-range steps					
1. Become more politically active and visible as professionals and as a profession.	X	X	X		X
2. Identify organizations that represent current and future demographics, and build and strengthen partnerships with those organizations.	X	X	X	X	X
Medium-range steps					
3. Commission statewide public opinion polls on voter attitudes regarding parks and recreation.			X		X
4. Strengthen strategic partnerships and collaborations with local and statewide organizations dealing with public safety, education, research and development, economic development, transportation, planning, and public health.	X	X	X	X	X

What possible steps (short, medium, or long range) could you and your agency undertake? Brainstorm with others, then list your ideas here and indicate the estimated time frame.

Idea	Time frame

8. Expand Resources

Identify new resources or strategic partners to move parks and recreation toward professional and community goals.

Trends Reference

External environmental factors

Organizational and operational changes

	Individuals	Agencies	Professional organizations	Allied professions	Educators/ academia
Short-range steps					
1. Develop a marketing plan to solicit sponsorships, secure grant money, and increase public awareness of the value of parks and recreation.		X	X		
2. Expand the use of technology to improve access, information, and services.		X	X	X	X
Medium-range steps					
3. Appoint park and recreation professionals' boards of directors to influence policy and generate resources.	X	X	X	X	X
4. Establish a fund to support implementation of the VIP Action Plan.	X	X	X		
5. Investigate organizational structures, operating models, and service delivery systems for parks and recreation that would increase effectiveness, resources, and partnerships.		X	X		X

What possible steps (short, medium, or long range) could you and your agency undertake? Brainstorm with others, then list your ideas here and indicate the estimated time frame.

Idea	Time frame

From California Park & Recreation Society, 2008, *Creating Community* (Champaign, IL: Human Kinetics).

Since the release of the VIP Action Plan in 1999, CPRS has focused time and resources toward its implementation. Progress has been made on many of the strategies:

• CPRS developed a VIP Ambassador training program and traveled throughout the state offering the free training program to members who wished to use the plan in their agencies. More than 100 members participated in the training.

• Agencies throughout California have adopted the vision statement of "We create community through people, parks, and programs" as their own. The vision is promoted on agency brochures, fliers, business cards, Web sites, staff shirts, activity guides, door mats, banners, and even vehicles. One department has the staff voice-mail greeting state that they are not currently available because they are out creating community through people, parks, and programs.

• Several agencies have used the VIP Action Plan framework to develop a strategic plan specific to their needs. One agency even applied the framework to the development of the municipal airport's strategic plan, which was also under the direction of the park and community services director.

• The California Park & Recreation Society has revamped its annual awards program to incorporate the values, vision, and mission as stated in the VIP Action Plan. The most coveted award is the Creating Community Award of Excellence, which recognizes those agencies that display a commitment to new directions, strategic action planning, and creating opportunities within the vision and mission of creating community through people, parks, and programs.

• CPRS developed a statewide public relations program (as seen in chapters 9 and 10) that provided agencies with tools to communicate the vision and mission of the profession.

VIP in Action

As a result of the CPRS VIP Action Plan, the City of El Cajon (California) Recreation Department has responded by embarking on and completing a three-year project that we call 3D: Determine, Deliver, and Demonstrate.

The purpose of our 3D Project and process was to identify the emerging needs of the community, its residents, and stakeholders; to realign department programs and services to reflect and incorporate the input and views of the community; and learn to demonstrate and measure outcomes of delivered services and programs. As outlined in the CPRS VIP Action Plan, our profession must be able to demonstrate the value of park and recreation services in order to remain essential for healthy, sustainable communities.

These were the intended outcomes of 3D:

• Strengthen the department's and city's relationships with the community.

• Use resources that are community centered and customer driven.

• Realign vision, mission, and values with those attributes, benefits, and issues identified as important to the community.

• Systematically align and refine programs, services, events, facilities, and activities around the attributes, benefits, and issues identified as important to the community.

• Expand government's capacity to address needs and issues important to the community and individual customers.

• Strengthen the department's and city's positions as essential components in the quality of life and continued viability of El Cajon.

With this shift in our culture, we now see that we are truly programming with a purpose. In short, identified VIP Action Plan strategies have been integrated into what our city is accomplishing via our 3D Project. For example, the following are identified VIP Action Plan strategies and derived outcomes as a result of our project.

• **Communicate the vision.** We completed a comprehensive marketing plan in which we identified target markets and target profiles, analyzed target market needs, identified competitors, created positioning statements unique to target markets, and developed marketing strategies and a branding style guide.

- **Form partnerships.** We work with and in the community. As an example, we are at the table with CBO El Cajon Collaborative and associated subcommittee work groups focused on youth violence prevention, after-school programming, and grant-funded programming. We also have formed staff liaisons with four city-appointed commissions (parks and recreation, aging, disabilities, and youth).

- **Expand professional competencies.** Professional enrichment opportunities for staff include the use of the Search Institute's 40 developmental assets as the adopted practice in youth development programs; focus on recruiting and training with the use of identified core competencies; and staff attendance at numerous trainings, seminars, and workshops in which topics involve leadership, youth development with middle school population, gang prevention, and marketing.

- **Demonstrate results.** We created a Program Planning and Documentation Form (PPDF) to be used as a tool in programming with a purpose and demonstrating those results. We created and used measurement instruments. To date, we have used this tool for three youth programs and one citywide project called Project Fit-Kids where a cross-sampling of programs were measured to demonstrate participants' developmental assets in constructive use of time, personal power, and caring adult relationships outside of family and school.

- **Document best practices.** Project Fit-Kids will be identified as a department best practice.

- **Expand resources.** Based on success of formed partnerships, we are now working with Cajon Valley Union School District in the opening of a new joint-use gymnasium and recreation center located in a neighborhood previously lacking in recreational facilities and programs. With this new joint use, both the school district and the recreation department have support from a community-based nonprofit organization known as Stoney's Kids, who will now fund a youth sports scholarship program for those targeted youth and families.

Our agency has proudly embraced the task that CPRS has asked us to do with the VIP Action Plan. We have also completed a summary report that specifically outlines what our department has done with the 3D Project and how it captures our organization's goals and objectives. Ultimately, the measure of our success is now based on our ability to measure program outcomes, demonstrate changes in participants, and share data in a way that is meaningful to the community and decision makers and is supportive of the mission of the department and to our profession.

Adapted, by permission, from City of El Cajon Recreation Department.

- CPRS conducted three benchmarking studies to determine the best practices in aerobic instructor training (promote health and wellness), playground safety inspection (strengthen safety and security), and youth development staff training (foster human development).

Does the VIP Action Plan work? That is a frequently asked question. There is no better answer to that question than one provided by a park and recreation professional who is using the VIP Action Plan to move the agency forward. The above box contains a statement from Lori Beliveau, director of recreation for the City of El Cajon (California) Recreation Department. She and her staff developed the "Determine, Deliver, and Demonstrate" project.

Figure 5.2 is the form that El Cajon staff used to guide the 3D process in their department. This form was used as a training tool for staff to make programs intentional, which includes clearly identifying the intended outcomes, which activities will lead to those outcomes, and what measurement tools will be used to demonstrate the outcomes to the stakeholders. The form is now used for designated programs and grant-funded programs.

In this chapter we provided updates on the projects undertaken by CPRS as well as how one agency used the VIP Action Plan for their program planning. While eight strategies were discussed, professionals and agencies may choose to focus on one or two strategies to adopt. Regardless of which implementation strategy you choose, it is

FIGURE 5.2

El Cajon Recreation Department 3D Program Planning and Documentation Form

First D: Determine

Community target issue:

Background information:

Related information:

Assumptions:

Second D: Deliver

Program or Service Description

Name of program: _____

Locations: _____

Starting and ending dates: _____ Hours of operation: _____

Age range of participants: _____ Gender breakdown: _____

% Male: _____ % Female: _____ Total available number of participant hours: _____

Overview of program: _____

Strategic goal: _____

Desired Program Outcome

What would you like to make happen for participants and the community as a result of this program or service? In what ways could this program or service contribute to youth development or sense of community?

Outcome 1

Outcome 2

Outcome 3

Program Activities Related to Target Issue

Activities and actions taken within the course of delivering the program or service will help participants and the community reach the desired outcomes. What would you do or what elements in the program would you change to make sure the desired outcomes are being worked on?

Activities related to outcome 1

Activities related to outcome 2

Activities related to outcome 3

Third D: Demonstrate

Proposed Measurement

Outputs: The outputs are about the programs, such as the number of participants, cost, and revenue.

Short-term outcomes: These short-term outcomes will relate specifically to the program activities related to target issue. Assume that you are observing this program. How could you observe or tell that the supportive activities were taking place?

Long-term outcomes: Note that you need to ask yourself how you would know that the important outcomes have been reached. List a few of those things. (We will refine the outcome measures and determine how we'll measure together. The following are just examples to get you thinking.)

Partners and Community Resources Involved

Partners	Current and potential	Resources

Accomplishments

Comments from staff

Feedback from parents

Comments from participants

Debriefing by staff to identify successes as well as changes to be made in the future

How Information Will Be Used (Marketing and Positional Strategies)

Quarterly reports

Year-end report

Budget and work plan

Article in newspaper

Presentation for community groups

Program brochure

Letter to council

Reprinted, by permission, from City of El Cajon Recreation Department. Created by Sheryl Gonzalez and Ellen O'Sullivan. From California Park & Recreation Society, 2008, *Creating Community* (Champaign, IL: Human Kinetics).

important that the values, vision, and mission are also engaged in this planning effort.

In chapter 6 we get more specific and discuss implementation steps you can undertake. We present ideas on a variety of performance measures you can develop for your own agency. Through implementation, the profession will be recognized for addressing communitywide concerns and societal trends.

6

Action Steps and Performance Measures

As you begin to think more broadly about the park and recreation profession by using the values, vision, and mission, you must also begin to craft specific goals that support your vision and strategies. Additionally, measuring your progress through regular assessments will keep you on track with your goals. This chapter covers getting started using the VIP Action Plan, writing VIP-based performance measures, and assessing your performance.

FORM AN ACTION TEAM

CPRS is the lead agency and sponsor of the VIP Action Plan, *Creating Community in the 21st Century*. The CPRS board of directors appointed an action team to implement the VIP Action Plan, to keep the project on track and alive with professionals, and to make recommendations to the CPRS board of directors.

Agencies or organizations wishing to implement the VIP Action Plan within their ranks should appoint such an action team—using both members (staff and board members) and nonmembers (partners, community leaders, commission and board members, and elected officials). Collaboration with strategic allies and partners allows the organization to shape its future using the VIP Action Plan.

Your participation as an individual professional is important to the plan's acceptance nationwide. The plan encourages you to conduct your own action-planning process in your organization or community (see appendix B) and participate individually in the project. Table 6.1 contains suggestions on how you, your agency, professional organizations, and educators and universities can get involved in the VIP Project. Be sure to come up with your own ideas as well; there is not one "right way."

DEVELOP ACTION STEPS

Any action team must start their work by developing the most important short-range (0 to 2 years to complete), medium-range (2 to 4 years to complete), and long-range (4 or more years to complete) action steps. Let's see the action steps chosen by the CPRS, then discuss how your action team might select their steps.

CPRS Action Steps

CPRS chose the following first goals, or action steps, in 2001. These are referred to as *clear first steps*. A more specific goal, or task, is also shown as an example of the type of activity that is needed

Table 6.1 VIP Project Participation Opportunities

	You	Agency	Professional organizations	Educators, universities, and students
Convene. Create a VIP Task Force to review the VIP Action Plan and to develop your plan for implementing it in your agency.	X	X	X	X
Align. Update your agency's strategic or master plan to incorporate the VIP Action Plan framework. Align your agency's vision, values, and mission with the VIP Action Plan. Identify how the key trends will affect your agency and its future plans.	X	X	X	
Join. Participate in a community task force that addresses one of the mission areas of the VIP Action Plan. For instance, ask the local chamber of commerce to assist you in evaluating the economic value of your agency's special events.	X	X		
Train. Coordinate, host, or attend educational sessions that develop the core competencies and skills outlined in the VIP Action Plan.	X	X	X	X
Benchmark. Produce or participate in benchmarking and standards development by contributing your agency's data.	X	X	X	X
Demonstrate and mentor. Declare your agency a VIP Project site. Agree to implement the plan with your colleagues. Be a resource to other agencies willing to join you. Share your successes and failures so others may learn.	X	X	X	X
Share. Write an article for your professional organization publication or Web site about what your organization is doing. Submit an educational session to your professional conference.	X		X	X
Join. Join your state and national professional park and recreation associations and encourage their adoption of the VIP Action Plan.	X	X		X
Spread the word. Read the VIP Action Plan and distribute a copy to your coworkers, city manager, county administrators, board, and commission. Make a presentation to them on how parks and recreation is addressing the future.	X	X		X

in order to reach the goal. The task relates to the work that CPRS undertook as it began its implementation of the plan.

1. Create an internal ambassador program to communicate the vision and value of parks and recreation and the VIP Action Plan to members of the profession.

   Task: By March 2002 develop a training program that introduces the values, vision, and mission to members and offer one training program in five locations.

2. Adopt and implement the VIP vision in individual agencies and organizations.

   Task: Recruit 50 park and recreation agencies in California to adopt the VIP vision as their agency's vision by March 2002.

3. Design and implement a phased-in statewide public relations program in public and professional media.

   Task: By March 2003 hire a communications consultant to develop a communications plan based on the VIP values, vision, and mission.

4. Develop core competencies and skills needed by park and recreation professionals.

   Task: At the 2002 conference, offer 20 educational sessions that address one or more of the core competencies identified in the VIP Action Plan.

5. Develop, gather, expand, and disseminate K-12 curriculum materials that demonstrate the value of parks, recreation, and leisure. Help children develop strong leisure skills; implement those in K-12 schools statewide by providing curriculum to teachers and through classroom presentations by recreation professionals, students, and educators.

   Task: By April 2003 assess the State Department of Education's willingness to accept curriculum materials from CPRS.

6. Develop an ongoing benchmarking program to establish performance standards for parks and recreation in California.

   Task: By March 2003 conduct two benchmarking projects that set performance standards for either a recreation program or a park practice.

Courtesy of the Department of Parks and Recreation, Lansing, Michigan

Agencies should consistently assess their performance in terms of their vision and mission. A variety of evaluation tactics should be implemented.

7. Establish criteria for identifying VIP demonstration projects related to each component of the mission.

   Task: By September 2002 add to the CPRS awards program criteria that entries must demonstrate how the program or design process used the values, vision, or mission of parks and recreation.

8. Become more politically active and visible.

   Task: By June 2002 conduct a member survey to assess the degree to which CPRS members are willing to increase their political knowledge and activity. This will identify barriers and create the baseline by which to measure changes.

9. Appoint park and recreation professionals to board of directors to influence policy and generate resources.

   Task: By June 2002 conduct a member survey to assess the degree to which CPRS members are currently engaged in community advisory or policy-making boards in their community and in the state. This will serve as the baseline by which to measure changes.

Creating Your Action Steps

Undertaking a major planning effort such as the VIP Action Plan requires the action team members to step back from their daily operations and challenges. It requires strategic thinking, the process of figuring out how to turn your vision into reality. It is done by maintaining focus, thinking long term, sorting out the important elements from the background noise, and developing the appropriate plan of action.

You can read many books about strategic thinking, but we have found that strategic thinkers do the following:

- Ask the right questions.
- Get and consider various perspectives.
- Have a clear sense of desired outcomes.
- Try to achieve multiple objectives through singular actions.
- Anticipate opponents' actions and develop contingency plans.
- Pick battles that can be won, and avoid those that cannot.
- Change or discard plans when they are not achieving the desired results.
- Form alliances.
- Question assumptions.
- Identify blind spots that may impede success.
- Ferret out unproductive habits.
- Think positively, not negatively.
- Identify core competencies necessary for success.
- Embrace change.

Table 6.2 shows the development of an action plan that uses planning a dream vacation and a dream home as examples.

Figure 6.1 is a worksheet with questions you can use during your action-planning sessions.

CHOOSE PERFORMANCE MEASURES AND SELECT GOALS

Performance measures are quantitative statistics or qualitative findings that provide information on how well we have completed tasks. Once you identify your strategies and actions, you must measure the outcomes you produce to demonstrate your value to policy makers, constituents, funding organizations, and partners.

Suppose that one of the implementation strategies is to develop strategic partnerships. You will select performance measures and create goals that are quantitative or qualitative. A quantitative measure might be the number of strategic partnerships developed. A qualitative measure might be analyzing the effectiveness of the strategic partnerships developed with questions such as these: Were the objectives of the partnership stated and met? Were more resources identified and applied? Is the community more knowledgeable about the agency? You might also measure the partnership outcomes that benefit the community or customers who are served by the agency, such as a decrease in juvenile crime during nonschool hours, an increase in the number of volunteers who volunteer regularly at the agency, or a decrease in the number of house calls made by the fire department to help seniors.

Table 6.2 Sample Action Plan Development

Strategic plan development	Planning a dream vacation	Planning a dream home
Vision	Destination	Mental picture or brief description of the home
Mission	Itinerary on arrival at destination	Artist's rendering
Strategic directions	Map of the route	Floor plan
Action plan	Detailed plan for pretrip preparations and journey	Complete blueprints, bid specs, contract agreements, and project plan—including the permit process, tools, and training necessary if you will do some of the work yourself

---

FIGURE 6.1

Questions for Action-Planning Sessions

1. What do the current policy makers expect of us?

2. What do our current customers expect of us?

3. Who could be our future customers and what do they want?

4. In the process of getting to where we want to go, what are the concerns of policy makers or customers, and will they still be with us when we achieve our vision and goals?

5. Who are our partners, what expectations do they have, and what resources do they have that we can use?

6. What are the barriers or obstacles that we must avoid or overcome?

7. Who are our competitors? Who are our opponents?

8. What strategies will we need in order to overcome our competition or opponents?

9. What core competencies will staff need as we move into new areas?

10. What else do we need in order to succeed?

11. How will we do all this?

12. What should our first steps be?

Finally, you could measure the outcomes for the park and recreation profession as a whole, looking at criteria such as the salaries earned by those professionals who apply the VIP Action Plan in their community or the degree [or frequency or ease] these professionals are hired versus those professionals who are not familiar with the principles of the VIP Action Plan.

You can collect performance data in a number of ways. You might be looking for information on the following (Riddick & Russell, 1999):

- *Attributes,* or specific characteristics about participants such as gender or age

- *Facts,* such as the number of program activities that participants have done in the past month

- *Attitudes,* or how people feel or think about a particular aspect of your programming

- *Preferences,* in which people can choose their most or least favorite from two or more choices

- *Opinions,* or what people think is true (such as their impressions of your agency) or is important to them

For quantitative studies, you'll generally use structured interviews or questionnaires. For qualitative studies, you'll use unstructured interviews, focus groups, or participant observations (Riddick & Russell, 1999). You also may be able to find data from other sources, such as public safety reports or crime statistics. When possible, use established assessment tools with proven validity and reliability (such as those shown in table 6.3. Or, you might seek out consultants or university faculty who specialize in public opinion research and can help you develop your own customized assessment tools.

Choose individualized performance measures based on the goals of your program, facility, or service. Then set specific annual numeric or qualitative goals for each performance measure when you develop work plans for your agency or organization. Examples of some standard

Table 6.3 Assessment Tools for Park and Recreation Agencies

Leisure interests and activity pursuits	Felt need		Expressed demand		For more information contact:
	Individual activity	Activity cluster	Individual activity	Activity cluster	
Leisure activities blank	X	X	X	X	Consulting Psychologists 380 3rd Ebayshore Road Palo Alto, CA 94300 650-969-8901
Leisure attitude measurement		X		X	Idlyll Arbor, Inc. PO Box 720 Ravensdale, WA 98051-0720 425-432-3231
Leisure diagnostic battery		X			Venture Publishing 1990 Caro Avenue State College, PA 16801 814-234-4561
Leisure interest measurement		X			Idlyll Arbor, Inc.
Leisurescope Plus		X	X		Idlyll Arbor, Inc.
Ohio functional assessment battery		X	X	X	Psychological Corporation 555 Academic Court San Antonio, TX 78204-2498 800-228-0752
State technical institute assessment process (STILAP)	X	X	X	X	Idlyll Arbor, Inc.
Affect					**For more information contact:**
Leisure attitude measurement					Idlyll Arbor, Inc.
Leisure motivation scale					Idlyll Arbor, Inc.
Leisure satisfaction scale					Idlyll Arbor, Inc.
Leisurescope Plus					Idlyll Arbor, Inc.
Self-perception for children					Susan Harter Department of Psychology University of Denver 2155 Race Street Denver, CO 80208-0201 303-556-8565

Adapted, by permission, from C. Riddick and R. Russell, *Evaluative Research in Recreation, Park, and Sport Settings: Searching for Useful Information* (Champaign, IL: Sagamore), 309-310.

measures would be to generate 50% of annual revenue through facility rental fees or recover 90% of direct programming costs.

A common tool used in writing goals is SMART:

S: Specific

What will happen as a result of your efforts? What will you see? Who will be involved? The more specific you are, the more likely you are to attain your goal.

M: Measurable

How will you know if you reached your goal? It can be quantity or quality.

A: Attainable

Is it reachable? If the goal is too easy, the motivation may be lower.

R: Realistic

Are you or your agency willing and able to do the work needed?

T: Timely

What time period will be applied?

You do not have to include this information in this specific order; just be sure it is listed within the goal statement.

To continue the partnership example, here are some sample SMART goals:

- By June 2009 the Youth Services Division will offer three new nonschool-hour programs in cooperation with the school district and the juvenile gang division targeting at-risk teens (as identified by the police department).

Writing a SMART Goal

Try writing a SMART goal for yourself by listing these key points:

Who?

What?

When?

With what results?

How will we know?

Your action team may choose to create community goals or professional goals for yourselves.

- By September 2008 the recreation superintendent will have a written joint-use agreement with the school district to expand the department's use of the sports fields by 40%.

Formulating Community Goals

An agency can adopt a variety of community goals as it implements the VIP Action Plan. The community goals will depend on a community needs assessment and recognition of the fiscal and human resources available.

Following are suggestions related to the VIP mission to get your thoughts going on creating your own community goals:

Recreational Experiences

- Percentage of community members who report being very satisfied with the quality of recreational experiences provided by the agency
- Per capita agency expenditures spent on park and recreation services

Human Development

- Percentage of community members who report improvements in physical, intellectual, or social abilities as a result of participating in recreation programs or using park facilities
- Increased recognition of the role of park and recreation agencies as facilitators of human development among the general public or policy makers
- Percentage of parents or caregivers who report child's participation in after-school program has positively affected child's behavior at home and at school

Health and Wellness

- Number of people who report improvements in health and wellness (lower blood pressure, improved cardiac performance, improvement in strength, endurance, or flexibility) from participating in park and recreation opportunities
- Number of recreation facilities developed and maintained that contribute to health and wellness, such as number of miles of trails, number of indoor gyms, number of swimming pools

Courtesy of California Park & Recreation Society

It is equally important to measure the number of attendees or participants and the effect the program or service had on the individuals. It is by understanding the outcome that park and recreation agencies will gain recognition.

- Improved perception among the general public, strategic partners, or policy makers of the importance of parks and recreation in promoting health and wellness

Cultural Unity

- Number of individuals who report increased cultural awareness through participating in park and recreation opportunities
- Reduction in reported social conflicts as reported by park and recreation staff or public safety departments

Community Problem Solving

- Number of community issues addressed or resolved through the use of park and recreation resources (programs, services, staff, leadership)
- Number of community or neighborhood councils established

- Increased perception among the general public of the role of park and recreation professionals as problem solvers within the community

Environmental Resources

- Number of projects undertaken to protect and enhance the community's natural resources
- Number of acres preserved as natural or open space

Safety and Security

- Decrease in juveniles arrested between 3 and 7 p.m.
- Improved perception among residents about the overall safety of the community
- Decrease in number of rescues or people drowning at publicly owned swimming or boating facilities

Community Image and Sense of Place

- Percentage of community members who report that the community has a very strong image and sense of pride
- Number of community volunteers and projects successfully completed

Economic Development

- Number of businesses or residents who report that the park and recreation services were a factor in their decision to move to a community
- Amount of money generated annually by tourism events and services offered by the park and recreation agency

- Number of full-time or part-time jobs provided by the park and recreation agency
- Amount of money generated by a community event organized or supported by the park and recreation agency

Formulating Professional Goals

Just as an agency needs to set community-wide goals, each professional and each park and recreation association should set professional goals. Here are suggestions to get you thinking about your own professional goals or ones that your professional park and recreation organization should adopt.

Here are the goals and strategies being used by the City of Concord, California, in implementing their strategic plan.

1. Share facilities with school district, neighborhood and youth groups, community and cultural organizations, churches, and businesses. (Mission: provide recreational experiences)

   Goal: Increase the use of facilities owned and operated by school districts, nonprofit organizations, churches, and businesses

   Measure: The number of joint-use agreements signed or renewed in one calendar year with the school district, community and cultural organizations, churches, and businesses that provide opportunities to offer recreation programs

2. Develop recreational, educational, community service, and cultural programs in partnership with the school district, neighborhood and youth groups, community and cultural organizations, churches, and businesses. (Mission: foster human development)

   Goal: Expand programs by partnering with other organizations within the community

   Measure: The number of recreational, educational, community service, and cultural programs conducted in partnership with an outside entity

3. Develop partnerships with transit operators and agencies (County Connection, Bay Area Rapid Transit [BART], school district) in order to develop new and creative solutions to transporting residents to recreational, cultural, and educational events and activities. (Mission: support economic development)

   Goal: Eliminate lack of transportation as a barrier to participation in recreation programs

   Measure: The number of participants who access recreational, cultural, and educational events and activities via public transit and partnerships with transportation providers

4. Develop partnerships to expand and promote volunteerism. (Mission: strengthen community image and sense of place)

   Goal: Increase the quantity of volunteers and the length of time they volunteer

   Measure: An increase in the number of volunteers recruited through partnerships and the length of time the volunteer continues to serve

5. Develop partnerships that enhance the department's ability to provide services to underserved neighborhoods. (Mission: facilitate community problem solving)

   Goal: Provide services to underserved neighborhoods

   Measure: The number of programs or participants in neighborhoods that have been identified as underserved through citizen surveys or neighborhood meetings

Adapted, by permission, from City of Concord, CA.

Strategic Partnerships

- Number of strategic partnerships with other professional organizations
- Quality (or effectiveness) of strategic partnerships as reported by the partner

Greater Perceived Community Value

- Percentage of increase in resources managed by parks and recreation
- Perceived political strength of the park and recreation profession by policy makers

Effective Facilities, Services, and Programs

- Percentage of stakeholders who are very satisfied with facilities, services, and programs
- Community perception of overall quality of facilities, services, and programs

As park and recreation professionals, we tend to rely on attendance numbers, revenues generated, acres of land purchased, or parks developed as performance measures. Those are adequate in certain circumstances, but as you consider the VIP Action Plan for your community, expand your thinking about performance measures and include such items as customer surveys, partner surveys, and leadership engagement in community organization.

Changing the way you do business is a tough job; however, it is worth the effort as you consider the gains the profession can make as it measures the qualitative results of programs and services in addressing the mission of parks and recreation. When you can show data that include performance measures that focus on promoting health and wellness, fostering human development, or increasing cultural unity, you will gain the support of policy makers and customers.

You've now come to the end of the VIP Action Plan. Hopefully you or your agency has formed an action team that's developed action steps and chosen goals and performance measures so you can track your progress. Next is part II, in which you'll learn more about the skill of communicating with your customers, other stakeholders, and your community about your work and how it improves people's lives.

II

Communications

One of the core competencies of our profession, as identified in the VIP Action Plan, is communication. External communication and outreach are essential in furthering our mission. Additionally, several of the key VIP Action Plan implementation strategies rely on skillful communication—communicating the vision, forming partnerships, strengthening the park and recreation ethic, affecting public policy, and expanding resources.

The chapters in this part will build your capacity to communicate the profession's vision of creating community through people, parks, and programs, as well as the themes and key messages of your public relations program. By being an effective communicator, you will make the value of parks and recreation more visible to policy makers, community residents, and others who influence decisions on resources. Through strategic communications, you can ensure that park and recreation professionals are recognized as a vital partner in building strong communities in the 21st century.

Strategic communications include many ways of reaching the public. In chapter 7 we recount how we researched the audience to determine how to communicate our vision through the appropriate theme of creating community through people, parks, and programs. Included are tips you can use for researching your local audience to develop appropriate programs and better communicate with those in your community.

In chapter 8 we get into the nuts and bolts of creating a communications plan. We describe seven steps to develop your plan, provide you with examples of how effective plans work, and briefly discuss evaluating your plan's results.

Chapter 9 concerns working with the press to gain publicity for your agency and its work. We cover choosing your stories and spokesperson, writing media releases and advisories, contacting the media, creating media kits, and setting up press conferences. We also offer tips on handling calls from reporters and interviews with them.

Newspaper reporting is not the only way to get a story out. In chapter 10 we review other media outlets: op-eds, letters to the editor, radio and TV talk shows, PSAs, paid media, and the Internet. You can explore these other methods of gaining publicity for your programs.

After reading through part II, you'll know how to improve your agency's communication practices. Use that information, along with what you develop through the VIP Action Plan, to communicate your agency's work and the profession to your community.

7

Researching the Audience

Local park and recreation agencies are integral to healthy urban, suburban, and rural communities. While we may have had victories in the past with local or state funding initiatives, our trends analysis shows we are in a constantly shifting economic and political environment. Park and recreation professionals must continually inform and educate the public about the value of our contributions and the ways in which we create community through people, parks, and programs.

The first step in developing any communications plan must be to determine the level of awareness among target audiences about the mission of their respective park and recreation agency. In 2000, i.e. communications, LLC, of San Francisco was retained by CPRS to create a research-based communications plan to further the vision "we create community through people, parks, and programs." The research included a written partner survey, a print media audit, a public opinion research review, and key informant interviews. A theme was derived from the research, which also offered a baseline for public relations campaigns.

RESEARCH HIGHLIGHTS OF PARTNER SURVEY

CPRS distributed a specific partner survey to 1,400 people with a response rate of over 5%. The focus was on foundations and partner organizations involved in promoting health, education, youth development, community building and economic development, law enforcement and violence prevention, seniors, and environmental protection.

Our survey respondents saw the following as the greatest strengths of parks and recreation:

- Being neighborhood based
- Facilities

Courtesy of the City of Eugene Parks & Open Space

Providing places for children to interact with others in an unstructured environment supports learning how to interact and problem solve with others.

The following were seen as the greatest weaknesses:

- Lack of engagement in collaborative efforts
- Identifying community needs
- Training staff in youth development

Respondents saw the greatest opportunities for impact in collaborating, providing more activities in low-income neighborhoods, and fostering community involvement.

RESEARCH HIGHLIGHTS OF PRINT MEDIA AUDIT

To better understand the media's portrayal of parks and recreation, i.e. communications searched six English-language daily newspapers in California, looking at editorials and news articles printed from June 1999 to December 2000. The print media audit included these publications:

- *Los Angeles Times*
- *Sacramento Bee*
- *San Diego Union Tribune*
- *San Francisco Chronicle*
- *San Jose Mercury News*
- *Fresno Bee*

Media stories portrayed parks and recreation as playing a significant role in just three of the nine mission components:

- Providing recreational experiences
- Fostering human development
- Strengthening community image and sense of place

The stories and editorials in the print media audit most frequently associated parks and recreation with these factors:

- Quality of life
- Places to play
- Time spent with family and friends
- Outdoor and physical activities
- Anchoring neighborhoods
- Preserving open space
- Resolving conflict between residents over different and incompatible uses

While the media overwhelmingly portrayed parks and recreation in a positive light, none of the stories developed the theme of parks as spaces in which to bring together people or neighborhoods. We found only one story or editorial that used the term *creating community*.

HIGHLIGHTS OF PUBLIC OPINION RESEARCH

Existing public opinion polling and other research on voters' attitudes was reviewed. We looked at the California Field Poll, a nonpartisan survey of public opinion for the comprehensive $2.1 billion Parks, Water, and Coastal Protection Bond Act that was passed by California voters in November 2000. Before the passage of the act, the California Field Poll found it was heavily supported by a margin of better than 3 to 1 (Field Poll, October 29, 1999).

The Trust for Public Land in San Francisco maintains a database, Public LandVote, which reveals voters support conservation-based ballot measures. In nearly all 50 states voters have approved conservation finance ballot measures that have funded parks and playgrounds, farmland preservation, trails and greenways, forests, and wildlife habitat protection (Trust for Public Land, 2006).

California's public opinion research revealed the following:

- Voters do not consider parks as a pressing environmental issue.

- The passage of California's Proposition 12 in 2000 (which was a $2.1 billion bond act for water, clean air, and parks) appears to be due more to its promise to protect air and water quality than to its promise to protect open space and improve the conditions of local parks.

- Voters consider parks a high priority when framed as safe places for children to play.

- Voters are very concerned about the lack of parental supervision of young people, and they see this as a major cause of problems facing young people in their communities.

HIGHLIGHTS OF THE INTERVIEWS

Thirty-one interviews were conducted with leaders from school boards, foundations, law enforcement, and local and state policy makers in California. These interviews found a high level of awareness of involvement in parks and recreation in eight of the nine mission components. Awareness was defined as "high level" when 50% or more of key informant respondents linked the mission area with their local park and recreation agency.

The interviews revealed the following as the greatest strengths of parks and recreation:

- Equality of access to facilities and programs
- Neighborhood based
- Reaching out to children and families
- Diverse staff
- Facilities

At the same time, these are the greatest weaknesses of parks and recreation:

- Inadequate participation in community meetings
- Not identifying community needs
- Needing better-trained staff

The following shows the level of awareness among our key informants of links between mission components and the local park and recreation agencies:

- Providing recreational experiences (100%)
- Fostering human development (88%)
- Strengthening community image and sense of place (82%)
- Strengthening safety and security (81%)
- Protecting environmental resources (71%)
- Increasing cultural unity (61%)
- Promoting health and wellness (61%)
- Facilitating community problem solving (54%)
- Supporting economic development (35%)

THEME AND VARIATIONS OF THE PUBLIC RELATIONS PLAN

Based on research, a theme was created that encompasses the mission of parks and recreation, translates well into Spanish, has the potential for powerful visual images, and allows for variations in order to communicate the mission components. Translating the public relation themes into Spanish opens the door for the profession to communicate to one of the fastest-growing population groups in the United States: Latinos.

After much research, the park and recreation theme for public relations is "Space to . . .," or in Spanish, "Espacio para . . .". Variations were created to reflect the mission of parks and recreation:

- Space to play and learn
- Space to be safe and secure
- Space to create and imagine

Each thematic variation relates to specific mission components.

Space to play and learn creates a reference to these aspects:

Park and recreation agencies offer a variety of classes and programs in the spaces that they manage (e.g., community centers, nature centers, fitness and wellness centers, and sport facilities).

- Providing recreational experiences (supporting education and lifelong learning)
- Fostering human development
- Promoting health and wellness
- Increasing cultural unity

Space to be safe and secure creates a reference to these aspects:

- Strengthening safety and security
- Protecting environmental resources
- Facilitating community problem solving

Space to create and imagine creates a reference to these aspects:

- Strengthening community image and sense of place
- Supporting economic development

These thematic variations form a base for the messages in your park and recreation public relations plan. Those messages can be repeated in printed materials (e.g., brochures and posters), press releases, opinion-editorials (also known as op-eds), and other communications tools that the agency itself can create.

RESEARCH SUMMARY

The research demonstrated that there were distinctly varied levels of understanding about the vision and mission of parks and recreation. The good news is that many of the mission components are well understood, and the public and its leaders believe parks and recreation are achieving those goals. It is also encouraging to realize that the mission components link well to the core values of both the general public and the media, which increases the likelihood of media coverage.

Based on the research and the resulting recommendations, communications tools were created for communicating the vision and mission of the park and recreation profession. We discuss those in the next few chapters. You can apply the tools anywhere you work.

8

Developing a Communications Plan

Take this quiz before you begin this chapter:

T F 1. Communications is a management function.

T F 2. My agency has a communications plan with measurable goals.

T F 3. My agency uses the same message regardless of the issue or audience.

T F 4. My agency views *everyone* as a target market.

The answers to these questions lie in this chapter. Most park and recreation professionals recognize the importance of public relations in promoting their activities and in generating support for their agencies. This is often viewed generically as marketing. But promoting an event or a public notice for a bond measure is only a small part of the picture. Agencies that incorporate strategic communications planning into their operations and management can enhance their success both inside and outside the organization. A good communications plan can improve morale, increase community participation, and help the agency's bottom line.

It is essential that management view communications as one of their key responsibilities. Communications is not a function that should be regulated to an entry-level position or given to a staff member who knows little about communications. The Commission for Accreditation of Park and Recreation Agencies (CAPRA, 2003) lists communications as one of the fundamental accreditation standards in public information, community relations, and marketing. CAPRA (2003) further states a person or unit within the agency should be designated with communications responsibilities, particularly with large agencies.

Let's take a look at the seven steps to a communications plan and how to execute each of them. We'll then examine how to combine them into a complete plan and how to assess the results after you've implemented the plan.

FOLLOWING THE STEPS OF THE PLAN

These are the steps we suggest for creating a communications plan:

1. Start with your vision and mission statement.
2. Set clear, measurable goals.
3. Identify your target audiences.
4. Develop your message.
5. Choose your tactics.
6. Create your communications tools.
7. Consider your timing.

Start With Your Vision and Mission Statement

All communications activities should enhance both the vision and the mission of your agency. Remember to start with your vision and mission statement.

The VIP vision (We create community through people, parks, and programs) and its mission components provide the focus for this communications plan. Write down your current personal or agency's vision and mission. Think about how this vision is consistent, complimentary, or in synch with the VIP vision.

Set Clear, Measurable Goals

Begin by identifying goals that are realistic and achievable. Base your communications plan on available data so that you have a baseline against which to measure your success and progress. Even data that are a few years old or anecdotal in nature can be used if none other are available.

The following are sample goals with measurable outcomes and referencing baselines:

> **Goal:** Enhance visibility of the agency among Latino residents.

- Raise Latino attendance or registration at our facilities by 15% within six months from current baseline of _____.

- Garner quarterly media coverage in the local Latino newspaper or television station regarding our agency's positive impact and services to the Latino community from current baseline of _____ per quarter.

> **Goal:** Increase participation of seniors in monthly community activities.

- Raise senior attendance at agency special events by 10% over the next six months.

- Offer one new program at the beginning of the next fiscal year that addresses the needs identified by the seniors living in our community.

> **Goal:** Generate positive media coverage of the agency following negative news coverage over a community dispute about the use of the local park for dogs.

- Garner quarterly coverage in local newspaper on collaborative efforts to resolve the dog–people conflict.

- Increase TV media coverage of programs that benefit the entire community from the current baseline of _____.

> **Goal:** Generate support from public opinion leaders and policy makers for an upcoming tax assessment. (A public opinion leader may be president of the local chamber of commerce, president of a local

community-based organization, or a faith-based leader.)

- Secure at least one endorsement from a local policy maker.

- Recruit a prominent public opinion leader to write an op-ed supporting the assessment.

- Meet with the editorial board of the local newspaper to obtain an editorial supporting the assessment. (See chapter 10 for more on meeting with an editorial board.)

> **Goal:** Encourage financial contributions for a capital campaign to build a new facility.

- Identify a specific amount of money from individual contributions as successful, and publicize results.

- Solicit contributions from various sectors of the community (private, individual, corporate) with targeted printed materials.

Identify Your Target Audiences

There is no such thing as "the public" these days; people and their communities are very diverse. Residents living across the street from each other might get their information from and be influenced by completely different sources. When thinking about communications strategies, you must specify which segments of the population you want to target. Note that the selected audience may affect the tactics you choose. For example, if you are opening a new senior center, a printed brochure mailed to residents over the age of 55 or an ad in the newspaper will better reach your target audience than an e-mail blast sent to everyone in your address book. Radio is a strong communications medium for Latinos, so a radio PSA sent to a Spanish-speaking radio station announcing a community-wide family festival will reach that audience better than an ad in the newspaper.

> ## TIP
>
> Communications should always answer the questions "For what?" and "So what?" Communications takes time and resources, so be sure that what you do will further your agency's objectives and enhance your agency's mission.

The following is a list of target audiences that influence the work of park and recreation agencies:

- Adults (who can be further segmented)
  - Generational differences (e.g., the GI generation, baby boomers, Generation X, and Generation Y)
  - Marital status
  - Lifestyle choices (e.g., WOOF are well-off older folks; DWK are dual income with kids; MOSS are middle-aged, overstressed, semiaffluent suburbanites, or seniors over 75) or frail elderly
- Business leaders
- Elected or appointed officials
  - City council or county board of supervisors
  - School boards
  - Park and recreation boards or commissions
  - State or federal legislators
- Public employees
  - City employees
  - County employees
  - Special district employees
  - State employees
  - Law enforcement
- Media (see note after this list)
  - Print
  - Radio
  - TV
  - Internet
- Faith-based community organizations
- School districts
  - Individual schools
  - School principals or superintendents
- Social service agencies
  - Organizations serving youth
  - Organizations serving ethnic populations or groups

Media is often considered just a means of distributing information. Also think of the media as a target market for communications and apply different tactics. For a TV station, you can send a video clip with a voiceover, or for a radio station you can send a podcast.

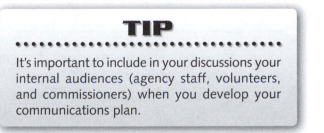

TIP

It's important to include in your discussions your internal audiences (agency staff, volunteers, and commissioners) when you develop your communications plan.

After you've identified the target audiences, the next step is to research who and what influence each target audience. You'll need this in order to determine the most effective ways of getting their attention. The following are sample questions for your target market research:

- Where do they get their information?
- What media do they watch?
- What do they read?
- Whom do they respect?
- Whom do they trust and listen to?

Answers to these questions can be gathered by one-on-one conversations, surveys, focus groups, and observations over time. Identify your target audience based upon your goal, measurable outcome, and referencing baseline.

Develop Your Message

An effective communications plan uses research in developing messages that will resonate with specific audiences. Facts and figures are worth inclusion, but the focus of each message should be something that matters to people in the community.

Our goal in this example is to communicate the vision "We create community through people, parks, and programs" and the ways in which the agency fulfills the mission of parks and recreation. The VIP Action Plan identified nine mission components for parks and recreation:

- Providing recreational experiences
- Fostering human development
- Promoting health and wellness
- Increasing cultural unity
- Facilitating community problem solving
- Protecting environmental resources
- Strengthening safety and security
- Strengthening community image and sense of place
- Supporting economic development

Courtesy of the City of Eugene Parks & Open Space

Protecting natural resources is important for environmental reasons. Parks and open spaces also strengthen the community's image and sense of place.

Fortunately, our research demonstrated that these mission components matter to the target audiences and supported their core values. However, the public does not always associate parks and recreation with addressing these community needs. The challenge for our communications efforts is to make that connection.

For the message development of the communications plan, specific questions were asked to determine how to best communicate the connection between parks and recreation and the mission components. Through our research, we found that the words and images that most frequently come to people's minds when they think about parks are trees, open spaces, grass, and the color green. After the natural settings, the public currently connects parks and recreation with relaxation, quiet and serenity, tranquillity, peacefulness, meditation, leisure time, and enjoying the sun. The asset that the public associates most with parks and recreation is its facilities (parks and buildings—that is, spaces).

Public-opinion polling showed that voters are concerned about the lack of safe places and spaces for children to play. They consider parks to be special natural places locally, and they think the disappearance of open space is a very or extremely serious issue. For these reasons, the communications plan includes the following themes and variations to frame the messages that reference each of the mission areas:

- Space to play and learn
- Space to be safe and secure
- Space to create and imagine

Beyond this theme and variations is the *specific* message development that each agency will need in order to tell and sell their local story to the media. We can offer broad themes for your communications planning, but remember that your message must be specific to your community's needs. It must be developed by *you* based on your goals.

TIP

You might want to conduct research on your own to determine what residents in your community rank as important issues or how the public reacts to the proposed messages. To see how your agency has been written about in the past and by whom, conduct a communications audit. A communications audit is broader than a simple review of news releases or stories printed in the newspaper. It is a review of your agency's past press releases (written by you or the local press), an assessment of where they were sent, where they were printed, what message was presented, and whether the release was read by the right audiences. It also looks at the agency's annual reports or other materials distributed to policy makers and the general public. An in-depth communications audit can also include a review of the agency's organizational issues; a situational analysis to assess your communication's strengths, weaknesses, opportunities, and threats; a review of your product and service descriptions; Web site analysis; a general survey of target audiences; and any implementation issues and evaluation issues (Full Circle Associates, 1999). Your research options are interviews of your key informants, survey residents, or users or a media audit of local papers (more on media audits in chapter 9).

When conducting local research, follow these guidelines:

- Ensure that your key informants or survey respondents represent your target audiences and your community. This means having a good cross section of age, gender, race, and socioeconomic background in your research samples.
- Word your questions carefully to avoid misinterpretation. For example, words such as *community* and *values* could be defined in different ways by different people.
- Ask the same questions each time you survey. This will allow you to compare responses and measure results over time.

A compelling message motivates your target audience. A message can be compelling only if it touches the audience's core values and beliefs, which is why your research is so important. Your message is not merely a restatement of your mission or goal. Frame your message in a way that makes it meaningful to the media and the audiences that you are trying to reach. The themes and variations for the park and recreation communications plan include messages that can be applied through your local communications plan.

For each communications goal, develop a phrase of about 4 to 10 words that you would like to see used *every time* a reporter conducts an interview on the subject or writes an article for the newspaper. What is the sound bite (or key message) you want to hear repeated again and again?

- Keep the message simple.
- Make the message relevant to your target audiences.
- Make the message quotable.

- Use facts and figures to back up your message points.
- Take cultural differences into account.

Here are some sample messages to consider:

- Parks and recreation keep youth safe.
- Park and recreation facilities are accessible to everyone.
- Parks and recreation enhances the good work already taking place in the community.
- Parks and recreation partners with schools, local organizations, and other outstanding community members.

A final note on the message is that it must be tied to your specific communications goal. Take your time when crafting your communications goal—it is not as easy as it appears.

Choose Your Tactics

Depending on your budget and goal, you can use a variety of tactics to communicate your message.

Crafting Your Communications Goal

As stated earlier, communications is more than marketing. First, think of an issue you are currently working on. For example, are you opening a teen center or other facility? Are you trying to eliminate graffiti in the parks? Write down your issue.

Second, think about what you want to tell others about what you are doing. Is the facility being opened in response to a community survey? Did you work with a partner to make the facility a reality? Were residents engaged in the planning of the facility? Write down what you are doing or did.

Third, craft your communications goal based on the issue and what you are doing to address it. For example, the new teen center is opening as a result of a community-wide teen survey that revealed teens are unhappy because there's no place for them to safely get together in the community.

Your communications goal is to garner media stories reassuring people that the teen center is a safe and fun place to meet. Write down your key message.

Tactics are the *ways* in which you will communicate. Remember to focus on tactics most likely to get the attention of your target audience.

The following are communications tactics available to you:

- Media relations (press conferences, press releases)
- Op-eds and letters to the editor
- Editorials
- Radio and television public affairs and talk or news shows
- PSA placements
- Paid advertising
- Policy-maker events (breakfasts, groundbreaking ceremonies, briefings)
- Private-sector partnerships
- Media partnerships
- Media roundtables
- Internet and blogs
- E-blasts (a method used to send a message to intended audiences electronically over a computer network)

We'll tell you more about these tactics in the next two chapters.

Create Your Communications Tools

Every agency needs to have a basic set of tools available to support the communications tactics listed previously. The tools you select must be appropriate to the selected tactics, which are tied to the selected audience based on the communications goal.

For our example of a teen center opening, possible tactics might be these:

1. Invite local media for a press conference and preopening tour of the center, and if possible, have your teens give the tour. This will present visual images that the reporter can use in the story.
2. Buy advertising in the public and private middle or high school bulletins. This will reach your target audience of teens.
3. Buy advertising at the local theater, particularly if there is a film showing that is popular with teens.
4. Place posters at businesses frequented by teens and families. This will present a colorful image of the center, especially if you feature local teens in the poster.

The following is a checklist of communications tools to consider:

- Fact sheet on the agency (preferably one page)
- Brochures
- One-paragraph bios on spokespeople and agency leaders
- Newsletters
- Copies of positive or noteworthy newspaper articles about the agency
- Web site
- Reports or studies
- Database (see Creating a Media Database on page 120 in chapter 9)
- Posters, postcards
- Press kit or information kit folders

Communications tools should be consistent in language, design, and messaging. Review the communications tools that you currently have. Suppose your agency has a newsletter, a Web site, and a brochure. Lay them out side by side and, as you look at each tool, ask these questions:

- Do they use similar language to describe your after-school or seniors programs?
- Do they have the same look? Do they have similar color schemes, fonts, and use of graphics?
- Do the newsletter and Web site contain the same theme and message?
- Do the readers come away with the sense that your park and recreation agency helps create community through people, parks, and programs?

As part of the public relations goal to communicate the VIP vision, the CPRS created a colorful brochure highlighting the nine mission components (figure 8.1). The brochure is easily adaptable to all agencies regardless of size. It is a tool used for informing and educating elected and appointed officials, policy makers, foundations, businesses, reporters, and other community partners about the contributions of local park and recreation agencies. A template (figure 8.2) allows each agency to insert specific information about its services and programs. The news release format (figure 8.3, see page 109) also highlights the VIP vision.

Consider Your Timing

Although it's important to have a strong message that resonates with your target audiences, it is equally important to understand when those messages will most likely be heard. In the case of the media, timing means being ready for the moment when a newspaper or television station is most likely to cover the issue or story. Given that there is news *every* day, note that not all topics are timing sensitive. As you draft your communications plan, be explicit about when each communications effort or tactic will be implemented. What time of the year will your communications efforts have the most impact?

Consider the following in timing elements of your communications plan:

- *Milestone events.* Anniversaries, commemorations, and other milestone events provide a focus for the media and a "hook" for your efforts. When building your communications efforts around milestone events, be clear how your message is connected to the milestone. For instance, how has your teen center program helped reduce conflicts among students before and after school?

- *Electoral and legislative cycles.* If policy decisions and resource distribution are what you want to influence, then pay attention to electoral and legislative cycles, because during elections and budget deliberations, policy makers are more attentive to constituents.

- *School calendar.* Report cards, exams, and session breaks offer opportunities to publicize programs for youth, highlighting your efforts at playground safety, employment opportunities, enrichment activities, and after-school tutoring.

- *Holidays.* There are always newspaper spreads or extended television coverage on volunteerism or charity during the Christmas and Thanksgiving seasons. The media allots space for such coverage each year. Smaller and sometimes less recognized holidays offer similar opportunities to a smaller degree. For instance, a news

Figure 8.1 Parks and Recreation in California brochure.

Parks and Recreation in California

City of Pleasant View Department of Recreation & Parks

We Create Community Through People, Parks and Programs.

Who We Are

The Department of Recreation & Parks maintains and operates more than 15 sites for recreational use. At the head of the Department is the Director who is appointed by the City Manager. A Recreation and Park Commission of seven members is appointed by the Mayor upon concurrence of the City Council. The Commission meets monthly providing valuable citizen input to the department's management. Commissioners are appointed for three-year terms.

Our Service Area

The Department of Recreation & Parks serves the 47,700 residents of Pleasant View as well as the thousands of visitors to the city each year.

Our Facilities

The Department operates 3 recreation centers, 2 swimming pools, 1 lake, 1 camp located in the Sierras, 1 historical museum, and hundreds of programs for youth, seniors, families, businesses, the disabled and volunteers. The responsibility for the total year-round recreation program is managed by professionally trained staff.

Our Professional Staff

Ella Marksbury, Director

Annual Funding

Our budget for FY 00-01 is $4,544,221.

Decision Makers in Our Community

William Kerman, Mayor
<u>City Council</u>
Michael Rosper
Leila Haas
Crystal Smith
Christina Gomez-Rodriguez
Mark Harrell

Space to learn & play

Space to be safe & secure

Space to create & imagine

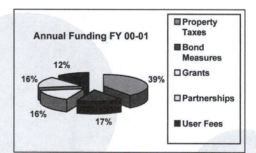

Contact Us:
1451 Light Street
Pleasant View, CA 99999
tel: 999.999.9999 fax: 999.999.9999
www.pleasantviewdrp.org

Figure 8.2 Template for City of Pleasant View.

FIGURE 8.3

Sample News Release

City of Pleasant View Department of Recreation & Parks — *We create community through people, parks, and programs.*
Opening of Senior Center Welcomed by Community

The Pleasant View Senior Center opened its doors on March 15, 2002. Located in the heart of downtown Pleasant View, the center offers resources and counseling for seniors. A library of information on services available to seniors in Pleasant View is available, as well as an on-site counselor to offer free advice on health coverage needs.

Currently, the center is surveying seniors in the community to identify pressing needs. The information will be used to guide future programming offered by the center. The center aims to survey 800 seniors by June 15, 2007. To receive a copy of the survey, visit the center's Web site or office.

Pleasant View Senior Center	**Hours of Operation**
652 Kearney Street	Monday to Friday: 8 a.m. to 7 p.m.
Pleasant View, CA 99999	Saturday: 10 a.m. to 6 p.m.
Phone: 999-999-9999	Sunday: 2 p.m. to 6 p.m.
Fax: 999-999-9999	
E-mail: info@pvsenior.org	
www.pvsenior.org.	

Space to learn and play — *Space to be safe and secure* — *Space to create and imagine*
Contact Us: 1451 Light Street, Pleasant View, CA 99999

---

release on a program reaching Latino community residents is more likely to get coverage around Cesar Chavez's birthday than during other times of the year. Pay attention to designated commemorative months, such as African American Heritage Month (February), Asian Pacific American History Month (May), and Hispanic Heritage Month (September).

Figure 8.4 (page 110) is a list of multicultural events grouped by month that you can use in finding connections between your message and relevant current events.

Finally, be sure to check whether something newsworthy has happened recently or is about to happen that affects your community and would relate to your message. Take advantage of the interest generated by such events to get media and audience attention.

PUTTING THE COMMUNICATIONS PLAN TOGETHER

Once you have planned the vision, mission, goals, baselines, target audiences, tactics, tools, and timing of your communications strategy, you are ready to put the pieces together to create a comprehensive communications plan.

Before you write your plan, assess your resources:

- What materials or information do you already have?
- What else do you need?
- How much time and which resources will you need in order to create the necessary tools?

- How much time will you and your staff need in order to implement the tactics you have chosen for your communications plan?

- Do you have dedicated staff for those responsibilities?

Make sure you have the staff and resources available to carry out the communications plan, and make sure your plan is easy to read. It's likely that other people will not be as knowledgeable or as enthusiastic about the topic as the writer! Also, your communications plan should present a case for why the organization requires the communications efforts the plan is proposing. Back up the plan with facts, figures, and charts.

Once your plan is written, you'll need to sell it internally. The first people to whom you must make your case is agency staff, elected officials or boards, and any other internal governing body. Having internal buy-in will help prepare staff and board members as frontline representatives or messengers of your agency.

FIGURE 8.4

Calendar of Multicultural Events

The following is an example of a calendar that references various cultural and recreation events. (Specific dates are not given because some vary based on the year. Consult the most current calendar to verify the date.)

January

New Year's Day: First day of the Gregorian calendar

Dr. Martin Luther King Jr. Day (1929-1968): Celebrates the birthday of African American civil rights leader

Tet begins: Vietnamese New Year (celebration lasts 7 days)

Day of remembrance for victims of Nazism

Tu B'Shevat: Jewish holiday to show respect and appreciation for plants and trees

February (African American Heritage Month)

National Freedom Day: Observes the 1865 abolition of slavery

Yuan Tan (Chinese New Year)

Valentine's Day

International Friendship Week

President's Day

National Day of Remembrance for Victims of the Japanese Internment

Birthday of W.E.B. Du Bois (1868-1963): African American leader and sociologist who helped found NAACP

March (Women's History Month)

International Women's Day: Widely observed holiday started by U.S. female garment workers demonstrating for the right to vote

Girl Scouts founded in 1912, Savannah, Georgia

Awwal Muharram: Begins the Islamic New Year

St. Patrick's Day

Purim: Celebrates the ancient rescue of the Jews from religious persecution

Passover begins at sundown: Jewish celebration of liberation from slavery

Birthday of Cesar Chavez (1927-1993): Mexican American labor leader who organized U.S. migrant farm workers

April (Child Abuse Prevention Month and Month of the Young Child)

Week of the Young Child begins

Earth Day: First celebrated in 1970 to honor the Earth and increase awareness and care for our planet and its people

Take Our Daughters to Work Day

Arbor Day: A special day for planting and caring for trees

May (Asian Pacific American Heritage Month)

Cinco de Mayo (Mexico)

Children's Day (Japan and Korea)

National Teacher's Day

Mother's Day

Memorial Day

World No Tobacco Day (U.N.)

June (Gay and Lesbian Pride Month)

Children's Day (China)

Stand for Children Day (U.S.)

Multicultural American Children's Awareness Day: Share the talents of all children

Children's Sabbath observed in Christian churches (U.S.)

Father's Day

Summer Solstice: First day of summer

July (Parks and Recreation Month)

Birthday of Thurgood Marshall (1908-1993): First African American Supreme Court Justice

Independence Day (U.S.)

Star Festival (Japan): Children tie poems to bamboo sticks and offer them to the stars

First Special Olympics held in Chicago, Illinois, in 1968

Parents' Day (U.S.)

August

Youth Day (Zambia)

Raksha Bandhan (Brother and Sister Day, India)

In 1963 Dr. Martin Luther King Jr. gave the "I Have a Dream" speech

September (Hispanic Heritage Month)

Childhood Injury Prevention Week

Labor Day (U.S. and Canada)

Rosh Hashanah: Jewish New Year begins at sundown

National Grandparents' Day (U.S.)

Yom Kippur: Jewish Day of Atonement begins at sundown

Mexican Independence Day

U.S. Constitution signed in 1787

Autumnal Equinox: First day of autumn

October (Child Health Month)

Universal Children's Day (U.N.)

National Day of Action to End Gun Violence

Indigenous People's Day (U.S.)

Lights On Afterschool! Celebrates after-school programs and publicizes the need for additional programs (U.S.)

Establishment of the United Nations in 1945

Halloween

November (Native American Indian Heritage Month)

Election Day (U.S.)

Veterans' Day (U.S.)

National Children's Book Week (U.S.)

Parent Involvement Day: Parents are encouraged to participate in the development and education of children

Thanksgiving (U.S.)

Education for all Handicapped Children Act passed in 1975

December

World AIDS Day

United Nations International Children's Emergency Fund (UNICEF) established in 1946

Winter Solstice: First day of winter

Christmas

Kwanzaa begins: Seven-day African American harvest festival

New Year's Eve

Courtesy of California Park & Recreation Society

Communication is more than writing a press release about who, what, why, and where. Promoting the message that community events provide opportunities for positive social interaction can enhance the public's perspective about the agency and its programs.

A sample communications worksheet is provided in figure 8.5.

EVALUATING RESULTS OF THE PLAN

Setting goals and establishing baselines will provide you with ways to measure whether your plan is successful. For the teen center, a goal might be to garner one positive news story per quarter about a program at the center from the current baseline of none. For the graffiti example, it might be to engage three community groups in your efforts to reduce graffiti from a baseline of no community engagement.

Go back and look at your goal and draft your baseline statement. Assuming that not all efforts will be equally fruitful, you can rely on evaluation results to help you develop future communications tactics. There are endless ways to evaluate the effectiveness of your efforts:

- Could the timing be better?
- Did we contact the media several times with no results?
- Are the tactics appropriate? If we used multiple tactics, did one tactic outperform the others? Did we ask the intended audience how they heard about the message?
- Did we have a target audience?
- Did we reach the target audience? If we did not reach them, what will we do differently next time to ensure we do?
- Did we have sufficient resources to carry out the effort? Was our staff fully trained? Was our time line realistic?

Include measures of accountability. Hold yourself accountable. Each person on staff should play a role in making your communications plan a success. Make evaluation of the plan mandatory. Involve everyone in the evaluation who had any part in the implementation. Take the time to measure your results—it will help ensure better ones next time.

FIGURE 8.5

Communications Worksheet

Name of agency: _____

Communications Goals

Goal 1: _____

Baseline data: _____

_____

Research to be done: _____

_____

Goal 2: _____

Baseline data: _____

_____

Research to be done: _____

_____

Target Audiences

List: _____ _____ _____

_____ _____ _____

_____ _____ _____

Messages: _____

_____

Inventory of Tools

What do we have?

What do we need?

Tactics and Timing

Base your tactics and timing on a quarterly basis (quarter 1, 2, 3, 4) starting with the first month of your fiscal year. For this example we use July as the first month of the agency's fiscal year:

First quarter: July, August, September   Third quarter: January, February, March

Second quarter: October, November, December   Fourth quarter: April, May, June

(continued)

From California Park & Recreation Society, 2008, *Creating Community* (Champaign, IL: Human Kinetics).

Figure 8.5 *(continued)*

First quarter: July, August, September		
July		
Tactic	Target audience	Outcome
August		
Tactic	Target audience	Outcome
September		
Tactic	Target audience	Outcome
Second quarter: October, November, December		
October		
Tactic	Target audience	Outcome
November		
Tactic	Target audience	Outcome
December		
Tactic	Target audience	Outcome

Third quarter: January, February, March		
January		
Tactic	Target audience	Outcome
February		
Tactic	Target audience	Outcome
March		
Tactic	Target audience	Outcome
Fourth quarter: April, May, June		
April		
Tactic	Target audience	Outcome
May		
Tactic	Target audience	Outcome
June		
Tactic	Target audience	Outcome

From California Park & Recreation Society, 2008, *Creating Community* (Champaign, IL: Human Kinetics).

A Recap of the Quiz

1. True. Communications is a management function that requires thought, planning, and resources.

2. True. Each agency, regardless of its size, should have a written communications plan with goals, messages, tactics, and tools.

3. False. Each agency should *not* use the same overall message regardless of the issue or audience. Tailor your message; what works for young mothers will not work for the frail elderly, and vice versa.

4. False. Each agency should *not* view everyone as one big target market. With the growing diversity in communities, you're wise to segment your market into groups (such as parents of children under 5, middle school–age youth, active seniors) and tailor your message to each group.

9

Working With the Press

Now that you understand the importance of communications and that it requires making decisions about your message, target audience, tactics, timing, and evaluation, you are ready to learn how you will get your communications noticed by your target market. We share ideas, resources, and tips on getting media coverage, which will help you position your agency with policy makers, the general public, and your partners. We explain how to choose your stories and spokesperson, develop a media database, and write media releases or advisories. We also explore contacting the media, creating media kits, and setting up a press conference. Finally, we talk about how to field calls and interviews from reporters.

IS YOUR STORY NEWSWORTHY?

To get media coverage, you need to promote something *newsworthy*. For park and recreation agencies, there may occasionally be bad news or controversy to manage (e.g., an accident or crisis), but most of the time park and recreation agencies generate good news, which can make it difficult to gain coverage.

If you're not sure whether a story is newsworthy, review the following list of questions and see if you can answer yes to one or more reasons your story may be newsworthy:

- Does it have an impact on the media outlet's readers or viewers?
- Is it local?

- Is there a controversy or conflict?
- Is someone prominent involved?
- Is something unusual involved?

The following are newsworthy items:

- New research: facts, figures, trends
- An award or honor
- An anniversary or milestone
- A visiting policy maker
- The opening of a facility
- A new partnership

Newsworthy events can be used for promoting any of the nine mission components for parks and recreation, each of which can be framed under one of the three "space to" themes mentioned in chapter 7. Following are some sample story angles that reinforce the VIP mission.

TIP

Bear in mind that generally, the larger the readership, the more difficult it is to get the attention of the newspaper, newsletter, or publication. Local community newspapers, television, or radio stations are more likely to cover local park and recreation events than regional publications such as the *Los Angeles Times, Chicago Tribune,* or *Miami Herald.*

Courtesy of California Park & Recreation Society

The opening of a new or remodeled facility may attract the media's attention, but if you tie the facility to addressing a need it becomes a front-page story.

Providing Recreational Experiences

In preparation for the summer months, the [park and recreation agency name] is expanding its [youth and family activities] program. Last year, [agency] served over 15,000 families through the program, which was initiated in response to residents' complaints about loitering teens two years ago. Since the start of the program, the city has seen a drop of [X]% in youth-related crime in the months of June, July, and August compared to two years ago.

Fostering Human Development

The [park and recreation agency name] is partnering with the public health department to offer parenting classes to local teen moms. The classes take place at the recreation center and give young mothers the chance to learn parenting skills without the worries of finding child care. Public health representatives have long been concerned about the lack of such education services for young mothers. Thus far, [XX] teen mothers have gone through the class and they report that attending the class has increased their knowledge of nutrition, age-appropriate behaviors, and parental responsibilities.

Promoting Health and Wellness

The senior center operated by [park and recreation agency name] has partnered with the local hospital and funders to create Aging With Energy. In this program, senior participants receive free pre- and postfitness testing and classes that increase fitness, strength, balance, and cardio-respiratory endurance. Seniors learn to monitor their own blood pressure and depression, two of the biggest health concerns among people ages 65 to 75. The program not only educates the elderly; it also empowers them by reminding them that they have control of their physical condition.

Increasing Cultural Unity

More than 60 ethnic communities participated in the International Friendship Festival, sponsored by the [park and recreation agency name]. City officials say that the festival is effective in building bridges in the community, reducing fear and intolerance, and motivating residents into lifelong learning. Since the recent suspected racially motivated attack of [name], the town had been stricken with suspicion, resentment, and pain. The festival attempted to open up dialogue once again among residents of the diverse community.

Facilitating Community Problem Solving

Amid recent public debates about skateboarding on city sidewalks and parking lots, the [local park and recreation agency name] has proposed construction of a skateboard park in a nearby park. Both sides agree that this is the right solution because of its proximity to the middle school and public transportation.

Protecting Environmental Resources

Eight youth from the local high school joined biologist [name] in a hike along a local stream to look for signs of an oil spill that occurred six months ago. The program was originally designed to involve local teens in cleaning up the spill, but it has evolved into an ongoing monitoring program. Representatives from the [park and recreation agency name] now routinely talk to the local high school's 9th- and 10th-grade biology classes to give students updates on the status of the stream.

Strengthening Safety and Security

Based on findings that youth ages 12 to 17 are at the highest risk of violence between the after-school hours of 3 p.m. to 7 p.m., the [park and recreation agency name] partnered with the local police department and [name] school district to design programs that provide youth with a safe place to be after school. The conversation resulted in the development of a teen program, which now serves [XX] youth. Youth-related crimes have decreased in the neighborhood by [XX]%, and residents, parents, and youth alike credit the teen program with contributing to the town's safety.

Strengthening Community Image and Sense of Place

To assist the community in remembering the September 11, 2001, attack, the [park and recreation agency name] will sponsor an annual candlelight vigil at a local park to commemorate the loss of lives.

Supporting Economic Development

A recent study conducted by the [name] Real Estate Agents Association showed that quality of life ranked in the top five most important factors in deciding to purchase a home in [city].

The [name] park and recreation agency recently received the highest award from [organization] for its efforts in attracting shoppers to the downtown shopping district during its remodeling. Owner of [name of store] stated that the Thursday night street fair organized by the [name] park and recreation department increased his sales in spite of the streets being under repair.

> **TIP**
>
> Another way you can get some press coverage is to ask your local paper if it wants to partner with you on a community survey to assess local needs for park and recreation services. A growing number of papers have an interest in civic journalism, in which they don't just sell papers but also provide a community service. This is one way they can show their commitment to creating community and demonstrate their corporate responsibility, and the survey results are more likely to be published.

WHO ARE YOUR SPOKESPEOPLE?

The people you choose to articulate the goals and accomplishments of the agency is important. The following are possible spokespeople for local park and recreation agencies:

- Park and recreation commissioners and board members
- City officials
- Department heads
- Staff
- Consumers (youth, seniors, volunteers)
- Local business leaders

Elected or appointed officials will likely welcome the opportunity to be associated with people, parks, and programs. Keeping them informed of your agency's activities and involving them in potential media events are great ways to enlist their support. Cultivating those relationships means keeping them informed, asking their advice, and providing them with opportunities to speak on your behalf.

Here are some suggested activities:

- Take Your Policy Maker to the Park Day gives you the opportunity to showcase your facilities and programs to your policy makers. Policy makers often like these events because they can portray themselves as caring and involved

> **TIP**
>
> When selecting a spokesperson, keep your target audience in mind. Think about whom the target audience will find credible. Whom would they believe? Whom would they look to? Whom would they trust?

in the community. Pick a day, create a series of events, invite the media, and award a plaque at the end.

• Feature a policy maker in your newsletter or magazine. In addition to familiarizing you with the policy maker, this gives you the opportunity to discuss your programs and facilities with him or her. Conduct an interview, include a photo, and highlight the person's support of the local agency and its programs.

Choose your spokesperson carefully, using these questions:

• Will the person attract positive attention based on his or her reputation in the community?

• Is the person well known in the community?

• Is the person seen as noncontroversial?

People to consider are the president of the local PTO (parent–teacher organization) or the local chamber of commerce or convention and visitors bureau, the valedictorian of the high school graduating class, or the CEO of a local business or hospital.

After you have selected a spokesperson, brief him or her on your communications goal and your key message and begin to engage that person in your communications work. Your spokesperson can attend an editorial board meeting, answer questions at a press conference or from reporters, and speak at community meetings. Be sure that your spokesperson can stay on message even when confronted with a question unrelated to the issue or topic. You may want to seek a public relations specialist or consultant to conduct your training. After each interview or presentation, debrief your spokesperson and

either strengthen your message or reaffirm your communications goals.

CREATING A MEDIA DATABASE

A media database that helps you contact the press can be a useful tool provided it is well organized and frequently updated. The following section provides some tips on setting up a media database, employing it, and ensuring that the information it contains continues to be valid and useful.

To begin forming your media database, think about what information you will need when you start to reach out. Contact information is a good first step. Also, consider including information that will help you work with individual news outlets, such as identifying the method in which the media outlet likes to receive stories (mail, fax, e-mail) and deadlines by which stories must be received in order to make it to print. Then consider the media environment for your area:

• How does the population in your area get news?

• Do more people read newspapers, watch television news broadcasts, or listen to the radio?

• If they listen to the radio, what stations have the most listeners?

• Do cultures in your area have media outlets in a language other than English?

Begin by examining population statistics of your area and the circulation numbers for local and regional media outlets. Using that information, create a list of media outlets you think can deliver your message to the entire range of your constituents.

Next, find out which reporters or editors cover issues that relate to possible story subjects. To accomplish this, perform a media audit of your area. A media audit is an analysis that gauges the way the media portrays the agency or the issue. It can show you how to frame an issue using language commonly used by the media, and it can identify what is "quotable" and "notable" about the issue. A media audit can be viewed as similar to a financial audit in that it gives you a snapshot at a certain point in time depicting how

TIP

Establishing a good relationship with individual journalists can be invaluable in getting your story to press. Before contacting reporters about a story, review their record in your media database to see what they have written in the past, and refer to those articles in your conversation.

your agency is being portrayed in the media. A media audit can be relatively informal, or it can be done in-depth. Assuming that you do not have the time or resources to hire a consultant to conduct a media audit, simply do a quick audit on your own by using online search engines (such as LexisNexis, http://global.lexisnexis.com/us) available for many newspapers and publications, make some phone calls, or take a trip to your local library. Subscribe to all local publications. Doing a media audit will reveal not only who is writing about issues relating to parks and recreation but also will give you an indication of the general tone that those writers lend to those issues.

Companies such as Cision (http://us.cision.com), Gebbie Press (www.gebbieinc.com), or News Media Yellow Book (212-627-4140, www.leadershipdirectories.com) provide media directories with comprehensive information about media outlets in your area, including contact information. Consult one of these, then contact

the individual news outlets to find out who should receive your submissions. This needs to be done often because of ongoing staff changes.

Finally, remember to keep the database current by recording any relevant stories posted by the various outlets and by periodically checking the contact information to ensure accuracy of delivery. Keep a written record of every personal contact with each journalist as well as the stories you submit.

WRITING A NEWS OR PRESS RELEASE

Ideally, a news or press release should read like a news story. It should include an attention-grabbing headline, facts, and quotes. These are written to encourage a journalist to develop articles on the subject. Many wire services and radio news departments rely heavily on the text of news or press releases for their stories, and in many instances they take the text verbatim. Descriptions should be as clear as possible because reporters are unlikely to call for clarification. In some cases the news or press release issued to the media can be referred to as a *media release*. The typical news or press release follows the format shown in figure 9.1.

While most news or press releases report on upcoming events, some can describe more general information or new trends, such as the emergency preparedness of park and recreation agencies. The information should always be relevant to recent events, and the message should always be clear. The sample news or press release in figure 9.2 pitches parks and recreation as a vital component of community emergency preparedness plans, announcing that they stand ready to assist in any incident involving human life or property damage.

WRITING A MEDIA ADVISORY

Sometimes it is advisable to alert the press a week or two before an event to attract coverage. A media advisory lets the media know when and where your event will occur and why they might want to attend. An advisory should not include every

TIP

Most newspapers have reporters assigned to cover specific topics, such as the environment, crime, and local politics. Parks and recreation may not be on the radar screen of those reporters. Part of your communications efforts should be to cultivate reporters by regularly sending them annual reports, fact sheets, and other materials to position yourself or your agency as a resource.

FIGURE 9.1

Headline: Keep It Short, Headline Capitalization

For immediate release _____

Contact [Name] _____

[Date of release] _____   [Phone number] _____

Paragraph 1: What is happening, who is involved, where and when

Paragraph 2: Why this event or news is significant and newsworthy

Paragraph 3: Quote from an expert involved that emphasizes how significant this event is

Paragraph 4: More details on where and when the event is happening

Paragraphs 5 and on: Other pertinent details:
- Speakers' names and affiliations
- Description of any photo opportunities
- Further quotes from other spokespeople

Final paragraph: One-sentence "boiler plate" description of the organizations involved in the event.

FIGURE 9.2

Parks and Recreation Staff Vital to Community Safety

For immediate release _____

Contact [Name] _____

[Date of release] _____   [Phone number] _____

(City), (State)–In response to the recent floods that affect one-third of the residents, [local park and recreation agency staff] assisted the community in the [disaster or incident]. It did this by [offering shelter for X number of days and organizing clean-up crews].

Residents in neighborhoods in Greenhaven, Land Park, and Curtis Park were affected due to streams overflowing. [The local park and recreation agency] was able to respond with crews and vehicles to help people vacate their homes in safety.

[Name], CEO of the [XX] chapter of the Red Cross, stated, "The response from the [XX] park and recreation agency staff was instrumental in our quick response. We work closely with the agency, ensuring their staff and our volunteers know each other and what our various responsibilities are. We are grateful for their expertise."

The effectiveness of this assistance is credited to the professional preparation of park and recreation staff and the availability of the community's facilities. Our town's recreation and community centers, senior centers, and parks serve as distribution points, administrative offices, or emergency housing during or after a disaster. The staff of the local park and recreation agency receive disaster-preparedness training with the Red Cross and the Office of Emergency Services, which enhances the agency's ability to coordinate information and provide assistance to disaster victims. This level of preparation makes parks and recreation a vital resource during any community disaster. "The high level of training received by our staff members makes us a natural component in a community's emergency preparedness plan," said [park and recreation director].

[One-sentence description of the local park and recreation agency mentioned.]

detail of the event; rather, it should give only a one-page overview that will inform at a glance. Figure 9.3 is a template for creating a media advisory; figure 9.4 is a sample advisory.

Keep in mind that the media likes to have time set aside to take pictures and ask questions of your spokesperson. Include a specific time on the media advisory for those activities. Media advisories can also be sent to nonmedia people (e.g., agency partners, the chamber of commerce, or community-based nonprofit leaders) whom you would like to attend your event. As always, if you have already made contact with the reporters or people to whom you are sending the advisory, include a personalized note explaining why their attendance is important to you.

FIGURE 9.3

Headline: Keep It Short, Headline Capitalization

For immediate release _____

Contact [Name] _____

[Date of release] _____ [Phone number] _____

What: [Two or three sentences on what is happening]

When: [Date and time as well as timing of press-related activities]

Where: [Address]

Who: [Names of people or organizations involved]

Why: [Two or three sentences that highlight why this event is important and newsworthy]

FIGURE 9.4

[Local Agency] Announces Seventh March for Parks

For immediate release _____

Contact [Name] _____

[Date of release] _____ [Phone number] _____

What: [Local park and recreation agency] is hosting its 7th annual March for Parks, a community event designed to acquaint local residents with [local park's] miles of trails while raising money for programs and awareness of this community's natural resources.

When: Registration 8:30 to 9:30 a.m.

Walk begins 10:00 a.m.

Press conference and photo opportunity 12:30 p.m.

Where: [Local park]

Who: [Names of local policy makers and other opinion leaders who will be available to the press]

Why: [Local park] has been a traditional meeting place and activity center for the

residents of [city] for over 45 years.

Come celebrate one of our largest local natural resources and find out more about the programs and activities that occur every week at [local park].

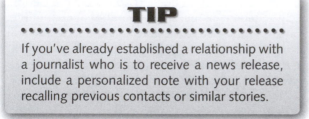

CONTACTING THE MEDIA

Once you have written a news release or a media advisory, spend time thinking about ways to get the attention of the media outlet. You may want to target a specific reporter. Each media outlet will often favor one method of contact or submission over another. It's a good idea to know the preferred method of each outlet before you begin to pitch your story. Working with the preferences of individual outlets or journalists is a sensible way to start a media relationship. Such preferences can easily be found with a phone call.

When submitting a story, remember that journalists are more apt to take interest if they are approached personally in addition to receiving a press release or informative materials.

FOLLOWING UP

After distributing a news or press release, follow up with the journalists in a timely manner to ensure that they received the story and to offer to answer questions. Try to call soon after the release has been sent to avoid having to resend materials.

When you call, keep the following in mind:

- Always start by asking if it is a good time to talk. If the reporter is working on deadline, offer to call back at a time convenient for him or her.
- Pitch to reporters you know (and get to know many reporters). Remember the basics of developing relationships. Journalists depend on sources they can trust for good information.
- Incorporate the elements of newsworthiness in your pitch. Emphasize its significance, timeliness, conflict, or controversy.
- Give reasons why the story is timely now.
- Create the broadest audience possible. Think of why it might be important to people who

drive, people concerned about their health, or people with children. The more people potentially affected, the better your story's prospects are of being covered.

- Pitch specific stories, not general issues. For example, don't talk about the problem of after-school violence, but do talk about specific programs that address the problem. Or give specific examples of people benefiting from those programs. Explain why those people's experience is representative. If possible, link your issue to some other current issue in the news. For instance, the recent news coverage about the prevalence of childhood obesity can be a tie-in to your youth sports, swimming instruction classes, or summer camps. Be sure you have the right activities, background information, and staff trained to lead the programs.
- Don't underprepare, but also don't read your pitch from a script.
- Remember that the person you pitch to might have to turn around and pitch it to his or her editor. Keep it simple and clear. Emphasize key points. For example, "Budget for Ohlone Park reduced. The budget cut will mean that the city's only after-school program will not be open starting [date]."
- Don't be discouraged if the first person you contact is not interested in your story. You might have to pitch it to several people.

Plan time for follow-up in advance to ensure that your story has the best chance of publication in a timely manner. Just sending out a news or press release is usually not enough to get the coverage you desire. You can improve any coverage received by making sure the journalist is familiar with the themes and what you hope to accomplish by telling your story.

Each publication has its own unique publication schedule. Ask the reporter specifically how much lead time he or she needs to cover your story. And, if you ask, be sure to meet that deadline.

CREATING MEDIA KITS

One way to organize your media release materials is by creating a media kit. A media kit is a packet of information designed to capture the media's attention for a project, an event, or a new initiative focused on solving a community need. A media kit typically includes the following:

- A media release that includes contacts' names, phone numbers, and fax numbers in appropriate languages for the media outlets you are targeting
- Your agency fact sheet
- A fact sheet on the programs, research, facilities, or activities that you are promoting
- Relevant bios for spokespeople or experts quoted in the release
- Copies of articles that have been written about your issue, program, or facility or op-ed pieces you have had published

Media kits may also include the following:

- A business card for your communications contact person
- Photos that highlight activities, facilities, or people mentioned in your media release
- Stickers or other giveaways created for promoting your story
- Relevant research

Print all media kit materials on agency letterhead and, if possible, use the same agency branding throughout the kit to enhance the presentation of your materials. Have enough media kits on hand so that you can give one to each reporter at a media event and have a few more for late arrivals. Also, save a media kit or two for your records to revisit when planning similar stories in the future.

In addition to using a media kit at a media event, the media kit can be the basis for collateral you leave behind when visiting a potential partner (such as a new school superintendent or principal), a policy maker (a new city council member or a state legislator), or a potential stakeholder (the CEO of the local chamber of commerce). When using the media kit in this fashion, be sure to delete the press release unless it is for a forthcoming event.

SETTING UP A PRESS CONFERENCE OR MEDIA EVENT

The first thing you should consider is whether a press conference or media event is the best way to present your story. A media event can focus on the opening of a new or renovated facility or park, the anniversary of an important community event, or a special event. Media events

When using a spokesperson to deliver your message, be sure he or she has been sufficiently trained and briefed about your key message.

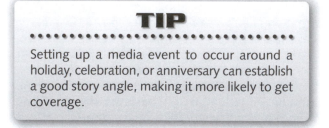

TIP

Setting up a media event to occur around a holiday, celebration, or anniversary can establish a good story angle, making it more likely to get coverage.

take a good deal of planning and strategy to be effective. Consider whether your message is best presented through a media event or simply through a press release and follow-up. Write out the specific objectives of the event and keep them in mind at all times. The press release, materials, spokespeople, and setting should all relate to one or a few clearly stated objectives. Trying to incorporate too many ideas into one event can result in a lack of focus, which might hurt your chances of coverage.

How do you know if a press conference or media event is appropriate?

Do it if . . .

- You have a series of influential speakers who are likely to draw media interest, such as the mayor and prominent business leaders or community members.
- You have new facts or research to reveal regarding your topic of interest.

Don't do it if . . .

- You don't have any new information to present.
- You don't have influential speakers at the conference.
- Your event coincides with an event likely to draw more attention than yours, such as the opening of a new store in your commu-

nity or a visit by a state or national political candidate.

Use figure 9.5 as a checklist with a time line as your media event approaches. Use figure 9.6 (see page 128) as a checklist for the news conference site itself.

FIELDING CALLS FROM REPORTERS

Reporters will typically call you for one of two reasons: when they have questions about a press release or materials or when there is a crisis or bad press that relates to your agency. Both of those instances are an opportunity to further the interests of parks and recreation. If a journalist has left you a message, respond in a timely manner—it could make the difference in getting coverage. If the press release is yours, you should already be prepared to answer questions, give quotes, or refer the journalist to other sources of information if necessary.

If a journalist calls you to ask you to respond to a crisis or bad press, start by assessing the situation. First, find out what story the journalist is researching. You cannot formulate a good response to a problem if you don't know what the problem is. Then, find out to whom the journalist has already spoken. Being aware of other sources of information can give you an idea of how the story is shaping up. Finally, find out what the journalist needs from you and when. Be courteous and direct. Cooperate, even when the story is not in your favor. Your openness can go a long way toward establishing a good relationship with the press.

TIP

A newly renovated park or recently established recreation center can make an excellent setting in which to host a media event. It can draw attention to the story at hand and make the resource visible to the community at large.

TIP

Too often, people feel pressured to speak to a reporter on the spot or to respond as soon as a reporter calls. That can lead you to say things you do not mean or cause you to deviate from your key message. Take your time! Ask the reporter if you can call him or her back within five minutes. Then, jot down the points you want to make. Think about your answers before you speak, making sure that you incorporate your key message.

FIGURE 9.5

Checklist for Media Event Planning

One Month in Advance

☐ Decide on objective and key message of the event.

☐ Decide on a newsworthy "hook" for the event.

☐ Find a site for the event.

☐ Come up with some interesting visual elements that will reinforce the key message of the event: charts, ads, demonstrators with signs.

☐ Arrange for speakers.

☐ Update media database, if necessary.

☐ Begin planning media kit materials.

Two Weeks in Advance

☐ Draft media advisory and news release.

☐ Draft fact sheets, speakers' bios, and other media kit materials.

☐ Assign roles for people at the event (media greeter, emcee, speakers).

☐ Work with speakers to draft talking points (related to objectives and your key message) and discuss possible questions from reporters.

One Week to Three Days Before

☐ E-mail or fax media advisory (including directions to event site) and news release.

☐ Follow up by calling journalists to pitch the story.

☐ Compile media kits.

☐ Conduct speaker training.

☐ Create sign-in sheet for attending journalists.

☐ Create table tents, name tags, or other means of identifying speakers.

The Day Before

☐ Make follow-up calls to media. E-mail or fax the advisory and news release to key media contacts again.

☐ Make sure media kits and all other conference materials are ready.

☐ Deliver media kits to any journalists who requested materials in advance. Make sure journalists have directions to the site.

☐ Rehearse the event with speakers, if possible. Ask every question that could possibly be important, and prepare for every possible problem.

At the Event

☐ Set up and check sound equipment, if needed.

☐ Introduce each speaker. Each speaker should limit his or her comments to 3 minutes.

☐ Leave time for questions after all speakers have presented.

☐ After the formal presentation, help reporters connect with individual speakers for one-on-one interviews.

After the Event

☐ Send media kits to any journalists who did not attend.

☐ Call journalists who attended, offering to answer further questions.

☐ Track and evaluate coverage to see what worked and how to improve.

From California Park & Recreation Society, 2008, *Creating Community* (Champaign, IL: Human Kinetics).

FIGURE 9.6

Checklist for News Conference Site

☐ Is your site large enough to hold the invited number of journalists, plus a few more?

Always leave yourself plenty of room for last-minute attendees.

☐ Is parking nearby for attendees?

If necessary, have signs, staff, or volunteers direct attendees from the parking lot to the conference site.

☐ Can the conference site accommodate TV cameras?

Are there enough (and powerful enough) electrical outlets and extension cords for cameras and lights? Is the podium positioned to offer an attractive background that helps tell your story? What will the cameras focus on?

☐ Will your office be staffed before, during, and after the conference?

The media can easily reach someone or get directions or additional information if necessary.

☐ Have you set up a check-in table near the entrance where you can greet arriving journalists?

Make sure you have extra media kits and other background materials.

☐ Have you compiled a complete list of invited media so you can check them off as they arrive, or created a sign-in sheet for names, addresses, and affiliations of all attendees?

Keep track of every media representative there and use the information to update your media database later.

☐ Have you prepared to give each attendee a press kit, including an agenda for the conference?

Have spare pens and paper available.

☐ Have you chosen an emcee to introduce all speakers?

Make your speakers and guests available for postconference interviews in person and by phone.

☐ Have you conducted a dress rehearsal?

Pretest the LCD slides or overhead projector or slide projector and have spare bulbs available. Have two copies of any video or audio tapes you are going to play in case one breaks.

☐ Will you need amplification for your speakers?

If so, check in advance to be sure your microphones work and are set to appropriate sound levels.

☐ Will refreshments be available?

Providing coffee, water, or light snacks for reporters is a nice touch, although not essential. At a minimum, be sure speakers have water available.

From California Park & Recreation Society, 2008, *Creating Community* (Champaign, IL: Human Kinetics).

BEING INTERVIEWED

Journalists seek good material for a story. They are not really interested in making you look good or bad. They are interested in telling an interesting story. Know your key messages well and be clear about your objectives for any interview. Many people want to tell the journalist everything they know in a short interview. Not only is that impossible, but it also increases the likelihood that you will dilute the power of your message and squander the opportunity to advance your objectives.

Remember, you are the expert. In most cases, the journalist has limited expertise on the topic and may have just been handed the story. Despite this, many people are intimidated by journalists, somehow believing that reporters are more knowledgeable than they are. Don't forget that you are the expert and that is why a journalist is talking to you.

An interview is not a conversation. In a conversation, it is easy to get drawn off your main point. In an interview, you must know the point you want to make.

Have your sound bites and a bottom-line message written down in front of you. You should be able to respond immediately in a single sentence if asked to sum up your story or position. Sound bites can also be considered your key message, as defined in chapter 8. Here are two examples of a sound bite:

- Parks and recreation keeps youth safe.
- Park and recreation facilities are accessible to everyone.

In addition, be careful to avoid the following potential pitfalls:

- Don't say too much. Make your point and stop. If you keep talking, you might say something you had not intended to say or dwell on a lesser point.
- Don't stray from your area of expertise. Don't fold under pressure from the reporter to give an opinion or fact in an area with which you are not familiar. State simply that you are not informed on the issue. If that uninformed opinion is printed, you could get in trouble with your supervisor or policy makers or lose credibility with the journalist when he or she finds out the information is incorrect.
- Don't relax too much, especially if you know the reporter. Don't accidentally provide some information that you did not want to become public.

CULTIVATING RELATIONSHIPS

A relationship with a reporter might get you an immediate response to your phone calls when pitching a story. A relationship with a local policy maker might get you an op-ed from an influential voice. A relationship with prominent community leaders might get you strong spokespeople to help deliver your message.

Most relationships are cultivated and require maintenance. Once you've established a relationship, keep in touch by sending newsletters or other publications on the progress of your agency's work. Think of cultivating relationships as building alliances with various segments of your community. Moving from a relationship to a partnership with members of the media and community leaders will provide you with a powerful resource for communicating your vision and mission.

Just like instituting a plan for a new season of recreation programs or for a park renovation, working with the media requires the same level of planning. Agencies that leave communications as an afterthought will be just that with the media—the agency will receive little or no media coverage. Understanding that the media is interested in newsworthy stories and learning how to write such stories will increase the likelihood of your agency receiving more positive press coverage. Tying your press releases to the mission of parks and recreation will gain the attention of the press, as you have moved beyond the basics of who, what, why, and when.

TIP

As a public agency in a city, county, or special district, you will likely have direct access to other agencies or departments, both formally and informally. Ask them to work with you to post announcements, include articles, and distribute brochures or other materials as part of your communications efforts. And offer them the same option for their announcements or materials!

Using Other Media Outlets

In this chapter we expand the opportunities you have to communicate your key message. We often rely on news or press releases, but there are many more ways to have the media cover your agency. Newspapers not only can supply feature stories but can also provide an opportunity for op-eds or letters to the editor as well as discussions with the editorial board about their upcoming editorials. Radio and TV shows, including culturally diverse media, can be a way to highlight your programs; so can public service announcements (PSAs). And don't forget the Internet and paid media as methods of getting the word out.

No matter which outlet you use, remember that you will be sending your materials to professionals. Therefore, you must know the right format and prepare your materials appropriately. While this might seem like a lot of work, the outcome may mean more resources, more partners, and greater visibility with policy makers and community residents.

OP-EDS AND LETTERS TO THE EDITOR

After the front page, the editorial page is the second most frequently read section of the newspaper. The editorial page is also the best place to reach policy makers and those who have an influence on public opinion—that is, your target audiences. There are two opportunities for pub-

lication on the editorial page: an op-ed piece or commentary and a letter to the editor.

Op-Ed Piece or Commentary

An opinion-editorial (op-ed) piece gives park and recreation agencies an opportunity to demonstrate the commitment to providing "Space to. . . ." Because the editorial page is so popular, there is competition for publication. Limit your submitted op-ed articles to approximately 450 words, although some papers will print longer articles. The pieces most likely to get printed are those that relate to breaking news. Figure 10.1 is a sample op-ed.

To get an op-ed or commentary placed, read those that were recently published in your paper. You may be able to tailor it to respond to a piece that has recently run. You may also want to pitch the piece to the editorial section editor before you send it in. When you send in your op-ed piece, include a cover note explaining the importance of the topic, and include your name and phone

TIP

Use op-eds and letters to the editor to respond to recent articles or editorials. These pieces increase your control over the content and boost your chances of getting published or aired.

FIGURE 10.1

Parks and Recreation: A Space for Youth to Feel Safe

Now More Than Ever, Youth Need Caring Adults

(City), (State)—Now more than ever, children need the support of caring adults to help them make sense of what is taking place in the world and help them incorporate current events into their young lives.

Since the September 11, 2001, terrorist attack on the United States and those in other countries, there is heightened awareness of the safety of Americans on American soil—in airports, at work, at school, on the street, and at home. It should not be forgotten, however, that not long before that horrendous event, Americans were already alerted to safety issues, particularly those of children. American youth at this moment are witnessing an enormous level of violence at their schools and in their communities. It is impossible, or maybe simply too frightening, for adults to know how our youth are interpreting and coping with all they are experiencing.

The hours between 3:00 p.m. and 6:00 p.m. continue to be a critical time for our youth, as violence involving them, either as victims or perpetrators, peaks during that time of day. How will our children respond to violence in their surroundings? This task is increasingly burdensome to many parents who work during the day and are unable to supervise or mentor their children until dinnertime. The responsibility of helping children to stay safe seems daunting for many parents.

Parks and Recreation Can Help

With numerous programs year round, [name of your agency] provides a secure place and caring adult supervision for youth during the critical after-school hours between 3:00 p.m. and 6:00 p.m. [Name of your agency] staff are well trained in [e.g., conflict management, youth development, leadership development] and serve as ideal mentors and supervisors for youth in our community. Each year, [name of your agency] serves more than [number] youth in its [number] programs. The programs include [names of specific programs]. For more information on out-of-school programs for your children, please contact [your agency's contact information].
Submitted by [name of park and recreation commissioner or director]
[One-sentence description of the local park and recreation agency]

---

number. You can e-mail it, fax it, or send it via regular mail. Also, follow up with a call to the editor once you've sent your op-ed piece. Editors rarely have your op-ed in hand. Also have a fax copy or e-mail ready to resend when you call.

Remember to include your name, title, and affiliation at the end of the op-ed. You will be notified if your article is accepted for publication. Note that it can take weeks for even a time-sensitive op-ed to appear, so be patient.

Letters to the Editor

Letters to the editor signal park and recreation agencies' concern and commitment. Start the letter with "Dear Editor," and include your name, address, and phone number. Draft sample letters for others to submit. Letters from elected or appointed officials, chamber of commerce leaders, or other community leaders may have a better chance of being published. Submit all letters on agency or professional letterhead. Be sure each

letter reaches the right editor by calling the paper beforehand to get the name of the letter section editor. Note that your letter might be altered without notice, especially if it is too long. You may want to track the length of the letters that are published in your paper and aim for that length.

TIP
....

Follow these guidelines for op-eds and letters to the editor:

- Your final piece should be no more than 450–700 words.
- You should follow up with editors and reporters, but do not badger the editorial staff.
- Do not despair if your piece is not accepted. Try another publication.

EDITORIAL BOARD MEETINGS

The goal of meeting with the editorial board is to get the staff at the paper to write an editorial supporting the policy or position of your agency. The support of a local media outlet can be invaluable in attracting the community's attention to your issue and securing support from policy makers.

Editorial boards vary considerably in terms of their composition. They may include as few as 2 people or more than 15. Commonly, the editorial board includes the editorial page editor, the letters editor, the op-ed page editor, the news director, and the city news director. Some editorial boards may have a representative from the community or an individual reporter assigned to the related beat.

To set up an editorial board meeting, get the editorial page editor's name from the paper's masthead and contact him or her, visit the paper's Web site for instructions, or call the newspaper and ask for information on how to meet with the editorial board. Work to gather influential representatives from your agency and the citizens you serve to join you. When you request a meeting, be prepared to describe the issue you want to discuss, your agency's position on the issue, and who will attend the meeting. It helps to write a letter describing the purpose of the meeting. Be sure to follow up by phone.

Before you set up a meeting with an editorial board, state what you want to say about why the board should meet with your agency. Editorial boards typically get many more requests for meetings than they can fulfill, so you should be prepared to make the strongest case possible for your issue. Use the worksheet in figure 10.2 to focus your thoughts and draft a letter describing your group's objectives. Figure 10.3 (see pages 135-136) is a checklist you can use in preparing for a meeting with a newspaper's editorial board.

ETHNIC MEDIA

Remember, the "general public" no longer exists. Our changing demographics nationwide have given rise to a number of media outlets serving communities in multiple languages and ethnic backgrounds. The increased presence and influence of ethnic media can be seen throughout the nation. In Los Angeles, a town once dominated by the *Los Angeles Times*, the most widely read newspaper is now *La Opinión* (www.laopinion. com). To communicate your message in today's world, you must engage ethnic media.

You are probably aware of the biggest ethnic media outlets covering your community. However, you can find more information on the Internet using search words such as *African media*, *African American media*, *Asian media*, *European media*, *Hispanic* or *Latino media,* and *Middle East media*.

Ethnic media outlets operate like any other media outlet. However, experience shows that ethnic media often is more likely to cover human interest stories and is more likely to do comparatively in-depth coverage. Like other media, however, ethnic media will not be interested in your story unless it is relevant to the media's audience. For instance, your best chance of getting coverage from the Spanish-language media is to demonstrate the impact of the subject on the Latino community. And, if you have a Spanish-speaking spokesperson available, especially for television coverage, it will make a huge difference in getting air time.

RADIO AND TV PUBLIC AFFAIRS AND TALK SHOWS

Radio and television provide an excellent opportunity to deliver your stories to the community in a personal format. Contact the stations in your area after you have developed your story or if you hear of a theme-oriented show that touches on an issue important to your park and recreation agency.

Also, consider the environment in which you will be interviewed. Make sure you have a good idea of what to expect before you arrive, because the situation may vary widely. Consider the following questions before you seek or respond to an interview request:

- What will be the position of the host? Have you heard him or her speak about the issue before? If possible, watch previously recorded interviews to assess the host's stance on similar issues.
- What is the style of the host? Does the host strive to create conflict and controversy? Again, watching the show can help you assess the host's style.
- Will someone else be on with you either in the studio or via remote setup? What can you find out about that person?

FIGURE 10.2

Planning Worksheet for Editorial Board Meeting

Newspaper we want to meet with: _____

Contact person for editorial board meetings: _____

Phone number and address: _____

_____

Dear [Name]: _____

　　We would like to meet with your editorial board to discuss an issue of great importance to your readers. We represent [park and recreation agency] in cooperation with [spokespeople, policy makers, and so on].

　　The specific issue we want to discuss is [issue]. This is an important issue in general because [reasons]. It is particularly urgent for your newspaper to take a stand on this issue at this time because [reasons].

　　We would be happy to provide you with additional materials on this issue. We look forward to hearing from you about when we can meet.

Sincerely,

_____

_____

_____

_____

[Name, address, and phone number]

From California Park & Recreation Society, 2008, *Creating Community* (Champaign, IL: Human Kinetics).

FIGURE 10.3

Editorial Board Checklist

Before the Meeting

☐ Decide who will attend the meeting. Editorial board members get a lot of requests for meetings. They are likely to give the highest priority to people they consider the significant players or who have special experience with the issue. You will probably have better luck being granted a meeting if your team includes high-profile members such as the executive director of a major agency, the head of a community coalition that represents significant numbers of community members, or the high school student body president (if appropriate).

List people whom you want to attend the meeting:

☐ Clarify how long the meeting will last. Reconfirm your appointment a few days in advance.

How long will your meeting last? Be sure to inform others joining you.

☐ Review the paper's previous editorials on your issue, if any, by searching at the library or in the newspaper's online archive. Be prepared to tell the board what is new since the last time they editorialized your issue and why now is an important time for them to take a stand.

What else has the paper printed on this or other related issues?

☐ Decide on the persuasive points you want to make and who among your spokespeople will make them. Try to limit your points to three key facts or statements, and practice making your case.

What key message or facts do you want to share?

☐ Consider tough questions on your issue. Part of the editorial board's job is to challenge your position. Be prepared to counter any arguments.

What questions might they ask you? Explore those aloud with others, some who are familiar with your issue and some who are not. Write possible questions here.

☐ Prepare materials to leave behind with the board. The materials should explain your position, provide facts on the issue, and contain a list of contacts for follow-up. Ask your editorial board contact whether you should send those materials before the meeting.

List the materials you want to leave behind or send before the meeting. Identify who will be responsible for preparing those materials.

(continued)

Figure 10.3 *(continued)*

At the Meeting

☐ Introduce all the members of your team (be sure to include their affiliation to the issue and why they are attending) and make sure you record the names and positions of all the editorial board members.

☐ Strongly advocate your position. Explain why an editorial would be timely and important at this time. Have a backup plan. If the board tells you during the meeting that they will not write an editorial on the issue, ask if they would print an op-ed piece written by a member of your team. Again, do not expect any commitments on the spot, but do get the name of the person to whom you should submit such a piece.

☐ Be honest. If you are asked something that you cannot answer, say that you do not know but will be happy to provide the information after the meeting is over. Be sure to follow through or you will lose credibility.

☐ Provide your key points and facts in writing. Give the members the materials you have prepared for their review.

☐ Be respectful of the board's time.

☐ Thank the participants for attending.

After the Meeting

☐ Follow up with a phone call, e-mail, or note to your contact. Thank him or her again for the meeting and use the opportunity to reiterate the importance of a timely editorial on the subject.

Who will be responsible for the follow-up?

☐ Honor commitments quickly. If you promised any follow-up materials or information during the meeting, provide them promptly. If you floated the idea of an op-ed piece, draft it quickly (within the paper's word limits) and submit it to the appropriate person.

Who will be responsible for the follow-up?

☐ Protect your investment of time and effort. Remember that even if you do not get an editorial at this time, the contacts you established with key editors will be invaluable in the future. Stay in touch with the editors through occasional phone calls or notes that provide additional information or perspectives.

Who is responsible for staying in touch?

From California Park & Recreation Society, 2008, *Creating Community* (Champaign, IL: Human Kinetics).

> ### TIP
>
> Before you contact any media, check your government's policy on granting interviews. Some government administrators require the approval of the city manager, county administrator, or elected policy maker before appearing.

- How does your interview advance the issue with which you are concerned?

- Do the show's producers have telephone call-ins? Is it aired at a time when you are sure you can get at least a few friends or colleagues to call in with supportive questions? Draft questions for your supporters to ask while you are on the air that allow you to deliver your key message.

- If possible, prepare for being on camera by setting up a mock interview and taping it. Remember that practice will make you more comfortable and confident in your delivery. Many local governments have public information offices that can be a valuable resource for you. Enlist their help as often as you can.

PUBLIC SERVICE ANNOUNCEMENTS

Public service announcements, or PSAs, are short messages produced on film, video, or audio that are aired by television or radio stations free of charge as a service to the community. Most PSAs are sent ready to air, but some stations prefer a script so their announcers may read it on air. Check with the intended station to know which format to use. Since television and radio stations are not required to air PSAs, do some research in advance and find out each station's requirements. For example, how long, what format, and how much advance time does an outlet need?

You have only 30 seconds (or less) to reach your audience with a PSA. Here are some tips to consider when writing your PSA:

- Brainstorm with others. If possible, bring in people from the target market you are trying to reach.

- Use vivid and simple language—for instance, "Friends don't let friends drive drunk."

- Make your message clear—for instance, "If you have asthma, don't smoke."

- Use words or phrases to grab attention. It can be funny, use catchy music, contain a shocking statistic, or involve children laughing.

- Give a number to call if specific action is desired.

- Check and double-check your facts.

Thirty seconds is not long; table 10.1 shows a guideline for the number of words according to the length of the PSA. When sending your PSA to a station, list these things on your document (Community Toolbox, 2007):

- The dates the PSA should run (e.g., "For use from November 18 to December 20" or "Immediate TFN" [till further notice])

- Length of the PSA

- What agency or group the PSA is for

- Title of the PSA

Also contact the radio station before you send in your PSA. Some stations have a community relations office. The key is to get the name of the person who will receive the PSA.

Find out what process you need to follow to ensure that your agency programs are consistently covered in the station's community calendar, if they have one, and whether you can post your information on their Web site. (Most newspapers also have community calendar pages or other sections devoted to promoting programs that serve their readers.) In addition, find out what they may have planned in the future for their own marketing efforts. For example, in its local news coverage and through PSAs, a local television station may focus on youth violence prevention as a topic for a given

Table 10.1   Guidelines for Length of PSA

Length of PSA	Number of words
10 seconds	20-25 words
15 seconds	30-35 words
20 seconds	40-50 words
30 seconds	60-75 words

month. They may also be looking for organizations and programs to feature in their coverage. A partnership with your agency could work well for both you and the television station.

PAID MEDIA

Depending on your communications budget and your goals, you might want to consider using paid ads. Many newspapers and radio and television stations have nonprofit rates, which can make that an affordable option. When you are negotiating ad rates, consider placement as well. Certain sections of the paper are read more frequently than others by various segments of the population. Ask the newspaper staff to provide you with readership data for the section you are considering. If that section does not attract your target audience, find the section that does. Always target your audience.

THE INTERNET

The Internet is the fastest-growing tool in media relations. In addition to faxing and mailing press releases, you can use the Internet to e-mail journalists with a link from which they can collect and disseminate information. Your agency's Web site should display descriptions of materials and topical information about local parks and recreation.

Create a "press room" on your Web site that can act as a single-stop portal for journalists interested in writing a story pertaining to your agency. A press room often includes press releases as well as staff bios, history of the department, awards or recognitions, stock photos, and other materials that journalists can access at any time. Many sites will post your press release along with other releases of a similar nature. Those sites are often viewed by journalists looking for other stories to pursue. Check with your city or county public information office to see what contacts they already have developed.

In this chapter, we explored other ways in which a park and recreation agency can obtain media coverage. We often ignore these methods because they may not be successful the first time they are used. Paying attention to the demographics of your community to ensure you are communicating to all of your residents may involve learning more about and engaging the ethnic media in your immediate area or region. Creating a press section on your agency's Web site (a media channel that is often overlooked) provides reporters with quick and easy access to the most current information about your programs and services. If you include a press section, be sure to update it daily or reporters will soon stop visiting your site.

A

Opportunities in Parks and Recreation

The following pages describe the opportunities mentioned in chapter 3 in greater detail. Those opportunities build on the core competencies of the park and recreation profession and respond to key trends. The opportunities are classified into four types:

1. Target markets
2. Social trends
3. Community planning and development
4. Environmental awareness and stewardship

Because trends, staff competencies, and partnership opportunities vary among agencies and across the nation, the role of individual agencies in addressing each opportunity will vary as well. An action-planning process for selecting the appropriate opportunities to pursue in the future and for determining the role of individual agencies in each market area is presented in appendix B.

TARGET MARKETS

Target markets in the future for parks and recreation include dependents, youth, seniors, ethnic populations, people with disabilities, and families.

Dependents: Children Under 12, People With Disabilities, and Frail Elders

In many households both parents or caregivers must work to support the family. Likewise, the number of single-parent households is also increasing. This group of middle-aged adults might also be called on to care for their own aging parents. These trends have created a growing demand for dependent care and child care. But good dependent-care services are typically expensive and inaccessible to many families. Parks and recreation already has facilities, staff, programs, and services that could be part of a successful delivery system of dependent-care services.

In the Future

In the future, parks and recreation will be recognized as a key partner, ensuring that all community residents have access to affordable care services for children and seniors.

Programs, Services, and Facilities

Programs and services will include elder care, before- and after-school care, nonschool day care, adult day care, respite care, parenting skill classes, caregiver skill classes, family and child leisure education, community centers, and dependent-care facilities.

Typical Clients

Typical clients will be children, frail elderly, and double-income or single-caregiver families in need of dependent care. Additionally, current dependent-care professionals could find a support network or training opportunities through parks and recreation.

Strategic Partners

Partners will be schools, health care providers, social service agencies, and nonprofit agencies that can collaborate in providing family services, facilities, staff, financial resources, and training.

Youth: Children to 18 Years Old

Our nation's population of individuals under 18 will increase in the coming years. Children are recognized as the future of our communities.

However, more young children in our communities are becoming involved with drugs and crime. As youth development and crime prevention continue to be political focal points, there will be an opportunity to increase services aimed at improving youth resiliency, maintaining healthy family relationships, developing self-esteem in young girls and boys, and preventing and reducing crime. Studies confirm that recreation programs demonstrate an ability to increase youth resiliency. As a major youth services provider, park and recreation professionals are already positioned to respond to this initiative.

In the Future

In the future, parks and recreation will be recognized as experts in youth development.

Programs, Services, and Facilities

Programs and services will include before- and after-school care, nonschool day care, parenting skill classes, child care and caregiver skill classes, family and child leisure education, referral services to drug and alcohol treatment, community centers and other youth facilities, jobs, skill training, and career development.

Typical Clients

Typical clients will be children, teenagers, and their families.

Strategic Partners

Partners will be schools, law enforcement and the criminal justice system, social service agencies, faith-based organizations, and nonprofit agencies involved with youth.

Seniors: Active to Frail

With the aging of the baby boomers, the number of people over 65 is expected to increase nationwide. Nationally, senior populations are expected to increase by over 90% by 2020. With life expectancy also increasing, there will be more people over the age of 70 as well. The senior population will range from active retirees to frail elderly. These varied senior populations will require services and activities focused on their needs. Parks and recreation is currently providing services for seniors and must continue to provide valuable community services for the range of seniors.

In the Future

In the future, parks and recreation will be recognized as a key partner in providing a continuum of services to seniors—from services for active seniors to services for frail elders. The services will promote healthy lifestyles among seniors and help them to remain in their homes and in their communities for as long as possible.

Programs, Services, and Facilities

Programs, services, and facilities will be senior centers, respite care facilities, staff training, recreation programs, volunteer opportunities, supportive community services, dependent care, and respite for caregivers.

Typical Clients

Clients will be care providers and frail, ambulatory, and active seniors.

Strategic Partners

Partners will be nonprofit agencies, social service providers, community and private senior centers, residential developers focused on the over-55 population, and other senior service providers.

Ethnic Populations

Park and recreation professionals will be called on to serve customers who are diverse in age, ability, income, and ethnicity. The ability to serve an increasingly diverse customer base will be necessary in order to meet recreation needs and maintain the support of policy makers and voters.

In the Future

In the future, parks and recreation will be recognized as a major force in meeting the recreational needs of diverse populations, in promoting the value of recreation and leisure, in serving as a unifying force in the communities and settings we serve, in serving as advocates for the underserved, and in celebrating the value of diversity.

Programs, Services, and Facilities

Programs and services will be tailored to diverse populations. Programming will emphasize the value of diversity, such as fairs and celebrations, language and arts classes, and mentoring programs. Facilities will incorporate use patterns of diverse groups in the design or celebrate diversity by using design elements and hiring and promoting diverse staff.

Typical Clients

Typical clients will be children, adults, seniors, immigrants, and tourists.

Strategic Partners

Partners will be nonprofit agencies, social service providers, faith-based organizations, neighborhood associations, and schools.

People With Disabilities

People with disabilities are leading active, independent lives and want to be involved with their communities as much as anyone else is. Park and recreation providers must offer accessible, inclusive facilities and programs, as they are mandated by law to do so. However, the cost of retrofitting facilities can be prohibitive, and funding sources are scarce. Also, many park and recreation staff are not knowledgeable about disabilities or adapting activities for people with various abilities. Because of that, agencies are hesitant to reach out to potential customers with disabilities. Making these changes will benefit not just people with disabilities—good design and programming techniques benefit everyone.

In the Future

In the future, parks and recreation will be known for making its facilities and programs universally accessible. Staff will have learned how to customize programming to meet individual needs of all types through this process. Everyone will benefit from new, improved universal designs and the upgrading of older facilities that have long suffered from a lack of maintenance.

Programs, Services, and Facilities

Accessible facilities, integrative programs, programs for target populations, advocate and support groups for people with disabilities, and family members are the focus of the programs, services, and facilities.

Typical Clients

Community residents and tourists will be the typical clients.

Strategic Partners

Nonprofit agencies, social service providers, schools, faith-based organizations, government agencies, and health care professionals will be strategic partners.

Families

Parks and recreation can play a major role in family development. Our people-oriented approach uniquely positions us to create a society of caring families. This market includes not only traditional families but new family types as well: families headed by single men and women, grandparents who are raising their grandchildren, parents by adoption, and other diverse family groups. Many of these emerging families currently feel isolated and unwelcome in family programs.

In the Future

In the future, parks and recreation will be known as the creator of strong families. All families will feel welcomed and supported by parks and recreation. Families will be prepared to raise resilient youth and lead healthy lifestyles.

Programs, Services, and Facilities

Family recreation programs, special events, and drop-in activities and facilities that serve families are the focus of the programs, services, and facilities.

Typical Clients

Typical clients will be children and their parents or guardians.

Strategic Partners

Nonprofit agencies, social service providers, faith-based organizations, and schools will be strategic partners.

SOCIAL TRENDS

Some of the major social trends that park and recreation agencies will need to address in their communities are health and wellness, lifelong learning, and technology-based recreation.

Health and Wellness

As the cost of health care increases, the medical community has prescribed regular physical activity as critical to disease prevention. At the same time, national and statewide statistics show that we spend an average of only 2.2 hours per week performing activities classified as recreation, sport, and outdoor pursuits; this is in comparison to the average of 12 hours we spend watching TV each week. More and more, people are looking for convenient opportunities for fitness- and sport-related activities. They want to be able to exercise while watching their children, visiting with family or friends, shopping, or doing other daily activities. Classes and group sports requiring a consistent time commitment have limited appeal, as evidenced by the increases in the number of people engaging in activities like walking and biking.

In the Future

In the future, parks and recreation will be known as the profession that educates the public about how they can achieve health and wellness and as the provider or partner in developing facilities and programs that support health and well-being.

Programs, Services, and Facilities

Programs and facilities will increase fitness, such as leisure education. Personal trainers, classes that last for a short duration, drop-in or programmed exercise, preschool gyms, adult fitness classes, athletic leagues, drop-in facility use, classes at businesses, and fitness for travelers and telecommuters will be the focus. Access should be increased through longer operating hours, night lighting for extended play, and neighborhood multiuse trails and sports fields.

Typical Clients

Children, adults, seniors, businesses, hospitals, health professionals, and health insurance agencies (such as HMOs) will be the typical clients.

Strategic Partners

Strategic partners will be the medical profession, nonprofit agencies, commercial health clubs, HMOs, insurance providers, and the media.

Lifelong Learning

Parks and recreation plays an important role in lifelong learning for both personal development and career change. In the past, people chose a career that they pursued for life. Today, people typically change careers several times during their lives (Munroe, 1999). Rapidly changing technology also requires those who do not change careers

to update their skills continuously. In addition, lifelong learning for personal development is an important form of recreation for many people. This trend is evident in the planning efforts of colleges and universities that are developing housing on campuses for seniors interested in learning-centered retirement.

In the Future

In the future, parks and recreation will be known for promoting lifelong learning, helping people adapt to changing careers and job requirements, and providing lifelong opportunities for personal development.

Programs, Services, and Facilities

Programs, services, and facilities will focus on classes and clinics to provide job skills for career changers or those who must improve their job skills, career counseling, and recreation programs that foster personal development.

Typical Clients

Typical clients will be adults and businesses.

Strategic Partners

Community colleges, universities, chambers of commerce, businesses, public television providers, Internet providers, online schools, elder hostel programs, and adult learners will be strategic partners.

Technology-Based Recreation

With the growing popularity of TV, computers, and video, park and recreation providers have an opportunity to reach out to the community with technology-based recreation media. The average American spends about 12 hours per week watching television. Park and recreation professionals can use a variety of media and technology to publicize traditional services as well as provide technology-based recreation for those with limited time, lack of transportation, or health issues that make participation outside the home difficult.

In the Future

In the future, parks and recreation will be known as the profession that uses technology to reach out to the community with their message and services.

Programs, Services, and Facilities

Programs, services, and facilities will be available through public television, public radio, the Internet, online registration, facility and program reservations, and access to public meetings concerning parks and recreation.

Typical Clients

Typical clients will be children, adults, seniors, families, and businesses.

Strategic Partners

Schools, community colleges, universities, businesses, corporations, and the media will be strategic partners.

COMMUNITY PLANNING AND DEVELOPMENT

Park and recreation agencies will be involved in shaping and developing their communities in the coming years. They will have input in park and recreation facilities, cultural arts, economic development and tourism, model neighborhoods, and partnerships with schools and libraries.

Park and Recreation Facilities

Citizens value open space and recognize the importance of parks as integral to a high quality of life. Parks and open space are primary factors in determining community livability and quality of life. Park and recreation facilities are also factors in deciding where to live or do business in a community. As our population and economy grow, we will need to expand park and recreation facilities to ensure that the community has accessible recreation opportunities. Older facilities that have suffered from a lack of maintenance will need to be upgraded to meet current standards and serve community needs. Park and recreation providers are also being called on to provide a wider variety of facilities to meet growing consumer demands. Skate parks, dog parks, active aquatic facilities, and other facilities that are common today were unheard of 20 years ago.

In the Future

In the future, parks and recreation will be known as the profession that provides spaces and places that determine quality of life, provides access to recreation opportunities, and develops partners in providing new facility types that meet changing needs.

Programs, Services, and Facilities

Development and operation of park and recreation facilities, neighborhood resources as an extension of the neighborhood backyard, community and

regional facilities, trails, aquatic facilities, joint-use facilities, revenue-generating uses, facilities for specific users (such as skate parks and dog parks), and indoor parks and gyms will be involved in the programs, services, and facilities.

Typical Clients

Residents, employees, and tourists will be the typical clients.

Strategic Partners

Government agencies that address economic development, developers, nonprofit land trusts, businesses, corporations, and private concession operations will be strategic partners.

Cultural Arts

Over the past few years, cultural arts have been eliminated from public schools and cut from local government budgets. In spite of those reductions, the arts community continues to grow through individual giving, estates, private and public foundations, and corporations. The National Assembly of State Arts Agencies economic study (2007) showed that in fiscal year 2007 state arts agencies invested $362.7 million in creating and sustaining arts infrastructures in communities across the nation. The National Endowment for the Arts (Nichols, 2006) indicated Americans spent $12.7 billion ($42.80 per person) on admissions to performing arts events in 2005. Local park and recreation agencies can be the catalyst for the arts in their communities either as the sole sponsor or by creating partnerships with businesses, nonprofit organizations, schools, and individuals.

In the Future

In the future, the park and recreation profession will be known as the profession that preserves our rich cultural heritage for all to enjoy, while enhancing our economy through the arts.

Programs, Services, and Facilities

Classes and performances of all types, special events, and facilities that support cultural programs will be involved.

Typical Clients

Community residents and visitors will be the typical clients.

Strategic Partners

Strategic partners will be developers, arts and cultural organizations, government agencies, chambers of commerce, economic development groups, schools, senior service providers, non-profit agencies, businesses, corporations, and foundations.

Economic Development and Tourism

Increasingly, communities are slowly recognizing the integral role that parks and recreation plays in community economic development and tourism. In addition, parks and recreation provides thousands of direct jobs, often to youth, contributing to the local economy. A major benefit of tourism is that local residents can realize an improved standard of living and take advantage of community enhancements, such as museums, zoos, and other recreation facilities (Canadian Parks & Recreation Association, 1997). Other benefits include preservation of cultural heritage, revival of traditional art, and growth of pride in the community.

In the Future

In the future, the park and recreation profession will be known as a partner in enhancing the economy and as the provider of facilities and programs that attract tourists and enhance quality of life for residents.

Programs, Services, and Facilities

Youth employment programs, farmers' markets, sports tournaments, small-business entrepreneurial opportunities for seniors and youth, and recreation and cultural facilities that support tourism will be the focus of programs, services, and facilities.

Typical Clients

Community members and tourists will be the typical clients.

Strategic Partners

Developers, government agencies, chambers of commerce, economic development groups, social service providers, private concessions, nonprofit agencies interested in community economic development, and businesses will be strategic partners.

Model Neighborhoods

Park and recreation facilities provide neighborhoods with a focal point for community interaction, foster a sense of community identity, and provide services to neighborhood residents. The neighborhood-based approach to planning and community services is gaining in popularity. This approach ensures that staff are familiar with the residents they serve and the issues residents face. Planning and community services are coordinated by interdisciplinary teams.

In the Future

In the future, park and recreation professionals will be key members of interdisciplinary teams that plan and design neighborhoods and provide services that meet residents' needs.

Programs, Services, and Facilities

Facilities and programs are part of an integrated neighborhood fabric. Joint-use facilities combine services, such as schools, community centers, libraries, and police and fire stations. Facilities also serve as a neighborhood "backyard."

Typical Clients

Neighborhood residents, planners, urban designers, businesses, and government agencies will be the primary clients.

Strategic Partners

Developers, nonprofit agencies, neighborhood associations, faith-based organizations, local businesses, social service providers, schools, community organizations, and government services will be strategic partners.

Partnerships With Education (K-12)

In the past several years, state and federal legislative initiatives have reduced class size, increased emphasis on test scores, and expanded before- and after-school care. Other initiatives that are changing education are home schooling, technology, and year-round schools. These changes, aimed at creating a more effective and efficient education system, are changing how and when learning occurs. The role of recreation in increasing children's educational skills and abilities, particularly in after-school programs, has been documented in recent studies (National Institute of Out-of-School Time, 2007). Recreation is already a recognized partner in providing enrichment through experiences that complement educational services.

In the Future

In the future, children will learn leisure skills and values along with other components of the curriculum. Recreation activities will be recognized as a modality for teaching curriculum concepts. Parks and recreation will continue to be a provider and partner in before-school, after-school, and intersession activities.

Programs, Services, and Facilities

Programs aimed at increasing education skills or enrichment programs; intersession programs; summer programs; before-, during-, and after-school programs; preschool development; literacy programs; facilities; staff training; parenting skill development; and family and child leisure education will be the focus of programs, services, and facilities.

Typical Clients

Children, their families, and education professionals will be the typical clients.

Strategic Partners

K-12 schools, law enforcement and the criminal justice system, social service agencies, faith-based organizations, and nonprofit agencies involved with youth will be strategic partners.

Partnerships With Libraries

Today's libraries are community meeting places as well as information providers. They offer information on site as well as off site through mobile programs and the Internet. The library is a source of community pride and a location for cultural and recreation programs. Lifelong learning also takes place at libraries, where literacy programs and computer training are frequently offered, in addition to special-interest programs. Libraries offer opportunities for joint facility development and enterprise programs through sharing facilities with coffee shops and bookstores, offering books and videos for rent, and sponsoring community events, such as youth flea markets.

In the Future

In the future, parks and recreation will be known as partners in providing information, preserving our culture, and creating economic development opportunities through and with libraries.

Programs, Services, and Facilities

Often libraries are operated under municipal community service departments along with recreation. Recreation providers could offer programs at libraries and could provide library services, facilities, and meeting space.

Typical Clients

Residents, businesses, and tourists will be the typical clients.

Strategic Partners

Government agencies, retail businesses, nonprofit "friends" groups, local organizations, and book and information technology advocates will be strategic partners.

Community Problem Solving

Park and recreation professionals have skills in facilitation and leadership that could be applied to community problem solving. As issues become more complex, residents need an opportunity to learn about issues and participate in developing solutions. The most effective solutions to community problems are developed when residents actively participate in decision making. Among residents there is a growing demand for information and a desire to become more involved in the community. In addition to government agencies, a variety of organizations would benefit from effective meeting facilitation and problem solving, including schools and nonprofit organizations. Park and recreation professionals also provide opportunities to volunteer and become involved, including mentoring or coaching youth, building trails, and visiting homebound seniors.

In the Future

In the future, the park and recreation profession will be known as facilitators of community involvement and problem solving for groups and individuals.

Programs, Services, and Facilities

Facilitator of local community groups who define and operate their own community services, community involvement opportunities, community-wide special events, and park stewardship opportunities will be the focus of programs, services, and facilities.

Typical Clients

Government agency staff, residents, neighborhood associations, nonprofit agencies, faith-based organizations, and families will be the typical clients.

Strategic Partners

Nonprofit agencies, social services, schools, government agencies, businesses, and interfaith organizations will be strategic partners.

ENVIRONMENTAL AWARENESS AND STEWARDSHIP

Park and recreation agencies can be the leaders in making community residents and visitors more aware of their environment through outdoor recreation and nature tourism and in developing programs that help to protect open spaces and the local environment.

Outdoor Recreation

As urban areas become further developed, opportunities for outdoor recreation are in greater demand (Munroe, 1999). Americans appreciate outdoor activities such as hiking, camping, and nature watching. Participating in those activities increases their appreciation of natural resources. These trends illustrate the growing demand for outdoor experiences.

In the Future

In the future, park and recreation professionals will be known as the provider of outdoor recreation experiences that increase residents' understanding and appreciation of natural resources.

Programs, Services, and Facilities

Informing people about the natural environment and providing outdoor recreation experiences will be the focus of programs, services, and facilities.

Typical Clients

Children, adults, seniors, businesses, and tourists will be the primary clients.

Strategic Partners

Nonprofit agencies; local, state, and federal natural resource agencies; environmental groups; businesses; chambers of commerce; school districts; open-space cooperatives; greenbelt alliances; land trusts; private concession operators; and water districts will be strategic partners.

Nature Tourism

Parks and recreation could be a leader in promoting nature tourism. According to the Nature Conservancy, tourism is now the world's largest industry, and nature tourism is the fastest-growing segment (Nature Conservancy, 2007).

Nature-based tourists represent a recent phenomenon in the tourism market and are big business, providing substantial economic rewards for many destinations. The USDA Forest Service's National Survey on Recreation and the Environment indicates that 207.9 million people age 16 or older are involved in some form of outdoor recreation. The five most popular activities are walking; family gathering; viewing natural scenery; visiting a nature center, nature trail, or zoo; and picnicking. Since many of our local, county, regional, state, and national parks manage and protect the spaces for those activities, park and recreation professionals are already positioned to be leaders in providing nature-based tourism activities that create advocates for our important natural resources.

In the Future

In the future, the park and recreation profession will be known as partners in building a strong economy through nature-based tourism opportunities.

Programs, Services, and Facilities

Environmental preservation or restoration, environmental education, interpretation, and creating volunteer experiences will be the focus of programs, services, and facilities.

Typical Clients

Children, adults, seniors, businesses, community organizations, and tourists will be typical clients.

Strategic Partners

Nonprofit agencies; natural resource agencies at the local, state, and federal level; chambers of commerce; tourism providers and organizations; environmental groups; public and private foundations; and businesses and corporations will be strategic partners.

Environmental Stewardship and Open Space

Because of the value Americans attribute to the natural environment and its importance in determining quality of life, open-space areas are being developed in urban areas as well as in natural and rural areas. These trends underscore the growing demand for outdoor experiences as well as the desire to preserve urban and rural natural resources. Open space protects habitat, biodiversity, and ecological integrity and improves air quality (Canadian Parks & Recreation Association, 1997).

In the Future

In the future, the park and recreation profession will be known as protectors of our natural environment and as providers of open space.

Programs, Services, and Facilities

Urban and rural open space, greenways, and wildlife refuges will be the focus of programs, services, and facilities.

Typical Clients

Typical clients will be children, adults, seniors, businesses, community organizations, and tourists.

Strategic Partners

Strategic partners will be nonprofit agencies; natural resource agencies at the local, state, and federal level; environmental groups; businesses; chambers of commerce; school districts; open-space cooperatives; greenbelt alliances; land trusts; private concession operators; and water districts.

B

Conducting an Action-Planning Process in Your Community

Because trends vary according to geographic locations, and each park and recreation agency fits into its local environment in a unique way, the market opportunities presented in chapter 3 and appendix A must be adapted for use in your own agency or organization. By conducting an action-planning process in your community or agency, staff will identify market opportunities that respond to local trends and needs and build on unique organizational competencies and available partnerships.

The following questions will assist staff in developing your own VIP Action Plan. Possible information sources and research activities for your agency's use are suggested. These sources and ideas are starting points for your work and are not intended to be all inclusive.

PART 1: YOUR ORGANIZATION

- What are the core values of your organization?

Hold a staff workshop and brainstorm core values. Compare the values identified by your staff with the core values presented in the VIP Action Plan. See figure 2.1, Discussion of Core Values, in chapter 2.

- What is the vision of your organization?

Discuss the VIP vision at a staff meeting and determine if it will fit your needs. Adopt the vision for your agency, department, division, or even program. A recreation supervisor decided to use the VIP vision for the summer day camp she supervised. Staff members were involved in determining the values they wanted to incorporate into their planning and interactions with the campers, and

they decided which of the mission components they thought were most important to the campers. They focused on promoting health and wellness and increasing cultural unity. The program received high evaluations from both the campers and the parents or caregivers. Many of the staff wanted to return the following year because they felt they were part of a community while working at the camp. This example shows that you can take a leadership role in bringing the VIP Action Plan to your agency regardless of your position. Remember, it can start with a conversation.

- What is the mission of your organization?

Hold a staff meeting to brainstorm your organization's mission. You can start with the mission statements identified in the VIP framework. Select the mission statements that address the needs of your community. Adopt those statements within your agency, department, division, or even program.

- Do your proposed values, vision, and mission meet the needs of your community?

Hold a community workshop, have a discussion with your strategic partners, and discuss with your board and commission to get feedback from your target markets, policy makers, customers, and partners.

PART 2: YOUR COMMUNITY

- How will the demographic makeup of your community or agency change in the next 5, 10, or 20 years?

Check the local government's planning department or U.S. Census Bureau, www.census.gov, for information.

- Will there be significant population growth?

Check the local government planning department or U.S. Census Bureau, www.census.gov, for information.

- Who are your community's leaders?

Identify community and business leaders and key stakeholders who are beneficial to your short- and long-range action-planning efforts.

- What social issues are affecting your community or agency?

Check with your planning, public health, public safety, and transportation departments. Talk to your local school superintendent, conduct a community survey or review the results of past surveys, talk to your staff, and conduct a focus group or workshop of current participants or potential new users. Interview your community leaders (chamber of commerce, real estate business owners, local nonprofit leaders, neighborhood associations). Talk to staff at partner agencies.

- What administrative or policy changes will affect your clients?

For example, are schools instituting a year-round schedule? Is your budget being reduced or increased? Is there governmental restructuring?

PART 3: YOUR COMPETENCIES

- What are the specific competencies and strengths of your organization and staff, including recognized skills, model programs, services, facilities, location, staff, partnerships, and funding sources?

Hold a staff meeting to identify your strengths. Look at letters of appreciation from customers or participant evaluations, review past awards, and ask customers and community leaders why they value the agency's staff. After you have determined the competencies needed for your future success, create staff development plans that focus staff training efforts on those necessary skills. Include those competencies in your job descriptions, job evaluations, and job announcements. Ask candidates about these skills in the interview process.

Barry Weiss, when recreation superintendent for the City of Palo Alto (California), was looking for a new recreation supervisor in youth development. He added this to the job announcement and recruitment efforts:

We are looking for someone to help the department foster youth development, strengthen community image and sense of place, reduce juvenile crime, and promote health and wellness. . . . The ideal candidate must possess skills in the following core competency areas: leadership, communications, partnerships and coalition building, outcome-driven management, resource development, and strategic thinking (City of Palo Alto, recreation supervisor—youth development job announcement, May 2000).

Reprinted, by permission, from B. Weiss, Recreation Superintendent for the City of Palo Alto, CA.

It was thought that the competency-based job announcement attracted a much higher quality of candidates than a traditional job announcement that refers to report writing, supervision of staff, or budget development. Barry further stated that candidates specifically mentioned the language and said that was one reason they were attracted to the position. The candidates thought it conveyed an organization that was operating in a strategic manner, and they liked that the mission of parks and recreation was communicated and seen as an important part of the department.

PART 4: YOUR STRATEGIC MARKET OPPORTUNITIES

- Who are your current and potential partners? What services do they provide? Are you duplicating efforts? What resources are they willing to share? What resources are *you* willing to share?

Inventory your current partnerships, survey other providers, and hold a focus group of potential partners. Identify overlapping resources and services and potential collaborations.

- What gaps (or opportunities) are notable in park and recreation services and facilities?

Review collected data and consider the type of service and outcome provided, location, and age group served. Assess whether your agency is the best agency to close the gap.

- Which of the opportunities identified in the trends analysis or opportunity section (chapter 3) matches well with your local trends, your unique strengths, and your current and future partnerships?

Review data with staff and select those that will strengthen your agency's position in the community.

- Are there market opportunities not presented in the VIP Action Plan that fit well with your situation?

Identify those with staff. Review the example of the City of San Carlos (chapter 3) and their identification of missed opportunities by not programming with active adults in mind.

- Which opportunities are the highest priorities based on community need and agency strengths? Of those, which are areas of your greatest strength?

Review data with staff, the board or commission, other department heads, and your policy makers.

PART 5: DETERMINE YOUR IMPLEMENTATION STRATEGIES

- For each identified opportunity, select your implementation strategies. You may need to redesign your programs, staff hiring procedures, budget development, or criteria to select partners in order to achieve your specific goals.
- Identify lead responsibilities and supporting responsibilities. Reassign staff if necessary.
- Identify agency needs for implementing your action plan. Consider internal and external communications (using the resources in chapters 7 through 10), your agency professional development needs, and resources needs. The City of Manhattan Beach organizes its commission report using the mis-

sion of parks and recreation as its format (see figure B.1).

PART 6: YOUR PERFORMANCE MEASURES

- Start by developing and writing down goals for your program (see chapter 6).
- Develop a means of measuring the attainment of goals as the plan is implemented. Conduct observational studies or customer surveys.
- Monitor your success. Use an established instrument to measure goal achievement, or work with educators or consultants to develop a customized instrument based on your needs.
- Establish a communications program to publicize your success using the resources in chapters 7 through 10.

Beginning this action-planning process will seem daunting to even the most seasoned park and recreation professional, but it is a process that begins with that one first step, which involves becoming familiar with the values, vision, and mission of parks and recreation as articulated in the VIP Action Plan. Where can you start? Figure B.2 (see page 152) presents ideas on where you can start talking about the mission of parks and recreation whether you are a student or a seasoned practitioner.

What will be the progressive impact of your outreach? Just as the single stone drops into the water and creates a ripple across the water, your words and actions will do the same. Figure B.3 (see page 152) gives you an idea of how your voice can be magnified throughout your agency, throughout your professional association, and to your peers. VIP begins with you.

Sample Commission Report

July 2006 commission report

To: Idris Jassim Al-Oboudi, recreation services manager

From: Cameron Harding, recreation supervisor

City of Manhattan Beach Department and Program Mission in Action

Strengthen community image and sense of place. The summer 2006 programs are in full swing, and they all contribute to this mission by providing events and services that strengthen community image and sense of place by taking pride in our community and providing recreation programs and services that address community needs.

Support economic development. All of the teen center's Rule Squad trips have sold out so far, and it looks as though we'll sell out the remaining 6 trips. Also, we have had more than 50 teens pay $5 each for the first two Discopooluzas as well as almost 60 kids paying $3 each at Begg Pool on Friday Funds Support the Pool program. Currently we have more than 80 teens signed up for the summer program at $16 each. The economic activity of the teen center helps to support recreation vendors and activity leaders and provide a proactive economical solution to issues of engaging youth in positive activities: Pay now or pay later.

Strengthen safety and security. The playground program and teen center, in collaboration with Aviation Cycle, put on a BMX stunt show and safety clinics for approximately 150 children. We gave out worksheets and stickers and put on an excellent show. Covers for the disc golf course baskets in Polliwog Park have been purchased. They will keep people from playing in busy areas on the weekends and during events such as concerts, Earth Day, and pet appreciation events.

Promote health and wellness. The teen center continues to implement healthy and active activities on a daily basis throughout the summer program. Examples are dodgeball, kickball, tag, skateboarding, rock wall climbing, and relay races. The teen center has also partnered with the playground program in getting fruits and vegetables from the farmers' market for distribution to its participants.

Foster human development. Customer service training for building attendant staff has helped in their communication skills when dealing with the public. This has proven to be extremely valuable when informing park patrons about rules and regulations they may not have been aware of.

Increase cultural unity. The teen center summer program and Rule Squad trips continue to serve a wide variety of demographics, giving the teens an opportunity to mix and play with other teens they may not have otherwise had a chance to get to know.

Protect environmental resources. Teen center participants conduct park clean-ups at the end of each day. This consists of picking up pieces of trash and wiping down picnic tables. Park patrol and building attendant staff also conduct park clean-ups at Heights, Marine, and Polliwog on a daily basis.

Facilitate community problem solving. Mira Costa High School student and Disc Golf Club president Nick Slobodian talked to MBMS physical education classes about proper etiquette when playing disc golf in Polliwog Park as well as the rules and regulations. We also took the opportunity to talk to the MBMS students about not playing disc golf during concerts, science camp, and other busy activities.

Provide recreational experiences. The teen center is offering the Fourth Annual Rule Squad trips. Members of the Rule Squad take trips to several local theme parks, Big Bear Lake, a three-day camping trip to San Onofre, and a three-day white-water rafting trip.

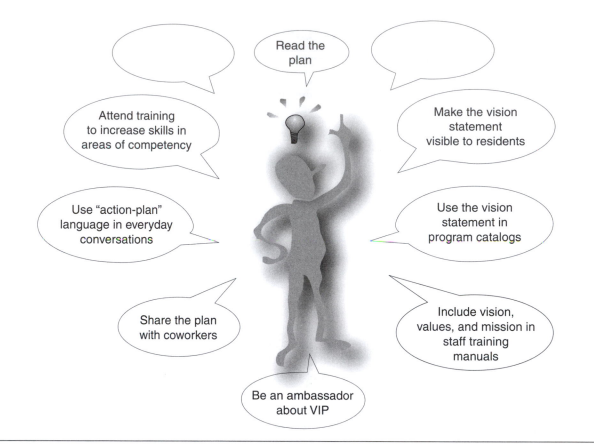

Figure B.2 Ideas for discussing the mission of parks and recreation.

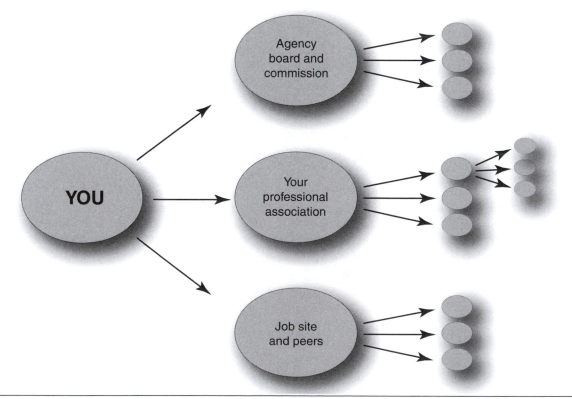

Figure B.3 The progressive impact of your outreach.

C

Evaluation and Research Methodology and Statistics

This section includes resources on action research, focus groups, and needs assessment.

Reprinted, by permission, from Betty van der Smissen, 2005, *Recreation and Parks* (Champaign, IL: Human Kinetics), 125-129.

Adler, E., and R. Clark. 2003. *How it's done: An invitation to social research.* Belmont, CA: Wadsworth/Thomson Learning.

Agere, S., and N. Jorm. 2000. *Designing performance appraisals: Assessing needs and designing performance management systems in the public sector.* London: Commonwealth Secretariat.

Alreck, P.L. 1995. *The survey research handbook.* 2nd ed. Chicago: Irwin Professional Publishing.

Altschuld, J.W., and B.R. Witkin. 2000. *From needs assessment to action.* Thousand Oaks, CA: Sage Publications.

Babbie, E. 1998. *The practice of social research.* 8th ed. Belmont, CA: Wadsworth.

Barnett, L.A. 1995. *Research about leisure: Past, present, and future.* 2nd ed. Champaign, IL: Sagamore Publishing.

Bartholomew, D.J. 1996. *The statistical approach to social measurement.* San Diego: Academic Press.

Baumgartner, T.A., C.H. Strong, and L.D. Hensley. 2002. *Conducting and reading research in health and human performance.* 3rd ed. New York: McGraw-Hill.

Bearden, W.O., R.G. Netemeyer, and M.F. Mobley. 1999. *Handbook of marketing scales: Multi-item measures for marketing and consumer behavior research.* 2nd ed. Newbury Park, CA: Sage Publications.

Berg, K.E., and R.W. Latin. 2004. *Essentials of research methods in health, physical education, exercise science, and recreation.* 2nd ed. Philadelphia: Lippincott, Williams & Wilkins.

Bickman, L., and D.J. Rog, eds. 1998. *Handbook of applied social research methods.* Thousand Oaks, CA: Sage Publications.

Biemer, P.P. and others, eds. 1991. *Measurement errors in surveys.* New York: Wiley.

Blaike, N. 2003. *Analyzing quantitative data from description to explanation.* Thousand Oaks, CA: Sage Publications.

Blalock, A.B., ed. 1990. *Evaluating social programs at the state and local level.* Kalamazoo, MI: W.E. Upjohn Institute for Employment Research.

Bogdan, R.C., and S. Knopp Biklen. 2003. *Qualitative research for education: An introduction to theory and methods.* 4th ed. Boston: Allyn & Bacon.

Browne, M.N., and S. Kelley. 2001. *Asking the right questions: A guide to critical thinking.* 6th ed. Upper Saddle River, NJ: Prentice-Hall.

Burdge, R.J. 1998. *A conceptual approach to social impact assessment.* Rev. ed. Middleton, WI: Social Ecology Press.

Burdge, R.J. 1999. *A community guide to social impact assessment.* Rev. ed. Middleton, WI: Social Ecology Press.

Burlingame, J., and T.M. Blascho. 2002. *Assessment tools for recreational therapy and related fields.* 3rd ed. Ravensdale, WA: Idyll Arbor.

Chambliss, D.F., and R.K. Schutt. 2003. *Making sense of the social world: Methods of investigation.* Thousand Oaks, CA: Sage Publications.

Chirban, J.T. 1996. *Interviewing in depth.* Thousand Oaks, CA: Sage Publications.

Church, A., and J. Waclawski. 1998. *Designing and using organizational surveys.* San Francisco: Jossey-Bass.

Churchill, G.A., Jr. 1999. *Marketing research: Methodological foundations.* 7th ed. Chicago: Dryden Press.

Coffey, A., and P. Atkinson. 1996. *Making sense of qualitative data: Complementary research strategies.* Thousand Oaks, CA: Sage Publications.

Coghlan, D., and T. Brannick. 2001. *Doing action research in your own organization.* Thousand Oaks, CA: Sage Publications.

Crabtree, B.F., and W.L. Miller, eds. 1999. *Doing qualitative research.* 2nd ed. Thousand Oaks, CA: Sage Publications.

Creswell, J.W. 1998. *Qualitative inquiry and research design: Choosing among five traditions.* Thousand Oaks, CA: Sage Publications.

Creswell, J.W. 2002. *Research design: Qualitative and quantitative approaches.* 2nd ed. Thousand Oaks, CA: Sage Publications.

Cunningham, J.B. 1993. *Action research and organizational development.* Westport, CT: Praeger.

Czarnecki, M.T. 1999. *Managing by measuring: How to improve your organization's performance through effective benchmarking.* New York: American Management Association.

Denzin, N.K., and Y.S. Lincoln, eds. 2005. *Handbook of qualitative research.* 3rd ed. Thousand Oaks, CA: Sage Publications.

Dillman, D.A. 2000. *Mail and Internet surveys: The tailored design method.* 2nd ed. New York: Wiley.

Donaldson, S., and M. Scriven, eds. 2003. *Evaluating social programs and problems.* Mahway, NJ: Lawrence Associates.

Dunaway, D.K., and W.K. Baum, eds. 1996. *Oral history: An interdisciplinary anthology.* 2nd ed. Walnut Creek, CA: AltaMira Press. Published in cooperation with the American Association for State and Local History and the Oral History Association.

Easterby-Smith, M., R. Thorpe, and A. Lowe. 1991. *Management research: An introduction.* Newbury Park, CA: Sage Publications.

Fern, E.F. 2001. *Advanced focus group research.* Thousand Oaks, CA: Sage Publications.

Fink, A., ed. 2002. *The survey kit.* 2nd ed. Thousand Oaks, CA: Sage Publications. The series is composed of nine small volumes.

Folz, D.H. 1996. *Survey research for public administration.* Thousand Oaks, CA: Sage Publications.

Gall, M.D., J.P. Gall, and W.R. Borg. 2003. *Educational research.* 7th ed. Boston: Allyn & Bacon.

Gray, S.T. and associates. 1998. *Evaluation with power: A new approach to organizational effectiveness, empowerment, and excellence.* San Francisco: Jossey-Bass.

Greenbaum, T.L. 2000. *Moderating focus groups.* Thousand Oaks, CA: Sage Publications.

Gubrium, J.F., and A. Sankar, eds. 1994. *Qualitative methods in aging research.* Thousand Oaks, CA: Sage Publications.

Gummesson, E. 2000. *Qualitative methods in management research.* 2nd ed. Thousand Oaks, CA: Sage Publications.

Hale, R., and P. Whitlam. 2000. *Powering up performance management.* Burlington, VT: Gower.

Harrington, H.J., and J.S. Harrington. 1996. *High performance benchmarking.* New York: McGraw-Hill.

Henderson, K.A. 1991. *Dimensions of choice: A qualitative approach to recreation, parks, and leisure research.* State College, PA: Venture Publishing.

Henderson, K.A. 2002. *Evaluating leisure services: Making enlightened decisions.* 2nd ed. State College, PA: Venture Publishing.

Henry, G.T. 1995. *Graphing data: Techniques for display and analysis.* Applied Social Research Methods Series, vol. 36. Thousand Oaks, CA: Sage Publications.

Holloway, J., J. Lewis, and G. Mallor. 1995. *Performance measurement and evaluation.* Thousand Oaks, CA: Sage Publications (with The Open University).

Huck, S.W. 2004. *Reading statistics and research.* 4th ed. Boston: Pearson Education.

Jason, L.A., et al., eds. *Participatory community research.* 2004. Washington, DC: American Psychological Association.

Jones, S. 1999. *Doing Internet research.* Thousand Oaks, CA: Sage Publications.

Kaydos, W. 1999. *Operational performance measurement.* Baton Rouge, FL: CRC Press.

Kelly, J.R., and R.B. Warnick. 1999. *Recreation trends and markets.* Champaign, IL: Sagamore Publishing.

Kraus, R., and L. Allen. 1997. *Research and evaluation in recreation, parks, and leisure studies.* 2nd ed. Columbus, OH: Publishing Horizons.

Kraut, A.I., ed. 1996. *Organizational surveys: Tools for assessment and change.* San Francisco: Jossey-Bass.

Krueger, R.A., and M.A. Casey. 2000. *Focus groups: A practical guide for applied research.* 3rd ed. Thousand Oaks, CA: Sage Publications.

Kvale, S. 1996. *InterViews: An introduction to qualitative research interviewing.* Thousand Oaks, CA: Sage Publications.

Malkin, M.J., and C.Z. Howe, eds. 1993. *Research in therapeutic recreation: Concepts and methods.* State College, PA: Venture Publishing.

Mangione, T.W. 1995. *Mail surveys: Improving the quality.* Applied Social Research Methods Series, vol. 40. Thousand Oaks, CA: Sage Publications.

Mark, M.M., G.T. Henry, and G. Julnes. 2000. *Evaluation: An integrated framework for understanding, guiding and improving public and nonprofit policies and programs.* San Francisco: Jossey-Bass.

Marshall, C., and G.B. Rossman. 1995. *Designing qualitative research.* 2nd ed. Thousand Oaks, CA: Sage Publications.

Martin, L.L., and P.M. Kettner. 1996. *Measuring the performance of human service programs.* Sage Human Services Guides, vol. 71. Thousand Oaks, CA: Sage Publications.

Maxwell, J.A. 1996. *Qualitative research design: An interactive approach.* Applied Social Research Methods Series, vol. 41. Thousand Oaks, CA: Sage Publications.

Merriam, S.B. and associates. 2002. *Qualitative research in practice: Examples for discussion and analysis.* San Francisco: Jossey-Bass.

Miles, M.B., and A.M. Huberman. 1994. *Qualitative data analysis: An expanded sourcebook.* 2nd ed. Thousand Oaks, CA: Sage Publications.

Miller, D.C., and N.J. Salkind. 2002. *Handbook of research design and social measurement.* 6th ed. Newbury Park, CA: Sage Publications.

Miller, G., and R. Dingwall, eds. 1997. *Context and method in qualitative research.* Thousand Oaks, CA: Sage Publications.

Miller, G.J., and M.L. Whicker. 1999. *Handbook of research methods in public administration.* New York: Marcel Dekker.

Miller, T.I., and M.A. Miller. 1991. *Citizen surveys: How to do them, how to use them, what they mean.* Washington, D.C.: International City/County Management Association.

Mitra, A., and S. Lankford. 1999. *Research methods in park, recreation, and leisure services.* Champaign, IL: Sagamore Publishing.

Mohr, L.B. 1992. *Impact analysis for program evaluation.* Newbury Park, CA: Sage Publications.

Morgan, D.L. 1997. *Focus groups as qualitative research.* 2nd ed. Qualitative Research Methods Series, vol. 16. Thousand Oaks, CA: Sage Publications.

Morgan, D.L., and R.A. Krueger. 1998. *The focus group kit.* Thousand Oaks, CA: Sage Publications. The kit contains six small volumes.

Morrow, J.R., et al. 2000. *Measurement and evaluation in human performance.* 2nd ed. Champaign, IL: Human Kinetics.

National Therapeutic Recreation Society (NTRS). 1996. *The best of the Therapeutic Recreation Journal: Assessments.* Ashburn, VA: National Recreation and Park Association.

Nicol, A.M., and P.M. Pexman. 2003. *Displaying your findings: A practical guide for creating figures, posters, and presentations.* Washington, D.C.: American Psychological Association.

Nicol, A.M., and P.M. Pexman. 2003 (updates). *Presenting your findings: A practical guide for creating tables.* Washington, D.C.: American Psychological Association.

Niven, P.R. 2002. *Balanced scorecard: Step-by-step.* New York: Wiley.

Noffke, S.E., and R.B. Stevenson, eds. 1995. *Educational action research: Becoming practically critical.* New York: Teachers College Press, Columbia University Press.

Organizations for Economic Cooperation and Development. 1996. *Performance auditing and the modernization of government.* Paris: OECD.

Patton, C.V., and D.S. Sawicki. 1986. *Basic methods of policy analysis and planning.* Upper Saddle River, NJ: Prentice-Hall.

Patton, M.Q. 2002. *Qualitative research and evaluation methods.* Thousand Oaks, CA: Sage Publications.

Popham, W.J., and K.A. Sirotnik. 1992. *Understanding statistics in education.* Itasca, IL: Peacock.

Posavac, E.J., and R.G. Carey. 1997. *Program evaluation, methods and case studies.* 5th ed. Upper Saddle River, NJ: Prentice-Hall.

Rea, L.M., and R.A. Parker. 1997. *Designing and conducting survey research: A comprehensive guide.* 2nd ed. San Francisco: Jossey-Bass.

Reason, P., and H. Bradbury, eds. 2001. *Handbook of action research: Participative inquiry and practice.* Thousand Oaks, CA: Sage Publications.

Riddick, C., and R. Russell. 1999. *Evaluative research in recreation, park, and sport settings: Searching for useful information.* Champaign, IL: Sagamore Publishing.

Ritchie, J.R.B., and C.R. Goeldner. 1994. *Travel, tourism, and hospitality research.* 2nd ed. New York: Wiley.

Robinson, J.P., P.R. Shaver, and L.S. Wrightsman, eds. 1991. *Measures of personality and social psychological attitudes.* San Diego: Academic Press.

Rosenthal, R., and R. Rosnow. 1991. *Essentials of behavioral research: Methods and data analysis.* 2nd ed. New York: McGraw-Hill.

Rossi, H.P., H.E. Freeman, and M.W. Lipsay. 2004. *Evaluation: A systematic approach.* 7th ed. Newbury Park, CA: Sage Publications.

Rubin, A., and E. Babbie. 2004. *Research methods for social work.* 5th ed. Belmont, CA: Wadsworth/Thomson Learning.

Rubin, H.J., and I.S. Rubin. 1995. *Qualitative interviewing: The art of hearing data.* Thousand Oaks, CA: Sage Publications.

Russ-Eft, D., and H. Preskill. 2001. *Evaluation in organizations.* Cambridge, MA: Perseus Publishing.

Schalock, R.L. 1995. *Outcome-based evaluation.* New York: Plenum Press.

Schuman, H., and S. Presser. 1996. *Questions and answers in attitude surveys.* Thousand Oaks, CA: Sage Publications.

Schut, R.K. 2001. *Investigating the social world: The process and practice of research.* 3rd ed. Thousand Oaks, CA: Sage Publications.

Seale, C. 1999. *The quality of qualitative research.* Thousand Oaks, CA: Sage Publications.

Shadish, W.R., Jr., T.D. Coo, and L.C. Leviton. 1991. *Foundations of program evaluation: Theories of practice.* Newbury Park, CA: Sage Publications.

Shaw, I. 1999. *Qualitative research.* Thousand Oaks, CA: Sage Publications.

Sheskin, D.J. 2000. *Handbook of parametric and nonparametric statistical procedures.* 2nd ed. Boca Raton, FL: CRC Press.

Shockley, J.M., Jr. 1995. *Research and data analysis in leisure, recreation, tourism and sport management.* Las Vegas, NV: Sigma Press.

Sirkin, R.M. 1995. *Statistics for the social sciences.* Thousand Oaks, CA: Sage Publications.

Stringer, E.T. 1999. *Action research: A handbook for practitioners.* 2nd ed. Thousand Oaks, CA: Sage Publications.

Templeton, J.F. 1994. *The focus group.* Rev. ed. Burr Ridge, IL: Irwin Publishing.

Thomas, J.R., and J.K. Nelson. 2001. *Research methods in physical activity.* 4th ed. Champaign, IL: Human Kinetics.

Thompson, N.J., and H.O. McClintock. 1998. *Demonstrating your program's worth.* Atlanta: National Center for Injury Prevention and Control.

United Way of America. 1996. *Measuring program outcomes: A practical approach.* Alexandria, VA: United Way of America.

Vaughn, S., J.S. Schumm, and J. Sinagub. 1996. *Focus group interviews in education and psychology.* Thousand Oaks, CA: Sage Publications.

Wallgren, A., et al. 1996. *Graphing statistics and data: Creating better charts.* Thousand Oaks, CA: Sage Publications.

Weisberg, H., and B. Brown. 1996. *An introduction to survey research polling and data analysis.* 3rd ed. Thousand Oaks, CA: Sage Publications.

Weiss, C.H. 1998. *Evaluation: Methods for studying programs and policies.* 2nd ed. Upper Saddle River, NJ: Prentice-Hall.

Wholey, J.S., H.P. Hatry, and K.E. Newcomer, eds. 1994. *Handbook of practical program evaluation.* San Francisco: Jossey-Bass.

Witkin, B.R., and J.W. Altschuld. 1995. *Planning and conducting needs assessment.* Thousand Oaks, CA: Sage Publications.

Wolcott, H.F. 2001. *Writing up qualitative research.* Thousand Oaks, CA: Sage Publications.

Worthen, B.R., J.R. Saunders, and J.L. Fitzpatrick. 1997. *Program evaluation: Alternative approaches and practical guidelines.* 2nd ed. White Plains, NY: Longman Publications.

Yin, R.K. 1994. *Case study research: Design and methods.* 2nd ed. Newbury Park, CA: Sage Publications.

Yow, V.R. 1994. *Recording oral history: A practical guide for social scientists.* Thousand Oaks, CA: Sage Publications.

Zalatan, A. 1994. *Forecasting methods in sports and recreation.* Toronto: Thompson Educational Publishing.

Zelazny, G. 1996. *Say it with charts: The executive's guide to visual communication.* 3rd ed. Chicago: Irwin Professional Publishing.

D

Portfolios and the Selection Process

Parks, recreation, and tourism is a diverse field that attracts students with varied backgrounds and career goals. Truth be told, most working professionals, along with academicians, believe that the field requires employees who have been involved in a multidisciplinary academic preparation and tested in a variety of field settings in order to understand the range of professional demands to which an employee might have to respond. It is impossible for people to experience everything before they set foot on a job. When both training dollars and time are in short supply, new employees have to be ready to hit the ground running.

This appendix offers an overview of the use, assessment, and interdependence among professional competencies, curriculum design, and portfolios as part of the employee selection process in parks, recreation, and tourism. Since many agencies now require full-time employees to hold at least a bachelor's degree in recreation or a related field, the chapter begins with a discussion of current professional competencies as they often are addressed in academic curriculums. Next, the role and pressures in higher education that shape curriculum design as it relates to this discipline are discussed. The third section describes the potential for portfolios to serve as a vehicle for documenting and sharing the interrelationship between employment criteria and academic preparation. Both strengths and weaknesses are presented.

This appendix was written by Veda E. Ward, department of recreation and tourism management, California State University at Northridge.

IDENTIFYING PROFESSIONAL COMPETENCIES

One of the best ways to illustrate how the profession identifies and disseminates the competencies required by entry-level employees is through professional organizations. The process of benchmarking (Ammons, 2001) suggests that when an organization cares about its performance and the quality of services it provides, it selects a comparable organization against which to compare its performance on a variety of criteria. This approach can be a cost-effective and time-saving way to determine how and where to improve performance instead of a random trial-and-error approach. The benchmark used to demonstrate this section is the California Park & Recreation Society's VIP Action Plan, the product of a strategic planning process that resulted in a long list of desired professional competencies along with goals and initiatives to showcase the people, parks, and programs that make the profession instrumental in the quality of life of the citizens of California.

In 2001, the California Park & Recreation Society published a fact sheet that identified and disseminated a set of professional competencies that were intended to trigger common understanding among park, recreation, and tourism educators; students; and practitioners. The list can be used in a variety of ways to articulate both educational and professional responsibilities to those interested in becoming high-performing members of the profession.

The following were the original competencies:

1. Action and strategic planning
2. Ecosystem management

3. Human development
4. Resource management and development
5. Strategic thinking
6. Technology
7. Communications
8. Facilitation
9. Mediation
10. Creator of experiences
11. Outcome-driven management
12. Prevention models (knowledge and use of)
13. Research and evaluation
14. Community knowledge
15. Community building
16. Partnering and coalition building
17. People orientation
18. Political dynamics and acumen
19. Flexibility
20. Leadership
21. Multitasking
22. Resourcefulness

How each of these terms is interpreted and applied by the local agency may vary. Similarly, some of the competencies may be more relevant at different stages in both the employment life of the employee and of the organization. For example, leadership is frequently expressed by employers as a desirable trait in employees, but it usually varies in scope and impact as one progresses from entry-level employee to senior executive. These competencies address the tripartite identity of the profession: *people, parks,* and *programs*.

Here are several practical ways that a list of desired competencies can be translated into components of the selection process:

- Use items to compose a self-assessment checklist to be administered to employees (or students) at the entrance and exit from their jobs (or the major).

- Use the list items as discussion points between supervisors and employees, or students and faculty advisors can use it to decide on training preferences or elective courses.

- Use the list to help identify matching preparation, whether in prior work experience or in courses.

- Employing agencies can use these to create target outcomes to be accomplished by student interns during field placement.

- Translate the competencies into selection criteria when hiring new full-time employees.

- Use this list as a part of the language in position descriptions when searching for new employees.

- Discuss these criteria with park, recreation, and tourism professors, using them as part of their self-assessment during retention, tenure, and promotion (RTP) or the post-tenure review process. This is a way of keeping academicians connected with the field and employers' expectations.

- Use the competencies as criteria to compare candidates competing for the same position.

- Use the competencies to identify training needs and priorities.

Everyone has probably already come up with several items to add to or to delete from this list. Today, the ability to use computers and word-processing programs is a very small part of an ever-changing world of technology. Should other emerging forms of technology be added? Those abilities may either be listed separately, thought of as part of communication, or considered as a tool that supports performance in the other areas. Similarly, grant writing can be viewed as a stand-alone skill or as one that is woven into resourcefulness, community building, or coalition development. One last example, developing a park and recreation master plan (Kelsey, 2002), is an important ability in placing parks and recreation as a key player in urban design and redesign and in deciding how and where to develop new housing, business industry, and transportation corridors. Or, is that simply a dimension of ecosystem management or research and evaluation?

Clearly, there is no one-size-fits-all model. The point is to use the approach and tailor it to suit the needs of each agency. Each competency could be analyzed as a set of specific skills to be acquired at various stages of one's career or as the employing agency shifts focus and priorities.

CURRICULUM DESIGN AND THE CHALLENGES OF HIGHER EDUCATION

Research findings on educational effectiveness can be applied to solving problems in business and industry, such as employee selection. Portfolios, for example, have been adopted by many colleges, universities, and even high schools as a means of assessing outcomes of student learning. According to Robert L. Linn (2001), assessment procedures can also be linked to a broader commitment to educational reform, by incorporating a performance-based approach focusing on concepts worth teaching, and addressing differential opportunities to learn among the nation's students.

EDUCATION AND CAREER PREPARATION

The mission, values, and purposes of institutions of higher learning vary widely. Even though assessment and evaluation of student learning are often mandated, standards, criteria, and procedures for accomplishing those are far from uniform. Similarly, reasons for obtaining an undergraduate degree vary from student to student, as do the ways in which the earned degree may be used to secure employment. The philosophy or purpose of a program or department may also shift, especially as influenced by economic and social changes.

The portfolio has evolved as a popular method of reporting performance-based learning outcomes, and it can be used to support student learning at all levels, extending from kindergarten through graduate school and into one's career. Portfolios are a systematic collection of evidence that teachers and students use in monitoring growth of students' knowledge, skills, and attitudes in a subject (San Diego County Office of Education, 1997). They were once common only in the arts, but now they have been adapted to a broad range of career assessment initiatives.

Throughout higher education, for example, portfolios are commonly used by faculty members to summarize and present professorial accomplishments as they progress through the retention, tenure, and promotion process. They may be called teaching portfolios, dossiers, or personal information files. As a result, faculty members, especially those who are also practitioners in their own field, also recognize the need for students to carefully and consistently document their achievements, both in and outside of the classroom.

Students and faculty seem to agree that collecting and presenting tangible examples of student work may be beneficial in either the college application process or in documenting one's capacity to fulfill responsibilities once employed. By assessing student progress from first-year matriculation through graduation, entrance and exit measures of professional competence go

hand in hand with other aspects of academic evaluation and fit well into the structure and hierarchy of higher education.

A parallel system can be identified in business and industry where competencies required at various levels of employee responsibility are aligned with specific education, training, and performance expectations that must be met in order to progress through the ranks. In parks, recreation, and tourism, for example, that progression might be from volunteer to aide to full-time professional to manager to CEO or CAO. Normally, applications, tests, transcripts, and diplomas are used in confirming acquisition of desired knowledge, skills, and experiences, leading to selection, retention, and promotion.

In the park, recreation, and tourism profession, portfolios can help demonstrate attainment of competencies agreed on by professional organizations through accreditation, certification, or other standards-identification procedures. Each academic program, however, has the option or mandate to design curriculums that include learning outcomes, objectives, assignments, and course-based experiential components that align with publicized professional standards. Campus policies may mandate course structure or formats that either complement or conflict with a department's ability to address professional standards.

Academic programs (regardless of discipline) may vary by size, expertise of the faculty, demands of the local employing market, and philosophy about professionalization. Since no two academic programs are exactly the same, it is unlikely that standardization of curriculums in a field as diverse as parks, recreation, and tourism will ever occur; in fact, it may be undesirable. Sports and games, travel and tourism, hobbies and arts, entertainment, fitness pursuits, social activities, and outdoor recreation make up the recreation sphere in the United States. Annual expenditures in recreation range from the Commerce Department's estimate of over $564.7 billion (U.S. Census Bureau, 2000) to as much as $1 trillion (Stynes, 1993).

It is difficult to imagine how a single set of courses or experiences could prepare all students majoring in parks, recreation, and tourism for such a diverse profession. In addition, students may further refine their career niche by population, geographic location, and sector through which programs and services are delivered (private, nonprofit, public, or government). At various stages of their careers, park, recreation, and tourism professionals may be required to focus on delivering economic, social, and political benefits to individuals, groups, or communities. The skill, knowledge, and experiential bases necessary for success in this field, therefore, may be both broad and deep.

Despite the diversity within a given field, all students enrolled in bachelor's degree programs clearly appreciate and expect consistency in the requirements established by those entities that will evaluate their credentials, whether for further education or fitness for work. Particularly at the undergraduate level, students want reassurance that there is a parallel between classroom expectations and qualifications identified by employers in entry-level position descriptions. This appendix provides recommendations on increasing compatibility and transferability between learning and professional expectations and performance, specifically by incorporating the academic or employment portfolio into the selection process.

Prospective employers may not recognize a connection between an applicant's major and the job duties (i.e., the relevance of specific courses to the job for which they are hiring). A portfolio can assist in making the case. According to Lankes (1995), businesses across the country are increasingly interested in viewing student portfolios in order to evaluate prospective employees' work readiness skills. The portfolio may help identify the relevance of degrees, majors, and courses by highlighting specific assignments through which job competencies were attained.

No matter how highly students and employers regard the formal academic degree, savvy prospective employers normally expect hands-on experience in one or more aspects of the field of practice. Unfortunately, field experience may be difficult to translate into career-related skills. The portfolio works well in demonstrating the applicant's ability to perform certain tasks or to achieve certain accomplishments (De Carlo, 1999) and may be used for documenting the student's ability to function in a professional setting or capacity.

Practical experience may seem straightforward, but it can present problems in the selection process, especially if reported only as a number of hours completed at a site. For example, the National Recreation and Park Association and American Alliance of Leisure and Recreation (Joint) Council on Accreditation has established 1,200 hours as a minimum number of field-placement hours to be amassed by undergraduate students in accredited programs. Students and academic departments, however, tend to document both the *content* of the student's experience and the quality of the student's actual *performance*

in a variety of ways, including written reports, on-site in-person assessments, and telephone conversations. As a result, it may be difficult for prospective employers to compare field work and internship evaluations across degree-granting programs, institutions, settings, and supervisors. By viewing additional forms of documentation in a portfolio, the prospective employer is better able to understand the range of experience, work skills, and level at which the student performed. De Carlo (1999), for example, recommends inclusion of seven types of materials in the portfolio: resume and cover letter; letters of recommendation from employers and professors; positive performance evaluations or reviews; college transcripts; training, certifications, or licenses; samples of work and relevant papers; and awards. The specific mix of these components may be tailored to reflect the unique aspects of each academic program.

When assessing the meaning of practicum hours or community-service learning projects, it may be difficult for reviewers to determine either the quality or quantity of tasks assigned a given student—especially when the student is working as a member of a team or group. Since students are often supervised by busy professionals or overworked university instructors, the portfolio can provide further documentation of actual on-site performance in the form of videos, photographs (where allowed by law), activity evaluations conducted by agency staff, written feedback from activity participants, or prose reports provided to the individual student by the course instructor. And when it comes to capturing the emotional responses of activity participants, clients, or visitors to the student or to the experience they provided, a picture might be worth a thousand words!

An increase in the number of accredited agencies—as well as the number of degreed, experienced practitioners supervising interns—may evolve into a common set of expectations for students at varying levels of field work, practicum, and internship. The quality of the experience is difficult to determine, so it may also be important to provide common criteria for intern supervisors and to develop a core training that would apply to all agency supervisors. Additional requirements could be tailored to the unique characteristics of the agency, state and local needs, or demographics.

Another perspective is introduced as one thinks about second-career or nontraditional employees. Because of health, family, career, and personal factors, today's baby boomers, along with other "intermittent" workers, may seek employment during nontraditional points in their lives. A common stereotype involves women or parents returning to work after an extended leave in which they took care of children or elderly parents. In the 21st century, however, there is much more concern about the potential impact on the quality of many organizations should those born between 1946 and 1964 all leave the workforce at one time ("Turning Boomers Into Boomerangs," 2006). Not only is there a concern about the loss of organizational history and intellectual capital, but there is also an absence of general maturity and problem-solving strategies. Some companies are recruiting mature adult "boomerangs" who may have retired elsewhere, or they are actively discouraging retirement by allowing their employees more flexible work patterns (telecommuting, flex weeks, more vacation days) to keep the stability and talents of that cohort in the workforce. The portfolio is an excellent way to address unique personal or career circumstances, such as gender (Sachs, 2006), as well as to showcase those sometimes intangible qualities that are transferable from one work environment to another.

Grades are perhaps the most familiar indicators of student academic achievement and may be assigned in percentages, letters, or narrative forms. Even when reported on the same 4.0 scale (where 4.0 means "outstanding"), however, the meaning of grades may vary greatly from institution to institution or from professor to professor. Similarly, course titles, descriptions, and content may be unclear or meaningless to practitioners unfamiliar with university and instructor standards as they assess a student applicant's readiness for future employment. The academic transcript is probably not the most reliable method available for documenting student competence. In fact, such limited information may lead to misinterpretation and possibly to an inaccurate prediction of the applicant's true capabilities.

One dimension of the educational process that remains unaddressed is the impact of differences in the awarding of grades and degrees. In this instance, ability, gender, socioeconomic status, culture and ethnicity, race, and sexual orientation may all come into play in the pursuit of a degree. All those factors can influence the meaning of grades, assignment to and acceptance at field placements, and many other supposedly "objective" criteria that are often considered in the selection process. Those biases may often be built into courses, testing items or methods, and a variety of other approaches to learning. Even authorities on higher education suggest that assessment strategies undertaken to provide evidence of student learning acknowledge the dangers of an overemphasis on outcomes (Wergin, 2005).

As Sterling (2001) states, "Leading businesses are beginning to put into practice a changed education and learning paradigm where organizations themselves are creative learning communities, and where people are valued as the prime resource. Further, they seek employees who can fully participate in a learning culture, who are adaptive, creative and flexible, rather than 'cogs' produced by mechanistic education systems and by narrow vocationalism and specialization. These businesses value diversity, and see it as essential to their own sustainability" (p. 46). How do park, recreation, and tourism curriculums assist students, as future practitioners, in valuing this range of ways of being, doing, and thinking in their courses? Certainly, the portfolio can provide that additional level of documenting intentionally innovative and inclusive approaches to program and facility design as well as to managerial philosophy and processes.

Figure D.1 illustrates the parallels between education and employment. Both end in an expectation of professional development, continuing education, and commitment to lifelong learning.

REASONS FOR NOT USING PORTFOLIOS IN THE SELECTION PROCESS

You've been given a lot of reasons for using portfolios in the selection of park, recreation, and tourism professionals. But it is only fair to identify potential weaknesses and pitfalls when using this tool.

Several types of portfolios exist: developmental, teacher planning, proficiency, showcase, employment skills, and college admissions (Lankes, 1995). In park, recreation, and tourism curriculums, the student portfolio may be a combination, or hybrid, of these types. For purposes of this discussion, however, the portfolio primarily assists students in securing employment, so we have called it the *academic-employment portfolio* because it is used in easing the transition from classroom to workplace.

Employers may resist using portfolios in the selection process for two major reasons. First, the portfolio may be believed to be a one-of-a-kind artifact that cannot be addressed by standardized selection review procedures that link content to job qualifications. Second, employers do not want to accept the responsibility of handling and

Department of Recreation and Tourism Management (RTM), California State University at Northridge

For each major core course, specify individual or group project and the domain in which learning outcomes fall: cognitive, affective, or psychomotor (describe or label).

Course number and title	Portfolio assignment	Domains	Identified competency or standard
RTM 278 Leisure in Contemporary Society			
RTM 202/L Planning Programs and Events for Recreation Experiences			
RTM 204 Foundations of Recreation Therapy & Special Populations			
RTM 300 Recreation and Community Development			
RTM 302 Dynamics of Leadership in Recreation & Human Services			
RTM 303 Promotion of the Recreation Experience			
RTM 304 Entrepreneurial Ventures in Recreation & Human Services			
RTM 402 Models of Play, Leisure & Recreation			
RTM 403 Evaluation Research in Recreation & Human Services			
RTM 490 Challenges in Leisure Services Seminar			
RTM 494 ABC Supervised (Senior) Internship (attach relevant pages from internship manual)			

securely storing portfolios. However, there are ways to overcome these perceived obstacles.

How Employers Can Use Portfolios in the Selection Process

Here are five questions that might be asked of any student applicant when a portfolio is introduced to supplement the hiring process.

1. How do the materials in the portfolio relate to your courses and to your preparedness to do this job? (Some universities provide students with a grid showing the interrelationships, as in figure D.1.)

2. Did you produce all of the materials in this portfolio yourself? Could you identify or clarify your contribution to group efforts or projects?

3. What did you learn from improving the work returned to you by your professors or field (agency) supervisors?

4. If you had the opportunity to add something to your portfolio that is not among the present materials, what would it be, and why?

5. Is there anything you would like to share about your portfolio that has particular relevance to this position or to your possible advancement in the future?

Just as with any selection procedure, a single method such as the portfolio might be used in establishing the level of competence of the applicant, but it is best used during, or as background for, the interview. In this situation students can convey enthusiasm for, and levels of understanding about, the work-relevant products to be presented. It is difficult for job applicants to rehearse answers to questions that might arise about the content of the portfolio, so applicants' responses to those types of questions tend to give interviewers a clear picture of how, as future employees, applicants will think on their feet as well as indicate how familiar they are with the portfolio contents.

Figure D.2 provides a comparison among common selection criteria, based on an analysis of the applicant's ability to document competence. The relative strengths and weaknesses of each method are apparent but must be evaluated based on each agency's ability and willingness to employ

---

FIGURE D.2

Matching Portfolio Assignments With Position Description and Selection Criteria

Title of position (attach published position description): _____

Date of review: _____

Qualification or criterion	Portfolio evidence (description and page)	Level of evidence (1, 3, 5*)
Degree in parks, recreation, and tourism or related field		
General recreation experience		
Experience specific to this position		
Activity or event programming		
Technological skills		
Language and communication		
Promotional skills		
Group and team skills		
Evaluation and research skills		
Other		

*Rating scale: 1= Does not meet expectations; 3 = Meets expectations; 5 = Far exceeds expectations.

a range of assessment strategies. Naturally, in an increasingly litigious society, it is often preferable to demonstrate that a variety of assessment tools were used so as not to unintentionally bias the outcome of the selection process. On the other hand, agencies do not wish to waste their time employing any method, no matter how tried and true, only to find employees unprepared for the myriad aspects of work life.

Including the portfolio in the selection process simply makes sense because portfolios establish the link between classroom assignments and career competencies. Few park, recreation, or tourism practitioners would hire an artist to paint a mural in a facility or hire a graphic artist to design a brochure or Web site for their agency without tangible evidence of the quality of the applicant's work. Usually this means the applicant is asked to produce examples of similar, successful projects completed elsewhere, commonly in the form of drawings or photographs. The student-applicant's portfolio provides a comparable place in which to showcase relevant work products (e.g., open-space plans, landscape designs, tournament ladders, assessments).

Professors generally believe that they require students majoring in parks, recreation, and tourism to complete numerous assignments that directly prepare them for professional practice; most of those assignments are evaluated by faculty and awarded a grade. Faculty members, however, often recommend that students revise portfolio assignments after graded work is returned so that students complete the learning cycle by perfecting their work based on professors' feedback. Thus, portfolio items are usually presented, if used in the selection process, without grades.

Today's faculty members are rarely so arrogant as to believe the only learning experiences relevant to the selection process are those they design, and most encourage students to continue learning once on the job, whether through continuing education, formal degree programs, or employer-sponsored training. In addition to required projects, students are often encouraged by faculty to add information gleaned from independent research, professional conference attendance, or volunteer experiences to supplement what was initiated through course design, assignments, and instruction.

Many state-supported institutions of higher education are facing numerous challenges triggered by lack of foresight in preparing for the onslaught of enrollment in higher education by the grandchildren of baby boomers, unstable economic climate, and increased demand for the bach-

elor's degree as the "ticket" to a lifelong ride as a paid employee. Therefore, the likelihood of going straight through undergraduate school in four years is increasingly low. According to Posnick-Goodwin and Martin (2004), "Some students are having to attend more than one college to get their classes. And students are working more hours and applying for financial aid in order to complete their studies" (p. 11). This only adds to the pressure to secure full-time employment with benefits upon graduation, just to get out of debt incurred while earning a degree. Few students think about or can even grasp the notion that in order to continue to grow in their field and to be promoted to higher levels of responsibility, they will have to continue to attend conferences, workshops, and trainings, often at their own expense. The stakes are high and the competition fierce in many parts of the country, so each candidate must present himself or herself in the best possible manner. That may mean presenting oneself in as comprehensive and concise a manner as possible.

One example of how the expectation for commitment to ongoing professional development is articulated to students embarking on the portfolio process is found at Queens College, where an introductory letter to students encourages continuous improvement based on reflection and self-evaluation (Hittleman, 2002). In fact, if carefully assembled, portfolios become an intersection of instruction and assessment; "they are not just instruction or just assessment. . . . Together, instruction and assessment give more than either gives separately" (San Diego County Office of Education, 1997). Once this process is mastered, it can be continued and modified throughout a career. Here the boundaries between classroom and work life expectations, such as professional development and continuing education, begin to fade.

How Employers Can Handle and Secure Portfolios

Many of the more common portfolio items can now be converted to an electronic format, so student applicants can present their e-portfolios to prospective employers before the interview. Prospective employers will recognize this as similar to the commonly exercised option of reviewing a resume in either hard-copy format or as an e-mail attachment. According to the San Diego County Office of Education (1997), the sheer volume of materials can make storage and retrieval of information in portfolios very difficult. Not only writing samples but also larger items such as audiotapes, videotapes, posters, and crafts projects need to be stored, retrieved, and preserved. Technology can ease the physical burden of storing large amounts of information.

Photos, video clips, musical performances, program outlines, treatment plans, research projects, PowerPoint presentations, and newsletters can all be produced on diskette or CD-ROM. Even with such a portable and flexible method, many students still prefer to cart around the hard-copy notebook as evidence of their ability to create high-quality work-related products. Unfortunately, this more

traditional "binder" method works best when there is a single interviewer or reviewer involved in the hiring process or when there is ample time for multiple members of the selection committee to review a hard-copy portfolio before the meeting. One clear benefit to the hard-copy version is that it can more effectively demonstrate the creativity (or lack thereof) of the person who produced it!

Figure D.3 offers a template that could be standardized to accommodate the preinterview evaluation of the single, hard-copy portfolio. In this instance, the figure uses the benchmark

FIGURE D.3

Documentation of Professional Competencies in the Portfolio

Competency clusters	Types of evidence or documentation of competence	Coursework, training, continuing education units (CEUs)	Experiential
People Human development Communications Facilitation Mediation Multitasking Leadership Flexibility Partnering and coalition building Political dynamism and acumen Community building Diversity and inclusion*			
Parks Ecosystem management Resource management Facility (universal) design, maintenance, and operations* Mapping systems* Safety, security, risk management, liability* Disaster preparedness*			
Programs Community knowledge Cultural awareness and sensitivity* Strategic thinking Action and strategic planning Technology (applications, promotion, delivery) Research and evaluation Resourcefulness, funding, grantsmanship* Prevention models Legislative mandates (ADA, HIPPA, JAHCO)* Multidisciplinary approaches			

*Indicates addition to or expansion of items on original VIP Action Plan professional competencies.

organization's competencies, sorts them into the three focus areas identified in the mission (people, parks, and programs), and offers a matrix for sorting portfolio evidence by course-work, training, and continuing education units, *or* by experience in the field (field work, practicums, internships).

Regardless of the awkwardness of the binder-style portfolio, if instructors have taught their students well, most know they should have a back-up version for all items included in the portfolio, just as students are warned to retain a copy of papers and projects they submitted for evaluation. This reduces the possibility of losing irreplaceable content. Selection procedures often require that applicant materials be stored in a confidential and secure space. While portfolios may require more physical space to review and store, it is difficult to argue that this constitutes a radical departure from more traditional human resource review procedures in many organizations.

ENSURING RELEVANT CONTENT

Thus far we have examined both pros and cons of including the academic and employment portfolio as a form of evaluation that complements other selection assessment tools and procedures when hiring entry-level professionals in parks, recreation, and tourism. Further, the portfolio can be adapted to the assessment of supervisory and administrative-level applicants. Based on years of experience, John Sullivan (1999) states, "As an HR (human resources) professor I get to review hundreds of resumes and I never have understood why any HR professional would rely on it as an accurate source of information about a candidate. If you really want to find out about a candidate, go beyond the resume and ask for a professional portfolio."

Similar to the "in-basket" technique commonly used in the 1980s, raters of applicants and inter-viewers have to be trained to know what they are seeing and how to compare student work with that of entry-level professionals already on the job. Any agency may develop their own form to help locate, check off, and evaluate portfolio materials that your organization believes are essential to providing services to your participants, clients, or visitors. Reviewers can assess the acquisition

and application of higher-level management or research skills in parks, recreation, and tourism based on portfolio evidence that the community group, agency, or individual requesting the work product is satisfied.

Decisions about appropriate portfolio assign-ments can, and should, become a component of the ongoing dialogue among practitioners, educators, and students. Artifacts, declarations, productions, and media (Hittleman, 2002), while less commonly associated with assignments that students might include in a portfolio, could enhance creative approaches to the design of both recreation programs and course assignments, especially in cultural or media arts programming or when park and recreation departments are charged with the selection and maintenance of art for public spaces. Academic departments can use their advisory councils or teams of invited practitioners to review student portfolios before graduation in order to become familiar with exist-ing content and expectations and to see the fit between curriculum and workplace readiness. In other words, practitioners and faculty members examine the relationship between assessment of student learning and professional employment preparation when they focus on the develop-ment and use of ambitious content standards as the basis for assessment and accountability, the dual emphasis on setting demanding performance standards and on the inclusion of all students, and the attachment of high-stakes accountability mechanisms for schools, teachers, and students (Linn, 2001). For many of today's students there are no higher stakes than the offer of full-time employment (with benefits) in a chosen field. And all the better if that field happens to be the one for which their academic program prepared them!

State and national professional governing bodies (associations), academic advisory coun-cils, and internship placement supervisors can all be involved in the establishment and monitoring of portfolio items required of, and produced by, students enrolled in park, recreation, and tour-ism curriculums. This interaction also increases common goals and strengthens the profession while reducing confusion for students about the continuity among academic assignments, learning experiences, and selection for entry-level, full-time positions. In other words, we're all working from the same page, but without adopting a cookie-cutter, one-size-fits-all approach.

Georgi and Crowe (1998) confirm that the use of portfolios is becoming commonplace in today's schools and universities, and they reflect a trend toward assessments that go "beyond the bubble" of such devices as multiple-choice exams. In fact, portfolio assessment is generally thought to be a more authentic way of demonstrating skills and experience. Research findings suggest that the portfolio may become the most fair, efficient, and effective tool for data collection and could replace, with equivalent reliability, other forms of assessment (San Diego County Office of Education, 1997).

Those hiring park, recreation, and tourism professionals can take advantage of this assessment strategy, whether they have a background in the field or not. Portfolios can assist with the search for best-prepared professionals—those who can and wish to meet the needs and challenges of a dynamic, constantly changing profession. Most important, the portfolio is not recommended as the sole basis for hiring a person, since successful selection processes usually combine multiple forms of assessment, just as more than one assignment usually informs the award of course grades.

REACHING BACK, REACHING FORWARD

Although the portfolio is one of the more powerful and adaptable assessment tools available because it can be tailored to meet specific employment situations and is an individualized representation of an applicant's skills, talents, and background, many other selection approaches are available to practitioners. All approaches should be carefully evaluated in order to produce the most effective combination. Although once perceived as too subjective to be incorporated into the selection process, organizations can design standardized questions and matrices to align portfolio contents with specific, publicized selection criteria.

There is no longer a good reason to exclude the portfolio from the selection process in parks, recreation, and tourism. In fact, more resumes are being delivered in Web-based electronic formats, with interview tutorials available online that teach applicants what to expect and how to conduct a successful interview (Smith, 2000). As a self-assessment and reflective process that is initiated during undergraduate studies, the portfolio can form the basis for continued professional development for many years to come.

Sterling (2001) suggests that the most effective and transformative education is one that focuses on change—a pervasive context in the lives of park, recreation, and tourism professionals. Strategies for predicting and dealing with change are often formulated by problem-solving approaches embedded in a well-designed curriculum, so when the curriculum is informed by and mirrors workplace expectations, employees will become lifelong learners and effective global citizens. The characteristics of global citizens are learning to look at problems in a global context, working cooperatively and responsibly, thinking in a critical and systematic way, solving conflicts nonviolently, changing lifestyles to protect the environment, defending human rights, and participating in politics (Sterling, 2001). Which employees have those traits and can provide supporting evidence of having acquired or practiced those perspectives before being hired?

The California Park & Recreation Society VIP Action Plan provides a benchmark set of career competencies around which the discussion points revolve. Each organization holds the potential to adapt selection criteria, portfolio design, review and interview, and eventual selection to its own culture. In the meantime, analyzing the efficacy of more traditional approaches in light of their impact on subsequent training needs, supervision, discipline, turnover, and recruitment is imperative not only in saving time and money, but in alleviating suspicions of bias, cronyism, and randomness in the selection within the profession.

Additional journal articles and background readings on portfolios and the assessment of learning outcomes are readily accessible on the Internet, at your local university office for excellence in teaching, or at your campus community service-learning office. You can also contact professors in park, recreation, and tourism programs at the closest college or university offering the course of study. National and state professional associations may also suggest specific strategies for learning about job openings and submitting credentials for consideration. The field of practice and higher education benefit from the increased accountability associated with producing and maintaining well-designed academic and employment portfolios that support and inform the selection process at various levels of employment.

VIP-Based Performance Evaluation

An important component of personnel management is measuring a person's performance based on that person's job description. A sample position evaluation tool based on several of the core competencies has been developed. This evaluation can be used with a 1-to-5 rating scale:

1 = unsatisfactory

2 = satisfactory, meets minimum position requirements

3 = good, clearly meets position requirements

4 = outstanding, clearly meets and often exceeds position requirements

5 = superior, consistently exceeds position requirements

FUNCTION I. PARTNERING AND COALITION BUILDING

Competency statement: Collaborations are maintained, enhanced, or increased in keeping with the partnering philosophy of the department. Is able to understand the qualities and communication that influence partnership success. Knows and applies interpersonal, organizational, operational characteristics, and communication.

Performance Criteria

1. Provides leadership to encourage alliances, cooperative ventures, and coalitions to further the services and programs of the organization.

2. Maintains contracts using city-sanctioned agreements.

3. Is able to generate clear and concise reports outlining the benefits of alliances from an economic and participant outcome perspective.

4. Works to reduce barriers to partnership when consensus and concession will not place organization in jeopardy.

5. Establishes policies and procedures for all collaborations.

6. Reviews staffing patterns and needs related to developing and maintaining collaborations.

FUNCTION II. COMMUNITY BUILDING

Competency statement: Has knowledge of governance, environment, process, and procedures and how decisions are made. Is able to understand community values, traditions, power structures, and roles. Demonstrates competence in communicating with stakeholders and constituents.

Performance Criteria

1. Leads division from a clear structure of governance.

2. Demonstrates ability to work within processes, procedures, and decision-making arms of governmental structure.

3. Has high level of comfort and effectiveness when communicating with stakeholders and constituents.

4. Is familiar with community's organizational structure.

5. Is able to establish effective working relationship with partnerships and collaborations in order to accomplish goals.

6. Has high level of sensitivity to the environment, culture, values, and traditions that are important to the community.

FUNCTION III. COMMUNICATION

Competency statement: Uses communication as a management tool supporting the organization's mission and strategic plan. Demonstrates competence in making decisions. Establishes effective relationships with multiple and diverse audiences. Communicates using a variety of media that enhance two-way and throughway communications.

Performance Criteria

1. Assists in efficient day-to-day operations.

2. Demonstrates ability to keep all persons within the organization abreast of progress, projects, and issues.

3. Communicates in a tactful and professional manner (verbally and in writing).

4. Resolves conflicts that interfere with the delivery of service.

5. Responds to e-mail and phone messages and correspondence in a timely manner in keeping with agency protocol and standards.

6. Maintains confidentiality according to human resource standards.

7. Effectively applies knowledge and skills with multicultural focus of the community including participants, staff, and volunteers.

8. Represents department at all council, advisory, and voluntary services organization meetings in the highest professional manner.

FUNCTION IV. STRATEGIC THINKING

Competency statement: Is able to analyze and evaluate all forms of data, information, and situations in order to complement agency mission, values, and goals. Is able to synthesize ideas from an inclusion perspective while integrating the best plans without isolating stakeholders.

Performance Criteria

1. Analyzes and evaluates data from research.

2. Demonstrates capabilities in problem solving and creates effective solutions based on analysis of data.

3. Integrates information from all divisions of organization into working plans and solutions to have an effect on the community as a whole.

4. Leads departmental efforts in strategic planning session.

5. Is able to conceptualize future trends and needs.

FUNCTION V. LEADERSHIP

Competency statement: Is able to commit people to action. Inspires followers within organization to become leaders and agents of change. Leads with vision and a philosophy of being an instrument of change. Sets high standards for accountability with a focus on the big picture. Encourages and insists on all decisions being made from the perspective of vision, integrity, and a reflection of the goals and mission of the agency.

Performance Criteria

1. Has a vision for the future.

2. Communicates the vision throughout the organization.

3. Is consistent in decisions to be aligned with mission.

4. Is able to take action and is accountable for decisions.

5. Commits people to action in the face of projects and priorities.

6. Demonstrates skill in focusing the organization on the future.

7. Models integrity in decisions, conversations, and communication.

FUNCTION VI. USE OF TECHNOLOGY

Competency statement: Embraces advances in technology and seeks resources internally and externally to position agency staff and programs to respond to the changes. Establishes departmental systems to enhance communication, work flow, and productivity through the use of electronic communication and devices. Works to create an environment that embraces the use of the Internet as a marketing, public relations, and educational tool.

Performance Criteria

1. Analyzes and evaluates data from research.
2. Demonstrates capability in problem solving and creating effective solutions.
3. Integrates use of Internet as a fully operating tool for the department and for the constituents to enhance communication and information exchange.
4. Integrates holistic planning versus fragmented planning with respect to budgetary and staffing resources related to technology.

FUNCTION VII. RESEARCH AND EVALUATION

Competency statement: Creates an environment that encourages obtaining objective data in order to improve organizational and management decision. Commits to determining the effectiveness of current practices, procedures, and plans from an outcome perspective.

Performance Criteria

1. Enhances services and programs after reviewing outcome data.
2. Makes decisions based on impact of programs and services on the preventive aspects of service delivery.
3. Establishes computer program or maintains reports for tracking evaluative processes for all programs and services offered.
4. Encourages collaborations with local colleges and universities to engage in research and program evaluation projects.
5. Encourages the participation of all commissions in the review of the analysis generated by research projects in the various program specialties.

FUNCTION VIII. OUTCOME-BASED MANAGEMENT

Competency statement: Demonstrates ability to focus efforts of agency on outcomes. Statistical measures will be determined from constituent programs, and results of services will be reported

based on quality indicator's effect of service on constituents. Focus will be on prevention and less on remediation of problems.

Performance Criteria

1. Has a clear plan for outcome measurement.
2. Is able to model and encourage employees to focus programming efforts in the area of prevention.
3. Writes reports that focus on outcomes achieved.
4. Identifies collaborations that support prevention outcomes.

FUNCTION IX. POLITICAL DYNAMICS OR ACUMEN

Competency statement: Has strong understanding and working knowledge of how decisions are made within the organization. Is able to track local, state, or national policies and decisions and their impact on the organization. Is capable of managing the relationship between community sectors, constituents, and stakeholders.

Performance Criteria

1. Effectively governs the organization at the division level.
2. Has clear understanding of the cultural climate of the organization.
3. Is able to generate strong working relationships with local, regional, state, or national organizations that directly affect the delivery of services.
4. Understands decision time lines and their impact on the organization, staffing, and resources.

FUNCTION X. USE OF PREVENTION MODELS

Competency statement: Has strong understanding of prevention models. Works to achieve effective intervention services and programs that directly contribute to the outcomes of constituents. Creates a top–down philosophy of developing and sustaining healthy citizens and communities.

Performance Criteria

1. Creates an organizational structure that supports the development of prevention programs and services.

2. Is able to budget for and calculate the long-term benefits of prevention and maintenance programs and services in the community.

3. Articulates and reports the cost savings of prevention programs.

4. Develops mechanism for community involvement and collaboration for the long-term health of the community as a whole.

5. Works with other city agencies to establish formal structures to respond to intervention needs as they arise.

6. Establishes annual system to gather data on social problems important to the community.

FUNCTION XI. KNOWLEDGE OF HUMAN DEVELOPMENT

Competency statement: Understands the lifelong development process of a person. Understands the complexities of physical, psychological, and sociological needs of individuals. Demonstrates leadership to bring that knowledge into program design and service.

Performance Criteria

1. Reviews programs on an annual basis, evaluating them for depth and breadth of programming along the developmental continuum.

2. Demonstrates competence in managing staff with strong consideration for the continuum within the developmental process.

3. Provides strong leadership in recognizing the community's demographic groups and facilitating positive outcomes.

4. Supports the advancement of staff knowledge in the importance that recreation plays in meeting the developmental needs of the community.

5. Communicates to the council and appropriate stakeholders the outcomes realized through programming within the developmental continuum.

6. Encourages staff to plan programs and services in keeping with appropriate developmental needs within groups served (preschool, youth, teens, adults, and seniors).

Tools for Implementation

CPRS has developed the following tools and resources to help individuals and agencies apply the values, vision, mission, core competencies, and implementation strategies of the VIP Action Plan. These tools are also available on the CPRS Web site at www.cprs.org.

VIP Planning Tools Help Agencies Position Parks & Recreation As Vital Component In Community

CPRS has developed a number of tools to help you communi-cate the vision "Creating Community Through People, Parks and Programs." Tools include: sample press releases, job descriptions, performance evaluations, benchmarking reports and the public relations program. All of these are available on the CPRS web site, www.cprs.org/creating-trends.htm.

"Space To..." Ads and Posters CD

CPRS recognizes the importance of effective communications to your policy makers and constituents. We also recognized two critical issues: (1) not all agencies have the resources to develop public relations messages and (2) that the delivery of consistent messages across the state will enhance visibility of parks and recreation – and your agency. CPRS created three easy-to-use ads and posters to help promote the value of your parks and recreation agency. For more information visit the CPRS Web site at www.cprs.org/creating-CDs.htm.

Health & Wellness Report

The first of a series of VIP Action Plan reports, this report provides background data, agency examples, and a wealth of information on how you can position your agency as a leader in this critical health area. Visit www.cprs.org/creating-trends.htm to download.

Public Relations Brochure

Designed to be easily used by agencies of all sizes, the brochure is an excellent tool to give to elected officials, policy makers, foundations, businesses, reporters and community partners. A template is provided for you to insert specific information about your agency. See www.cprs.org/public-prbrochure.htm more information and an order form.

Media Releases

On the CPRS web site you can download tips and tools for placing an opinion-editorial piece (op-ed) with your local newspaper. We have also included a sample op-ed for you to adapt. The goal is to communicate your agency's role and promote **local activities for youth,** which tie to the public's concern about violence prevention.

Core Competencies Defined

In order for park and recreation professionals to perform their work effectively in the 21st century, they must possess certain competencies. The competencies have been grouped into five "meta" categories: Business Acumen, Communications & Marketing, Planning & Evaluation, Community Relations and Leadership & Management. To view the 22 competencies visit the CPRS web site.

Job Descriptions

Job descriptions using language from the "Creating Community" VIP Action Plan are available. These descriptions are created in Microsoft Word® format for easy download and editing. The job titles currently available include:

- Recreation Division Manager
- Aquatics Supervisor
- Parks Maintenance Supervisor
- Recreation Therapist
- Youth Development Program Coordinator
- Director Parks and Recreation or Community Services

Sample Job Interview Questions

Preparing for the job interview can be a stressful time. What will they ask me? How can I prepare? What should I be thinking about as I go into the interview? CPRS became interested in what questions were being asked of today's candidates and we sent out a general call for interview questions. We have compiled over 400 questions that are being asked in job interviews. www.cprs.org/JobCenter-interviewquestions.htm

Core Competencies Performance Evaluations

Examples of how to design a performance evaluation using the core competencies is outlined in the "Creating Community" VIP Action Plan. This gives examples of Competency Statements and Performance Criteria for many competencies including: Communications, Community Building, Human Development, Leadership, Strategic Thinking and more. Go to www.cprs.org/creating-trends.htm to download a Microsoft Word® document for easy editing.

Benchmarking/Best Practices

Benchmarking allows park and recreation professionals to position the profession more effectively with policy makers, collect data to improve agency operations, stimulate strategic planning, forecast industry trends and identify best practices. CPRS has produced three benchmarking reports:

1) Playground Safety Inspection
2) Low Impact Aerobics Instruction for Adults 55+, and
3) Training of Youth Development Staff.

Each report includes: Study Methodology, Best Practices Findings, Detailed Appendices and Questionnaire Results. The reports are available online at www.cprs.org/publications-benchmarking.htm.

RFP for Consultant Services

If your agency is preparing to write a strategic plan, general plan or master plan and you will be hiring a consultant, you will want to see the RFP Guide. Developed to help agencies write a RFP for professional service in preparing a strategic plan, general plan or master plan. Go to www.cprs.org/creating-trends.htm to download an editable word document.

Youth Sports & Fitness Initiative

CPRS began exploring options for creating a more positive youth sports climate in California. CPRS in partnership with the National Alliance for Youth Sports, created the Youth Sports and Fitness Initiative with the intention of developing a model plan for implementing a model plan. The task force created a CD with numerous tools, real examples, and resources to help agencies create a strong and positive youth sports environment in your community. Call CPRS for more information on ordering the CD, 916/665-2777.

References and Resources

Allen, L. (1998). *Benefits-based programming of recreation services: Training manual.* Ashburn, VA: National Recreation and Park Association.

Ammons, D.N. (2001). *Municipal benchmarks: Assessing local performance and establishing community standards.* Thousand Oaks, CA: Sage.

Annie E. Casey Foundation. (2004). *KIDS COUNT data book: Moving youth from risk to opportunity.* Baltimore, MD: Author.

Beliveau, L. (2007). *Program planning and documentation form.* El Cajon, CA: Author.

Bossidy, L., & Charan, R. (2002). *Execution: The Discipline of Getting Things Done.* New York: Crown Business.

Bureau of Justice Statistics. (1992). *Uniform crime report for the United States.* Washington, DC: Federal Bureau of Investigation, U.S. Department of Justice.

Bureau of Justice Statistics. (2004). Direct expenditure for each of the major criminal justice functions (police, corrections, judicial) has been increasing. www.ojp.usdoj.gov/bjs/glance/exptyp.htm.

Burns, M., Soderberg, P., & Dangermond, P. (1997). *California parks & recreation entering the 21st century: A discussion paper* (unpublished).

Cairncross, F. (1997). *The death of distance.* Boston: Harvard Business School Press.

California Park & Recreation Society. (March 1995). *Phoenix project handbook.* Sacramento: Author.

California Park & Recreation Society. (2001). *CPRS fact sheet of professional competencies.* Sacramento: Author.

Canadian Parks & Recreation Association. (1997). *The benefits catalogue.* Ottawa, ON: Author.

Cauchon, D. (May 24, 2006). Retiree benefits grow into "monster." *USA Today.*

Celente, G. (1997). *Trends 2000.* New York: Warner.

Centers for Disease Control and Prevention. (2007). Diabetes disabling disease to double by 2050. www.cdc.gov/nccdphp/publications/aag/ddt.htm.

Chapman, D.P, Perry, G.S., & Strine, T.W. (2005). The vital link between chronic disease and depressive disorders. *Prev Chronic Dis* [serial online]. www.cdc.gov/pcd/issues/2005/jan/04_0066.htm.

Commission for Accreditation of Park and Recreation Agencies. (2003). *Self-Assessment Manual for Quality Operation of Park and Recreation Agencies,* 3rd ed. Ed. Dr. Betty van der Smissen, CPRP. Ashburn, VA: National Recreation and Park Association.

Community Toolbox. (2007). University of Kansas. http://ctb.ku.edu.

Crompton, J. (2000). Repositioning leisure services. *Managing Leisure, 5,* 65-75.

Crompton, John L. (2007). *Community benefits and repositioning: The key to a viable future for parks and recreation.* Ashburn, VA: National Recreation and Parks Association.

De Carlo, L. (1999). Designing an employee portfolio. Gonyea & Associates. www.acompetitiveedge.com/a designing.html.

Facts on File. (May 10, 2001). 2000 census: Racial, ethnic minority populations surge. www.facts.com/2001213270.htm.

Field Poll. (October 29, 1999). Parks/water bond heavily favored: Majority supports lowering approval threshold for school construction bonds. Release #1938. San Francisco.

Frumkin, H., Frank, L., & Jackson, R. (2004). *Urban sprawl and public health: Designing, planning, and building for healthy communities.* Washington, D.C.: Island Press.

Fulbright, L. (May 17, 2007). Minority population grows to 100 million. *San Francisco Chronicle.*

Full Circle Associates. (1999). Communications audit. www.fullcirc.com/rlc/commaudit.htm.

Georgi, D., & Crowe, J. (Winter 1998). Digital portfolios: A confluence of portfolio assessment and technology. *Teacher Education Quarterly.* www.csubak.edu/~dgeorgi/projects/digital.htm.

Harnik, P. (2006). *The excellent city park system: What makes it great and how to get there.* Washington, D.C.: Trust for Public Land.

Hittleman, D.R. (2002). *Student handbook for preparing a professional portfolio.* City University of New York, Queens College, Division of Education, Department of Educational and Community Programs, Literacy Education Program. www.qc.edu/ECP/LITERACY/professionalportfolio.htm.

Howe, N., & Strauss, W. (2006). *Millennials rising: The next generation.* New York: Random House.

International City/County Management Association and National Association of Counties. (2004). *Active living approaches to local government.* Washington, D.C.: Author.

Kaihia, P. (November 1, 2005). The next real estate boom. *Money.*

Kaiser Family Foundation. (2003). New study finds children age zero to six spend as much time with TV, computers and video games as playing outside. www.kff.org/entmedia/entmedia102803nr.cfm.

Kelsey, C. (Spring 2002). Developing a parks and recreation master plan: Seven important factors for you to consider. *Parks and Recreation, 58*(2): 26-28.

Kotlikoff, L.J., & Burns, S. (2005). The coming generational storm, welfare entitlements, Social Security, Medicare, Medicaid. Book review. www.futurecasts.com.

Kraemer-Sadlik, T. & Paugh, A. (2004). *Everyday moments: Finding quality time & working families.* UCLA Sloan Center on Everyday Lives of Families, Working Paper No. 32. http://celf.ucla.edu/pages/view_abstract.php?AID=39.

Lankes, A. (1995). Electronic portfolios: A new idea in assessment. *ERIC Digest.* http://searcheric.org/digests/ed390377.html.

Library Index. (2004). The increasing cost of health care: How much does health care cost? www.libraryindex.com/pages/1845/Increasing-Cost-Health-Care-HOW-MUCH-DOES-HEALTH-CARE-COST.html.

Linn, R.L. (2001). Assessments and accountability (condensed version). *Practical Assessment, Research & Evaluation, 7*(11): 1-5. http://pareonline.net/getvn.asp?v=7&n=11.

Mandel, M. (1996). *High-risk society.* New York: Time/Random House.

Mishel, L., Bernstein, J., & Allegretto, S. (2005). *The state of working America, 2004/2005.* Ithaca, NY: IRL Press.

Morrison J., & Schmidt, G. (1994). *Future tense: The business realities of the next ten years.* New York: Morrow.

Munroe, T. (1999). *Trends analysis for parks & recreation: 2000 and beyond.* Moraga, CA: California Park & Recreation Society.

Murphy, J.F., Niepoth, E.W., & Williams, J.G. (1991). *Leisure systems: Critical concepts and applications.* Champaign, IL: Sagamore.

National Assembly of State Arts Agencies. (2007). *Legislative appropriations annual survey, FY 2007.* Washington, D.C.: Author.

National Institute of Out-of-School Time. (2007). *Making the case: A fact sheet on children and youth in out-of-school time.* Wellesley Centers on Women, Wellesley College: Author.

The Nature Conservancy. (2007). What is ecotourism. www.nature.org/aboutus/travel/ecotourism/about/art667.html.

Nichols, B. (2006). *Consumer spending on performing arts: Outlays flat for 2005; Non-spectator categories show growth.* Washington, D.C.: National Endowment for the Arts.

O'Sullivan, E. (1999). *Setting a course for change.* Ashburn, VA: National Recreation and Park Association.

O'Sullivan, E., & Spangler, K. (1998). *Experience marketing—Strategies for the new millennium.* State College, PA: Venture.

Pew Center on Global Climate Change. (2006). Pew Center on Global Climate Change releases first comprehensive approach to climate change. www.pewclimate.org/press_room/sub_press_room/2006_releases/agenda_release.cfm.

Pichly, A. (2004). *Internship interview evaluation sheet.* West Sacramento, CA: Author.

Pichly, A. (2004). *Interview questions for recreation interns.* West Sacramento, CA: Author.

Pichly, A. (2004). *Interview questions for senior recreation supervisor.* West Sacramento, CA: Author.

Pichly, A. (2004). *Resource exercise for recreation interns.* West Sacramento, CA: Author.

Pink, D. (2005). *A whole new mind: Moving from the information age to the conceptual age.* New York: Riverhead Books.

Pizor, A.G., & Tindall, B.S. (1992). *Preventing delinquency, an assessment of park & recreational actions. Program of research on the causes and correlates of delinquency.* Washington, D.C.: Congressional briefing, Office of Juvenile Justice and Delinquency Prevention A.G.

Popcorn, F., & Marigold, L. (1996). *Clicking—16 trends to future fit your life, your work and your business.* New York: Harper Collins.

Posnick-Goodwin, S., & Martin, D. (December 2004). Is there a "perfect storm" brewing in higher education? *California Educator.*

Putnam, R. (2000). *Bowling alone.* New York: Simon & Schuster.

Riddick, C.C., & Russell, R. (1999). *Evaluative research in recreation, park, and sport settings: Searching for useful information.* Champaign, IL: Sagamore.

Robinson J., & Godbey, G. (1997). *Time for life.* University Park, PA: Pennsylvania State University Press.

Sachs, A. (2006). Women and money. *Time, 167*(6), 67.

San Diego County Office of Education. (1997). Notes from research: Portfolio assessment. www.sdcoe.net/pdop/rise/support/html/rs_mods_2a.html.

Simple Living Network. (2004). Challenging time poverty. www.timeday.org.

Smith, A.K. (November 6, 2000). Charting your own course: The new workplace is risky, rugged and rewarding. *US News and World Report*, 56-65.

Sterling, S. (2001). *Sustainable education: Re-visioning learning and change*. Devon, United Kingdom: Green Books.

Stynes, D.J. (1993). Leisure—the new center of the economy? Academy of Leisure Sciences White Paper. *SPRE Newsletter, XVII* (3): 15-20.

Sullivan, J. (1999). Resumes stink, start asking for a portfolio. *Electronic Recruiting Exchange.* www. driohnsullivan.com/articles/1999/o30599.htm.

Tapscott, D. (1995). *The digital economy—Promise and peril in the age of networked intelligence.* New York: McGraw-Hill.

Trust for Public Land. (1996). *Protecting the land where we live: A report on the need for urban parks in America's cities.* San Francisco: Author.

Trust for Public Land. (October 2006). *Land vote 2006.* San Francisco: Author.

Trust for Public Land. (2004). *Voters approve $3.25 billion in open space funding.* San Francisco: Author.

Turning boomers into boomerangs. (February 2006). *The Economist, 378,* 8465, p. 65.

U.S. Census Bureau. (2003). Statistical Abstract of the United States. Section 26. No. 1234. Washington, D.C. www.census.gov/prod/2004pubs/03statab/arts.pdf.

USDA Forest Service. (2002). National survey on recreation and the environment. The Interagency National Survey Consortium, coordinated by the USDA Forest Service, Recreation, Wilderness, and Demographics Trends Research Group, Athens, GA and the Human Dimensions Research Laboratory, University of Tennessee, Knoxville, TN.

Wallis, C. (March 19, 2006). The multitasking generation. *Time.* www.time.com/time/magazine/article/0,9171,1174696,00.html.

Weiss, B. (2000). Recreation supervisor—youth development job announcement, Palo Alto Community Services Department. Palo Alto, CA: Author.

Wergin, J.F. (2005). Higher education: Waking up to the importance of accreditation. *Change, 37*(3), 35-41.

Zolli, A. (March 2006). Demographics—The population hourglass. Issue 103. p. 56, 67. New York: FastCompany.

About the California Park & Recreation Society

The California Park & Recreation Society (CPRS) is the largest state park and recreation professional association in the United States. CPRS, with its headquarters in Sacramento, represents more than 400 local and state park and recreation agencies, colleges and universities, therapeutic recreation agencies, and companies providing products and services to the profession. CPRS is a significant information source and an effective service provider to its more than 4,000 members. CPRS offers professional development and networking opportunities; leadership development; resources, tools, and publications; legislative advocacy; awards and recognitions; and specialty membership sections.

The CPRS Board of Directors has identified three organizational goals:

1. To ensure members have educational opportunities to develop the skills and knowledge to succeed within the park and recreation profession

2. To help members understand, articulate, and operate from the core values, vision, and mission set out in their VIP Action Plan, and to provide members with the tools to brand parks and recreation as an essential community service

3. To ensure members' concerns are heard by legislators in the creation of relevant public policies that affect parks and recreation, and that they are informed of proposed public policies of substantial importance to the profession

If you are interested in joining CPRS, visit www.cprs.org.

About the Editor

Jane H. Adams, MS, is executive director of the California Park & Recreation Society (CPRS). Ms. Adams was heavily involved in seeing the VIP concept become a reality in CPRS. As a member of the VIP Steering Committee, she participated in creating the vision, values, and mission of the plan as well as in the training and education of CPRS members about the plan. In addition, she made more than 50 VIP plan presentations to the CPRS, the National Recreation & Park Association (NRPA), and state associations.

Ms. Adams is a long standing member of the National Recreation & Park Association (NRPA) and the American Academy for Park & Recreation Administration, for which she served as president in 1998-99. In her leisure time, she enjoys participating in sprint triathlons, traveling to national and international parks, and cooking.

About the Contributors

Veda Ward has been a member of the recreation profession for more than 30 years. She has worked for the Baltimore City Department of Parks and Recreation and in the fitness and hospitality industries. She has taught at the University of Maryland and at California State University at Northridge. Veda has been professionally certified since 1992 and has assumed leadership roles on campus committees, in the California Park & Recreation Society, and with the National Recreation and Park Association (NRPA) (as trustee, Society of Park and Recreation Educators, accreditation site visitor, Aging Section Board). She has published numerous articles and presented papers and workshops at international, national, and regional conferences on immigrant elders; higher education administration; assessment of student learning in parks, recreation, and tourism; and the role of recreation in urban community development.

Ellen O'Sullivan, **PhD, CPRP,** is a longtime park and recreation professional who began as a camp counselor and community recreation director and advanced to university professor and consultant. Ellen has long believed in the power and promise that parks and recreation holds for individuals, communities, and society overall. Her contributions to the field include authorship of several books on marketing, extensive work in the benefits movement, groundbreaking applied research in health using the innovative magnet center approach, and her role in supporting and sustaining community agencies as they strategically alter the course to create a viable future in the health, livability, and vitality of communities. Ellen is CEO of Leisure Lifestyle Consulting, where she assists agencies in understanding their role in creating community through people, parks, and programs. She writes *TrendScan*, a quarterly publication focused on trends and their impact on parks and recreation. *TrendScan* is published by several state park and recreation associations.

Having been in the field since 1990, **André Pichly** is currently the recreation superintendent for the City of West Sacramento (California) Parks & Recreation Department. He has both a bachelor's and master's degree in recreation administration from Sacramento State University. He is a certified park and recreation professional and a lecturer in the park, recreation, and tourism administration department at Sacramento State University.